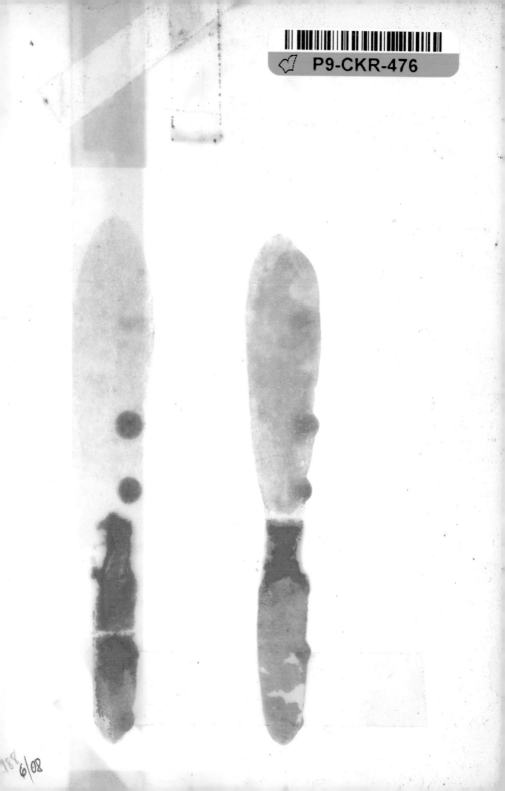

Also by the Author:

ANGELA DAVIS: AN AUTOBIOGRAPHY

WOMEN, RACE & CLASS

WOMEN, RACE & CLASS

ANGELA Y. DAVIS

 Random House ✐ New York

Library of Congress Cataloging in Publication Data

Davis, Angela Yvonne, 1944–
  Women, race and class.
    1. Racism—United States. 2. United States—Race
relations. 3. Sexism—United States. 4. United States—
Economic conditions—1961–   I. Title.
HT1521.D38   305.4'2   81–40243
ISBN 0–394–51039–9   AACR2

Manufactured in the United States of America
98765432
First Edition

To my mother,
Sallye B. Davis

I want to thank the following people for their help:
Kendra Alexander; Stephanie Allen; Rosalyn Baxandall;
Hilton Braithwaite; Alva Buxenbaum; Fania Davis; Kipp
Harvey; James Jackson; Phillip McGee, Dean of the School
of Ethnic Studies, San Francisco State University; Sally
McGee; Victoria Mercado; Charlene Mitchell; Toni Morrison;
Eileen Ahearn; the Women's Studies Program of San
Francisco State University.

Contents

WOMEN, RACE & CLASS

1 ~ The Legacy of Slavery: Standards for a New Womanhood

When the influential scholar Ulrich B. Phillips declared in 1918 that slavery in the Old South had impressed upon African savages and their native-born descendants the glorious stamp of civilization,[1] he set the stage for a long and passionate debate. As the decades passed and the debate raged on, one historian after another confidently professed to have deciphered the real meaning of the "peculiar institution." But amidst all this scholarly activity, the special situation of the *female* slave remained unpenetrated. The ceaseless arguments about her "sexual promiscuity" or her "matriarchal" proclivities obscured, much more than they illuminated, the condition of Black women during slavery. Herbert Aptheker remains one of the few historians who attempted to establish a more realistic basis for the understanding of the female slave.[2]

During the 1970s the slavery debate reemerged with renewed vigor. Eugene Genovese published *Roll, Jordan, Roll: The World the Slaves Made.*[3] John Blassingame's *The Slave Community*[4] appeared, as did Fogel and Engerman's ill-conceived *Time on the Cross*[5] and Herbert Gutman's monumental *Black Family in Slavery and Freedom.*[6] Responding to this rejuvenated debate, Stanley Elkins decided it was time to publish an expanded edition of his 1959 study *Slavery.*[7] Conspicuously absent from this flurry of publications is a book expressly devoted to slave women. Those of us who have anxiously awaited a serious study of the Black woman during slavery remain, so far, disappointed. It has been equally disappointing to discover that with the exception of the traditionally debatable questions of promiscuity versus marriage and forced versus voluntary sex with white men, scant attention has been focused on women by the authors of these new books.

The most enlightening of all these recent studies is Herbert Gutman's investigation of the Black family. In furnishing documentary evidence that the family's vitality proved stronger than the dehumanizing rigors of slavery, Gutman has dethroned the Black Matriarchy thesis popularized by Daniel Moynihan et al.[8] in 1965. Yet, since his observations about slave women are generally designed to confirm their wifely propensities, the implication is easily drawn that they differed from their white counterparts only to the extent that their domestic aspirations were thwarted by the exigencies of the slave system. According to Gutman, although institutionalized slave norms accorded women a great degree of premarital sexual freedom, they eventually settled into permanent marriages and built families based as much on their husband's input as on their own. Gutman's cogent and well-documented arguments against the matriarchy thesis are extremely valuable. But how much more powerful his book might have been had he concretely explored the multidimensional role of Black women within the family and within the slave community as a whole.

If and when a historian sets the record straight on the experiences of enslaved Black women, she (or he) will have performed an inestimable service. It is not for the sake of historical accuracy alone that such a study should be conducted, for lessons can be gleaned from the slave era which will shed light upon Black women's and all women's current battle for emancipation. As a layperson, I can only propose some tentative ideas which might possibly guide a reexamination of the history of Black women during slavery.

. . .

Proportionately, more Black women have always worked outside their homes than have their white sisters.[9] The enormous
space that work occupies in Black women's lives today follows a
pattern established during the very earliest days of slavery. As
slaves, compulsory labor overshadowed every other aspect of
women's existence. It would seem, therefore, that the starting
point for any exploration of Black women's lives under slavery
would be an appraisal of their role as workers.

The slave system defined Black people as chattel. Since women,
no less than men, were viewed as profitable labor-units, they
might as well have been genderless as far as the slaveholders were
concerned. In the words of one scholar, "the slave woman was
first a full-time worker for her owner, and only incidentally a wife,
mother and homemaker."[10] Judged by the evolving nineteenth-
century ideology of femininity, which emphasized women's roles
as nurturing mothers and gentle companions and housekeepers
for their husbands, Black women were practically anomalies.

Though Black women enjoyed few of the dubious benefits of
the ideology of womanhood, it is sometimes assumed that the
typical female slave was a houseservant—either a cook, maid, or
mammy for the children in the "big house." Uncle Tom and
Sambo have always found faithful companions in Aunt Jemima
and the Black Mammy—stereotypes which presume to capture
the essence of the Black woman's role during slavery. As is so
often the case, the reality is actually the diametrical opposite of
the myth. Like the majority of slave men, slave women, for the
most part, were field workers. While a significant proportion of
border-state slaves may have been houseservants, slaves in the
Deep South—the real home of the slaveocracy—were predominantly agricultural workers. Around the middle of the nineteenth
century, seven out of eight slaves, men and women alike, were
field workers.[11]

Just as the boys were sent to the fields when they came of age, so too were the girls assigned to work the soil, pick the cotton, cut the cane, harvest the tobacco. An old woman interviewed during the 1930s described her childhood initiation to field work on an Alabama cotton plantation:

> We had old ragged huts made out of poles and some of the cracks chinked up with mud and moss and some of them wasn't. We didn't have no good beds, just scaffolds nailed up to the wall out of poles and the old ragged bedding throwed on them. That sure was hard sleeping, but even that felt good to our weary bones after them long hard days' work in the field. I 'tended to the children when I was a little gal and tried to clean house just like Old Miss tells me to. Then as soon as I was ten years old, Old Master, he say, "Git this here nigger to that cotton patch."[12]

Jenny Proctor's experience was typical. For most girls and women, as for most boys and men, it was hard labor in the fields from sunup to sundown. Where work was concerned, strength and productivity under the threat of the whip outweighed considerations of sex. In this sense, the oppression of women was identical to the oppression of men.

But women suffered in different ways as well, for they were victims of sexual abuse and other barbarous mistreatment that could only be inflicted on women. Expediency governed the slaveholders' posture toward female slaves: when it was profitable to exploit them as if they were men, they were regarded, in effect, as genderless, but when they could be exploited, punished and repressed in ways suited only for women, they were locked into their exclusively female roles.

When the abolition of the international slave trade began to threaten the expansion of the young cotton-growing industry, the slaveholding class was forced to rely on natural reproduction as the surest method of replenishing and increasing the domestic slave population. Thus a premium was placed on the slave woman's reproductive capacity. During the decades preceding the Civil War, Black women came to be increasingly appraised for their fertility (or for the lack of it): she who was potentially the mother of ten, twelve, fourteen or more became a coveted treasure indeed. This did not mean, however, that as mothers, Black women enjoyed a more respected status than they enjoyed as workers. Ideological exaltation of motherhood—as popular as it was during the nineteenth century—did not extend to slaves. In fact, in the eyes of the slaveholders, slave women were not mothers at all; they were simply instruments guaranteeing the growth of the slave labor force. They were "breeders"—animals, whose monetary value could be precisely calculated in terms of their ability to multiply their numbers.

Since slave women were classified as "breeders" as opposed to "mothers," their infant children could be sold away from them like calves from cows. One year after the importation of Africans was halted, a South Carolina court ruled that female slaves had no legal claims whatever on their children. Consequently, according to this ruling, children could be sold away from their mothers at any age because "the young of slaves . . . stand on the same footing as other animals."[13]

As females, slave women were inherently vulnerable to all forms of sexual coercion. If the most violent punishments of men consisted in floggings and mutilations, women were flogged and mutilated, as well as raped. Rape, in fact, was an uncamouflaged expression of the slaveholder's economic mastery and the overseer's control over Black women as workers.

The special abuses inflicted on women thus facilitated the ruthless economic exploitation of their labor. The demands of this exploitation caused slaveowners to cast aside their orthodox sexist attitudes except for purposes of repression. If Black women were hardly "women" in the accepted sense, the slave system also discouraged male supremacy in Black men. Because husbands and wives, fathers and daughters were equally subjected to the slavemasters' absolute authority, the promotion of male supremacy among the slaves might have prompted a dangerous rupture in the chain of command. Moreover, since Black women as workers could not be treated as the "weaker sex" or the "housewife," Black men could not be candidates for the figure of "family head" and certainly not for "family provider." After all, men, women and children alike were all "providers" for the slaveholding class.

In the cotton, tobacco, corn and sugar-cane fields, women worked alongside their men. In the words of an ex-slave:

> The bell rings at four o'clock in the morning and they have half an hour to get ready. Men and women start together, and the women must work as steadily as the men and perform the same tasks as the men.[14]

Most slaveowners established systems of calculating their slaves' yield in terms of the average rates of productivity they demanded. Children, thus, were frequently rated as quarter hands. Women, it was generally assumed, were full hands—unless they had been expressly assigned to be "breeders" or "sucklers," in which case they sometimes ranked as less than full hands.[15]

Slaveowners naturally sought to ensure that their "breeders" would bear children as often as biologically possible. But they never went so far as to exempt pregnant women and mothers with infant children from work in the fields. While many mothers were forced to leave their infants lying on the ground near the area where they worked, some refused to leave them unattended and tried to work at the normal pace with their babies on their backs. An ex-slave described such a case on the plantation where he lived:

> One young woman did not, like the others, leave her child at the end of the row, but had contrived a sort of rude knapsack, made

of a piece of coarse linen cloth, in which she fastened her child, which was very young, upon her back; and in this way carried it all day, and performed her task at the hoe with the other people.[16]

On other plantations, the women left their infants in the care of small children or older slaves who were not able to perform hard labor in the fields. Unable to nurse their infants regularly, they endured the pain caused by their swollen breasts. In one of the most popular slave narratives of the period, Moses Grandy related the miserable predicament of slave mothers:

> On the estate I am speaking of, those women who had sucking children suffered much from their breasts becoming full of milk, the infants being left at home. They therefore could not keep up with the other hands: I have seen the overseer beat them with raw hide, so that the blood and milk flew mingled from their breasts.[17]

Pregnant women were not only compelled to do the normal agricultural work, they could also expect the floggings workers normally received if they failed to fulfill their day's quota or if they "impudently" protested their treatment.

> A woman who gives offense in the field, and is large in a family way, is compelled to lie down over a hole made to receive her corpulency, and is flogged with the whip or beat with a paddle, which has holes in it; at every stroke comes a blister. One of my sisters was so severely punished in this way, that labor was brought on, and the child was born in the field. This very overseer, Mr. Brooks, killed in this manner a girl named Mary. Her father and mother were in the field at that time.[18]

On those plantations and farms where pregnant women were dealt with more leniently, it was seldom on humanitarian

grounds. It was simply that slaveholders appreciated the value of
a slave child born alive in the same way that they appreciated the
value of a newborn calf or colt.

When timid attempts at industrialization were made in the
pre-Civil War South, slave labor complemented—and frequently
competed with—free labor. Slaveowning industrialists used men,
women and children alike, and when planters and farmers hired
out their slaves, they found women and children in as great
demand as men.[19]

> Slave women and children comprised large proportions of the work
> forces in most slave-employing textile, hemp and tobacco factories.
> . . . Slave women and children sometimes worked at "heavy"
> industries such as sugar refining and rice milling. . . . Other heavy
> industries such as transportation and lumbering used slave women
> and children to a considerable extent.[20]

Women were not too "feminine" to work in coal mines, in iron
foundries or to be lumberjacks and ditchdiggers. When the San-
tee Canal was constructed in North Carolina, slave women were
a full fifty percent of the labor force.[21] Women also worked
on the Louisiana levees, and many of the Southern railroads
still in use today were constructed, in part, by female slave
labor.[22]

The use of slave women as substitutes for beasts of burden to
pull trams in the Southern mines[23] is reminiscent of the horrendous utilization of white female labor in England, as described in
Karl Marx's *Capital:*

> In England women are still occasionally used instead of horses for
> hauling canal boats, because the labor required to produce horses
> and machines is an accurately known quantity, while that required
> to maintain the women of the surplus population is below all
> calculation.[24]

Like their British counterparts, the Southern industrialists made no secret of the reasons motivating them to employ women in their enterprises. Female slaves were a great deal more profitable than either free workers or male slaves. They "cost less to capitalize and to maintain than prime males."[25]

Required by the masters' demands to be as "masculine" in the performance of their work as their men, Black women must have been profoundly affected by their experiences during slavery. Some, no doubt, were broken and destroyed, yet the majority survived and, in the process, acquired qualities considered taboo by the nineteenth-century ideology of womanhood. A traveler during that period observed a slave crew in Mississippi returning home from the fields and described the group as including

> . . . forty of the largest and strongest women I ever saw together; they were all in a simple uniform dress of a bluish check stuff; their legs and feet were bare; they carried themselves loftily, each having a hoe over the shoulder, and walking with a free, powerful swing like chasseurs on the march.[26]

While it is hardly likely that these women were expressing pride in the work they performed under the ever-present threat of the whip, they must have been aware nonetheless of their enormous power—their ability to produce and create. For, as Marx put it, "labor is the living, shaping fire; it represents the impermanence of things, their temporality."[27] It is possible, of course, that this traveler's observations were tainted by racism of the paternalistic variety, but if not, then perhaps these women had learned to extract from the oppressive circumstances of their lives the strength they needed to resist the daily dehumanization of slavery. Their awareness of their endless capacity for hard work may have imparted to them a confidence in their ability to struggle for themselves, their families and their people.

When the tentative pre-Civil War forays into factory work

gave way to an aggressive embrace of industrialization in the United States, it robbed many white women of the experience of performing productive labor. Their spinning wheels were rendered obsolete by the textile factories. Their candlemaking paraphernalia became museum pieces, like so many of the other tools which had previously assisted them to produce the articles required by their families for survival. As the ideology of femininity —a by-product of industrialization—was popularized and disseminated through the new ladies' magazines and romantic novels, white women came to be seen as inhabitants of a sphere totally severed from the realm of productive work. The cleavage between the home and the public economy, brought on by industrial capitalism, established female inferiority more firmly than ever before. "Woman" became synonymous in the prevailing propaganda with "mother" and "housewife," and both "mother" and "housewife" bore the fatal mark of inferiority. But among Black female slaves, this vocabulary was nowhere to be found. The economic arrangements of slavery contradicted the hierarchical sexual roles incorporated in the new ideology. Male-female relations within the slave community could not, therefore, conform to the dominant ideological pattern.

Much has been made of the slaveholders' definition of the Black family as a matrilocal biological structure. Birth records on many plantations omitted the names of the fathers, listing only the children's mothers. And throughout the South, state legislatures adopted the principle of *partus sequitur ventrem*—the child follows the condition of the mother. These were the dictates of the slaveowners, who fathered not a few slave children themselves. But were they also the norms according to which the slaves ordered their domestic relationships among themselves? Most historical and sociological examinations of the Black family during slavery have simply assumed that the masters' refusal to acknowledge fatherhood among their slaves was directly translated into a matriarchal family arrangement of the slaves' own making.

The notorious 1965 government study on the "Negro Family" —popularly known as the "Moynihan Report"—directly linked the contemporary social and economic problems of the Black community to a putatively matriarchal family structure. "In essence," wrote Daniel Moynihan,

> the Negro community has been forced into a matriarchal structure which, because it is out of line with the rest of the American society, seriously retards the progress of the group as a whole and imposes a crushing burden on the Negro male and, in consequence, on a great many Negro women as well.[28]

According to the report's thesis, the source of oppression was deeper than the racial discrimination that produced unemployment, shoddy housing, inadequate education and substandard medical care. The root of oppression was described as a "tangle of pathology" created by the absence of male authority among Black people! The controversial finale of the Moynihan Report was a call to introduce male authority (meaning male supremacy of course!) into the Black family and the community at large.

One of Moynihan's "liberal" supporters, the sociologist Lee Rainwater, took exception to the solutions recommended by the report.[29] Rainwater proposed instead jobs, higher wages and other economic reforms. He even went so far as to encourage continued civil rights protests and demonstrations. But, like most white sociologists—and some Black ones as well—he reiterated the thesis that slavery had effectively destroyed the Black family. As a result, Black people were allegedly left with "the mother-centered family with its emphasis on the primacy of the mother-child relation and only tenuous ties to a man."[30] Today, he said,

Men often do not have real homes; they move about from one
household where they have kinship or sexual ties to another. They
live in flop houses and rooming houses; they spend their time in
institutions. They are not household members in the only "homes"
they have—the homes of their mothers and of their girlfriends.[31]

Neither Moynihan nor Rainwater had invented the theory of
the Black family's internal deterioration under slavery. The pioneering work to support this thesis was done in the 1930s by the
renowned Black sociologist E. Franklin Frazier. In his book *The
Negro Family*,[32] published in 1939, Frazier dramatically described the horrendous impact of slavery on Black people, but he
underestimated their ability to resist its insinuations into the
social life they forged for themselves. He also misinterpreted the
spirit of independence and self-reliance Black women necessarily
developed, and thus deplored the fact that "neither economic
necessity nor tradition had instilled (in the Black woman) the
spirit of subordination to masculine authority."[33]

Motivated by the controversy unleashed by the appearance of
the Moynihan Report, as well as by his doubts concerning the
validity of Frazier's theory, Herbert Gutman initiated his research
on the slave family. About ten years later—in 1976—he published
his remarkable work *The Black Family in Slavery and Freedom*.[34] Gutman's investigations uncovered fascinating evidence
of a thriving and developing family during slavery. It was not the
infamous matriarchal family he discovered, but rather one involving wife, husband, children and frequently other relatives, as well
as adoptive kin.

Dissociating himself from the questionable econometric conclusions reached by Fogel and Engerman, who claim that slavery
left most families intact, Gutman confirms that countless slave
families were forcibly disrupted. The separation, through indiscriminate sales of husbands, wives and children, was a terrifying

hallmark of the North American variety of slavery. But, as he points out, the bonds of love and affection, the cultural norms governing family relations, and the overpowering desire to remain together survived the devastating onslaught of slavery.[35]

On the basis of letters and documents, such as birth records retrieved from plantations listing fathers as well as mothers, Gutman demonstrates not only that slaves adhered to strict norms regulating their familial arrangements, but that these norms differed from those governing the white family life around them. Marriage taboos, naming practices and sexual mores—which, incidentally, sanctioned premarital intercourse—set slaves apart from their masters.[36] As they tried desperately and daily to maintain their family lives, enjoying as much autonomy as they could seize, slave men and women manifested irrepressible talent in humanizing an environment designed to convert them into a herd of subhuman labor units.

> Everyday choices made by slave men and women—such as remaining with the same spouse for many years, naming or not naming the father of a child, taking as a wife a woman who had children by unnamed fathers, giving a newborn child the name of a father, an aunt or an uncle, or a grandparent, and dissolving an incompatible marriage—contradicted in behavior, not in rhetoric, the powerful ideology that viewed the slave as a perpetual "child" or a repressed "savage." . . . Their domestic arrangements and kin networks together with the enlarged communities that flowed from these primordial ties made it clear to their children that the slaves were not "non-men" and "non-women."[37]

It is unfortunate that Gutman did not attempt to determine the actual position of women within the slave family. In demonstrating the existence of a complex family life encompassing husbands and wives alike, Gutman eliminated one of the main pillars on which the matriarchy argument has stood. However, he did not substantially challenge the complementary claim that where there were two-parent families, the woman dominated the man. Moreover, as Gutman's own research confirms, social life in the slave quarters was largely an extension of family life. Thus, women's role within the family must have defined, to a great extent, their social status within the slave community as a whole.

Most scholarly studies have interpreted slave family life as elevating the women and debasing the men, even when both mother and father were present. According to Stanley Elkins, for example, the mother's role

> . . . loomed far larger for the slave child than did that of the father. She controlled those few activities—household care, preparation of food and rearing of children—that were left to the slave family.[38]

The systematic designation of slave men as "boys" by the master was a reflection, according to Elkins, of their inability to execute their fatherly responsibilities. Kenneth Stampp pursues this line of reasoning even further than Elkins:

> . . . the typical slave family was matriarchal in form, for the mother's role was far more important than the father's. In so far as the family did have significance, it involved responsibilities which traditionally belonged to women, such as cleaning house, preparing food, making clothes, and raising children. The husband was at most his wife's assistant, her companion and her sex partner. He was often thought of as her possession (Mary's Tom), as was the cabin in which they lived.[39]

It is true that domestic life took on an exaggerated importance in the social lives of slaves, for it did indeed provide them with the only space where they could truly experience themselves as human beings. Black women, for this reason—and also because they were workers just like their men—were not debased by their domestic functions in the way that white women came to be. Unlike their white counterparts, they could never be treated as mere "housewives." But to go further and maintain that they consequently dominated their men is to fundamentally distort the reality of slave life.

In an essay I wrote in 1971[40]—using the few resources allowed me in my jail cell—I characterized the significance of the slave woman's domestic functions in the following way: "In the infinite anguish of ministering to the needs of the men and children around her . . . , she was performing the *only* labor of the slave community which could not be directly and immediately claimed by the oppressor. There was no compensation for work in the fields; it served no useful purpose for the slaves. Domestic labor was the only meaningful labor for the slave community as a whole. . . .

"Precisely through performing the drudgery which has long been a central expression of the socially conditioned inferiority of women, the Black woman in chains could help to lay the foundation for some degree of autonomy, both for herself and her men. Even as she was suffering under her unique oppression as female, she was thrust into the center of the slave community. She was, therefore, essential to the *survival* of the community."

I have since realized that the special character of domestic labor during slavery, its centrality to men and women in bondage, involved work that was not exclusively female. Slave men executed important domestic responsibilities and were not, therefore—as Kenneth Stampp would have it—the mere helpmates of their women. For while women cooked and sewed, for example, men did the gardening and hunting. (Yams, corn and other vegetables, as well as wild animals such as rabbits and opossums, were always a delicious addition to the monotonous daily rations.) This sexual division of domestic labor does not appear to have been hierarchical: men's tasks were certainly not superior to and were hardly inferior to the work performed by women. They were both equally necessary. Moreover, from all indications, the division of labor between the sexes was not always so rigorous, for men would sometimes work in the cabin and women might tend the garden and perhaps even join the hunt.[41]

The salient theme emerging from domestic life in the slave quarters is one of sexual equality. The labor that slaves performed for their own sake and not for the aggrandizement of their masters was carried out on terms of equality. Within the confines of their family and community life, therefore, Black people managed to accomplish a magnificent feat. They transformed that negative equality which emanated from the equal oppression they suffered as slaves into a positive quality: the egalitarianism characterizing their social relations.

Although Eugene Genovese's major argument in *Roll, Jordan, Roll* is, at best, problematic (i.e., that Black people accepted the paternalism associated with slavery), he does present an insightful, though abbreviated, picture of the slaves' home life.

The story of the slave women as wives requires indirect examination. To deduce it from an assumption that the man was a guest in the house will not do. A review of the actual position of the men as husbands and fathers suggests that the position of the women was much more complex than usually credited. The women's attitude toward housework, especially cooking, and toward their own femininity by itself belies the conventional wisdom according to which the women unwittingly helped ruin their men by asserting themselves in the home, protecting their children, and assuming other normally masculine responsibilities.[42]

While there is a touch of male supremacy in his analysis, implying, as he does, that masculinity and femininity are immutable concepts, he clearly recognizes that

> What has usually been viewed as a debilitating female supremacy was in fact a closer approximation to a healthy sexual equality than was possible for whites and perhaps even for postbellum blacks.[43]

The most fascinating point Genovese raises here—although he does not develop it—is that women often defended their men from the slave system's attempts to demean them. Most women, perhaps a substantial majority, he says, understood that whenever their men were degraded, so too were they. Furthermore,

> [t]hey wanted their boys to grow up to be men and knew perfectly well that, to do so, they needed the example of a strong black man in front of them.[44]

Their boys needed strong male models to the very same extent that their girls needed strong female models.

If Black women bore the terrible burden of equality in oppression, if they enjoyed equality with their men in their domestic environment, then they also asserted their equality aggressively in challenging the inhuman institution of slavery. They resisted the sexual assaults of white men, defended their families and participated in work stoppages and revolts. As Herbert Aptheker points out in his pioneering work *American Negro Slave Revolts*,[45] they poisoned their masters, committed other acts of sabotage and, like their men, joined maroon communities and frequently fled northward to freedom. From the numerous accounts of the violent repression overseers inflicted on women, it must be inferred that she who passively accepted her lot as a slave was the exception rather than the rule.

When Frederick Douglass reflected on his childhood introduction to the merciless violence of slavery,[46] he recalled the floggings and torture of many rebellious women. His cousin, for example, was horribly beaten as she unsuccessfully resisted an overseer's sexual attack.[47] A woman called Aunt Esther was viciously flogged for defying her master, who insisted that she break off relations with a man she loved.[48] One of Frederick Douglass' most vivid descriptions of the ruthless punishments reserved for slaves involved a young woman named Nellie, who was whipped for the offense of "impudence":

> There were times when she seemed likely to get the better of the brute, but he finally overpowered her and succeeded in getting her arms tied to the tree towards which he had been dragging her. The victim was now at the mercy of his merciless lash. . . . The cries of the now helpless woman, while undergoing the terrible infliction, were mingled with the hoarse curses of the overseer and the wild cries of her distracted children. When the poor woman was untied, her back was covered with blood. She was whipped, terribly whipped, but she was not subdued and continued to denounce the overseer and to pour upon him every vile epithet of which she could think.[49]

Douglass adds that he doubts whether this overseer ever attempted to whip Nellie again.

Like Harriet Tubman, numerous women fled slavery for the North. Many were successful, though many more were captured. One of the most dramatic escape attempts involved a young woman—possibly a teenager—named Ann Wood, who directed a wagonload of armed boys and girls as they ran for their freedom. After setting out on Christmas Eve, 1855, they engaged in a shoot-out with slavecatchers. Two of them were killed, but the rest, according to all indications, made their way to the North.[50] The abolitionist Sarah Grimke described the case of a woman whose resistance was not so successful as Ann Wood's. This woman's repeated efforts to escape from the domination of her South Carolina master earned her so many floggings that "a finger could not be laid between the cuts."[51] Because she seized every available opportunity to break free from the plantation, she was eventually held prisoner in a heavy iron collar—and in case she managed to break the collar, a front tooth was pulled as an identification mark. Although her owners, said Grimke, were known as a charitable and Christian family,

> . . . this suffering slave, who was the seamstress of the family was continually in (their) presence, sitting in (the) chamber to sew, or engaging in . . . other household work with her lacerated and bleeding back, her mutilated mouth and heavy iron collar without, so far as appeared, exciting any feelings of compassion.[52]

Women resisted and advocated challenges to slavery at every turn. Given the unceasing repression of women, "no wonder," said Herbert Apthcker, "the Negro woman so often urged haste in slave plottings."[53]

> Virginia, 1812: "she said they could not rise too soon for her as she had rather be in hell than where she was." Mississippi, 1835: "she wished to God it was all over and done with; that she was tired of waiting on *white folks* . . ."
> One may better understand now a Margaret Garner, fugitive slave, who, when trapped near Cincinnati, killed her own daughter and tried to kill herself. She rejoiced that the girl was dead—"now she would never know what a woman suffers as a slave."—and pleaded to be tried for murder. "I will go singing to the gallows rather than be returned to slavery."[54]

Maroon communities, composed of fugitive slaves and their descendants, could be found throughout the South as early as 1642 and as late as 1864. These communities were "havens for fugitives, served as bases for marauding expeditions against nearby plantations and at times supplied leadership to planned uprisings."[55] In 1816 a large and flourishing community was discovered: three hundred escaped slaves—men, women and children —had occupied a fort in Florida. When they refused to surrender themselves, the army launched a battle which lasted for ten days and claimed the lives of more than two hundred fifty of the inhabitants. The women fought back on equal terms with the men.[56] During the course of another confrontation in Mobile, Alabama, in 1827, men and women alike were unrelenting, fighting, according to local newspapers, "like Spartans."[57]

Resistance was often more subtle than revolts, escapes and sabotage. It involved, for example, the clandestine acquisition of reading and writing skills and the imparting of this knowledge to others. In Natchez, Louisiana, a slave woman ran a "midnight school," teaching her people between the hours of eleven and two until she had "graduated" hundreds.[58] Undoubtedly many of them wrote their own passes and headed in the direction of freedom. In Alex Haley's Roots[59]—his fictionalized narrative of his ancestors' lives—Kunta Kinte's wife, Belle, painfully taught herself to read and write. By secretly reading her master's newspapers, she stayed abreast of current political events and communicated this knowledge to her sister and brother slaves.

No discussion of the part played by women in resisting slavery would be complete without paying tribute to Harriet Tubman for the extraordinary feats she performed as the conductor for over three hundred people on the Underground Railroad.[60] Her early life unfolded in a manner typical of most slave women's lives. A field hand in Maryland, she learned through work that her potential as a woman was the same as any man's. Her father taught her to chop wood and split rails, and as they worked side by side, he gave her lessons which would later prove indispensable during the nineteen trips she made back and forth to the South. He taught her how to walk soundlessly through the woods and how to find food and medicine among the plants, roots and herbs. The fact that she never once suffered defeat is no doubt attributable to her father's instructions. Throughout the Civil War, Harriet Tubman continued her relentless opposition to slavery, and even today she still holds the distinction of being the only woman in the United States ever to have led troops into battle.

Whatever the standards used to judge her—Black or white, male or female—Harriet Tubman was indeed an exceptional individual. But from another vantage point, what she did was simply to express in her own way the spirit of strength and perseverance which so many other women of her race had acquired. This bears repeating: Black women were equal to their men in the oppression they suffered; they were their men's social equals within the slave community; and they resisted slavery with a passion equal to their men's. This was one of the greatest ironies of the slave system, for in subjecting women to the most ruthless exploitation conceivable, exploitation which knew no sex distinctions, the groundwork was created not only for Black women to assert their equality through their social relations, but also to express it through their acts of resistance. This must have been a terrifying revelation for the slaveowners, for it seems that they were trying to break this chain of equality through the especially brutal repression they reserved for the women. Again, it is important to remember that the punishment inflicted on women exceeded in intensity the punishment suffered by their men, for women were not only whipped and mutilated, they were also *raped*.

It would be a mistake to regard the institutionalized pattern of rape during slavery as an expression of white men's sexual urges, otherwise stifled by the specter of white womanhood's chastity. That would be far too simplistic an explanation. Rape was a weapon of domination, a weapon of repression, whose covert goal was to extinguish slave women's will to resist, and in the process, to demoralize their men. These observations on the role of rape during the Vietnam War could also apply to slavery: "In Vietnam, the U.S. Military Command made rape 'socially acceptable'; in fact, it was unwritten, but clear, policy."[61] When GIs were encouraged to rape Vietnamese women and girls (and they were sometimes advised to "search" women "with their penises"[62]) a weapon of mass political terrorism was forged. Since the Vietnamese women were distinguished by their heroic contributions to their people's liberation struggle, the military retaliation specifically suited for them was rape. While women were hardly immune to the violence inflicted on men, they were especially singled out as victims of terrorism by a sexist military force governed by the principle that war was exclusively a man's affair. "I saw one case where a woman was shot by a sniper, one of our snipers," a GI said.

> When we got up to her she was asking for water. And the lieutenant said to kill her. So he ripped off her clothes, they stabbed her in both breasts, they spread her eagle and shoved an E tool (entrenching) up her vagina. And then they took that out and used a tree limb and then she was shot.[63]

In the same way that rape was an institutionalized ingredient of the aggression carried out against the Vietnamese people, designed to intimidate and terrorize the women, slaveowners encouraged the terroristic use of rape in order to put Black women in their place. If Black women had achieved a sense of their own strength and a strong urge to resist, then violent sexual assaults —so the slaveholders might have reasoned—would remind the women of their essential and inalterable femaleness. In the male supremacist vision of the period, this meant passivity, acquiescence and weakness.

Virtually all the slave narratives of the nineteenth century contain accounts of slave women's sexual victimization at the hands of masters and overseers.

> Henry Bibb's master forced one slave girl to be his son's concubine; M.F. Jamison's overseer raped a pretty slave girl; and Solomon Northrup's owner forced one slave, "Patsy," to be his sexual partner.[64]

Despite the testimony of slaves about the high incidence of rape and sexual coercion, the issue of sexual abuse has been all but glossed over in the traditional literature on slavery. It is sometimes even assumed that slave women welcomed and encouraged the sexual attentions of white men. What happened between them, therefore, was not sexual exploitation, but rather "miscegenation." In the section of *Roll, Jordan, Roll* devoted to interracial sex, Genovese insists that the problem of rape pales in relation to the merciless taboos surrounding miscegenation. "Many white men," the author says, "who began by taking a slave girl in an act of sexual exploitation ended by loving her and the children she bore."[65] "The tragedy of miscegenation lay," as a consequence,

> not in its collapse into lust and sexual exploitation, but in the terrible pressure to deny the delight, affection and love that often grew from tawdry beginnings.[66]

Genovese's overall approach hinges on the issue of paternalism. Slaves, he argues, more or less accepted the paternalistic posture of their masters, and masters were compelled by their paternalism to acknowledge slaves' claims to humanity. But since, in the eyes of the masters, the slaves' humanity was childlike at best, it is not surprising that Genovese believes he has discovered a kernel of that humanity in miscegenation. He fails to understand that there could hardly be a basis for "delight, affection and love" as long as white men, by virtue of their economic position, had unlimited access to Black women's bodies. It was as oppressors—or, in the case of non-slaveowners, as agents of domination—that white men approached Black women's bodies. Genovese would do well to read Gayl Jones' *Corregidora* [67], a recent novel by a young Black woman which chronicles the attempts of several generations of women to "preserve the evidence" of the sexual crimes committed during slavery.

E. Franklin Frazier thought he had discovered in miscegenation Black people's most important cultural achievement during slavery:

> The master in his mansion and his colored mistress in her special house nearby represented the final triumph of social ritual in the presence of the deepest feelings of human solidarity. [68]

At the same time, however, he could not entirely dismiss the numerous women who did not submit without a fight:

> That physical compulsion was necessary at times to secure submission on the part of black women . . . is supported by historical evidence and has been preserved in the tradition of Negro families. [69]

He cites the story of a woman whose great-grandmother always described with enthusiasm the battles which had earned her the considerable scars on her body. But there was one scar she persistently refused to explain, saying, whenever she was asked about it, "White men are as low as dogs, child, stay away from them." After her death, the mystery was finally solved:

> She received that scar at the hands of her master's youngest son, a boy of about eighteen years at the time she conceived their child, my grandmother Ellen. [70]

White women who joined the abolitionist movement were especially outraged by the sexual assaults on Black women. Activists in the female anti-slavery societies often related stories of brutal rapes of slave women as they appealed to white women to defend their Black sisters. While these women made inestimable contributions to the anti-slavery campaign, they often failed to grasp the complexity of the slave woman's condition. Black women were women indeed, but their experiences during slavery —hard work with their men, equality within the family, resistance, floggings and rape—had encouraged them to develop certain personality traits which set them apart from most white women.

One of the most popular pieces of abolitionist literature was Harriet Beecher Stowe's *Uncle Tom's Cabin*, a book which rallied vast numbers of people—and more women than ever before— to the anti-slavery cause. Abraham Lincoln once casually referred to Stowe as the woman who started the Civil War. Yet the enormous influence her book enjoyed cannot compensate for its utter distortion of slave life. The central female figure is a travesty of the Black woman, a naïve transposition of the mother-figure, praised by the cultural propaganda of the period, from white society to the slave community. Eliza is white motherhood incarnate, but in blackface—or rather, because she is a "quadroon," in just-a-little-less-than-white-face.

It may have been Stowe's hope that the white women readers of her novel would discover themselves in Eliza. They could admire her superior Christian morality, her unfaltering maternal instincts, her gentleness and fragility—for these were the very qualities white women were being taught to cultivate in themselves. Just as Eliza's whiteness allows her to become the epitome of motherhood, her husband, George, whose ancestry is also predominantly white, comes closer than any other Black man in the book to being a "man" in the orthodox male supremacist sense. Unlike the domestic, acquiescent, childlike Uncle Tom, George is ambitious, intelligent, literate, and most important of all, he detests slavery with an unquenchable passion. When George decides, very early in the book, to flee to Canada, Eliza, the pure, sheltered houseservant, is terribly frightened by his overflowing hatred of slavery:

> Eliza trembled, and was silent. She had never seen her husband in this mood before; and her gentle system of ethics seemed to bend like a reed in the surges of such passions.[71]

Eliza is practically oblivious to the general injustices of slavery. Her feminine submissiveness has prompted her to surrender herself to her fate as a slave and to the will of her good, kind master and mistress. It is only when her maternal status is threatened that she finds the strength to stand up and fight. Like the mother who discovers she can lift an automobile if her child is trapped underneath, Eliza experiences a surge of maternal power when she learns that her son is going to be sold. Her "kind" master's financial troubles compel him to sell Uncle Tom and Eliza's son Harry—despite, of course, the compassionate and maternal pleas of his wife. Eliza grabs Harry and instinctively runs away, for "stronger than all was maternal love, wrought into a paroxysm of frenzy by the near approaches of a fearful danger."[72] Eliza's mother-courage is spellbinding. When, in the course of her flight, she reaches an impassable river of melting ice, the slavecatcher hot on her heels, she spirits Harry across

> . . . nerved with strength such as God only gives to the desperate. . . . (S)he vaulted sheer over the turbid current by the shore and on to the raft of ice beyond. . . . With wild cries and desperate energy she leaped to another and still another cake;—stumbling,—leaping,—slipping,—springing upwards again! Her shoes are gone,

—her stockings cut from her feet,—while blood marked every step; but she saw nothing, felt nothing, till dimly, as in a dream, she saw the Ohio side, and a man helping her up the bank.[73]

The implausibility of Eliza's melodramatic feat matters little to Stowe—because God imparts superhuman abilities to gentle Christian mothers. The point, however, is that because she accepted wholesale nineteenth-century mother worship, Stowe miserably fails to capture the reality and the truth of Black women's resistance to slavery. Countless acts of heroism carried out by slave mothers have been documented. These women, unlike Eliza, were driven to defend their children by their passionate abhorrence of slavery. The source of their strength was not some mystical power attached to motherhood, but rather their concrete experiences as slaves. Some, like Margaret Garner, went so far as to kill their children rather than witness their growth to adulthood under the brutal circumstances of slavery. Eliza, on the other hand, is quite unconcerned about the overall inhumanity of the slave system. Had she not been threatened with the sale of her son, she would have probably lived happily ever after under the beneficent tutelage of her master and mistress.

The Elizas, if they indeed existed, were certainly oddities among the great majority of Black women. They did not, in any event, represent the accumulated experiences of all those women who toiled under the lash for their masters, worked for and protected their families, fought against slavery, and who were beaten and raped, but never subdued. It was those women who passed on to their nominally free female descendants a legacy of hard work, perseverance and self-reliance, a legacy of tenacity, resistance and insistence on sexual equality—in short, a legacy spelling out standards for a new womanhood.

2 ⌒ The Anti-Slavery Movement and the Birth of Women's Rights

> When the true history of the anti-slavery cause shall be written, women will occupy a large space in its pages; for the cause of the slave has been peculiarly women's cause.[1]

These are the words of an ex-slave, a man who became so closely associated with the nineteenth-century women's movement that he was accused of being a "women's rights man."[2] Frederick Douglass, the country's leading Black abolitionist, was also the most prominent male advocate of women's emancipation in his times. Because of his principled support of the controversial women's movement, he was often held up to public ridicule. Most men of his era, finding their manhood impugned, would have automatically risen to defend their masculinity. But Frederick Douglass assumed an admirably anti-sexist posture and proclaimed that he hardly felt demeaned by the label "women's rights man. . . . I am glad to say that I have never been ashamed to be thus designated."[3] Douglass' attitude toward his baiters may well have been inspired by his knowledge that white women had been called "nigger-lovers" in an attempt to lure them out of the anti-slavery campaign. And he knew that women were indispensable within the abolitionist movement—because of their numbers as well as "their efficiency in pleading the cause of the slave."[4]

Why did so many women join the anti-slavery movement? Was

there something special about abolitionism that attracted nineteenth-century white women as no other reform movement had
been able to do? Had these questions been posed to a leading
female abolitionist such as Harriet Beecher Stowe, she might have
argued that women's maternal instincts provided a *natural* basis
for their anti-slavery sympathies. This seems, at least, to be an
implication of her novel *Uncle Tom's Cabin*, [5] whose abolitionist
appeal was answered by vast numbers of women.

When Stowe published *Uncle Tom's Cabin*, the nineteenth-
century cult of motherhood was in full swing. As portrayed in the
press, in the new popular literature and even in the courts of law,
the perfect woman was the perfect mother. Her place was at
home—never, of course, in the sphere of politics. In Stowe's
novel, slaves, for the most part, are represented as sweet, loving,
defenseless, if sometimes naughty children. Uncle Tom's "gentle
domestic heart" was, so Stowe wrote, "the peculiar characteristic
of his race."[6] *Uncle Tom's Cabin* is pervaded with assumptions
of both Black and female inferiority. Most Black people are docile
and domestic, and most women are mothers and little else. As
ironic as it may seem, the most popular piece of anti-slavery
literature of that time perpetuated the racist ideas which justified
slavery and the sexist notions which justified the exclusion of
women from the political arena where the battle against slavery
would be fought.

The glaring contradiction between the reactionary content and
the progressive appeal of *Uncle Tom's Cabin* was not so much a
flaw in the author's individual perspective as a reflection of the
contradictory nature of women's status in the nineteenth century.
During the first decades of the century the industrial revolution
caused U.S. society to undergo a profound metamorphosis. In the
process, the circumstances of white women's lives were radically
changed. By the 1830s many of women's traditional economic
tasks were being taken over by the factory system. True, they were

freed from some of their old oppressive jobs. Yet the incipient industrialization of the economy was simultaneously eroding women's prestige in the home—a prestige based on their previously *productive* and absolutely essential domestic labor. Their social status began to deteriorate accordingly. An ideological consequence of industrial capitalism was the shaping of a more rigorous notion of female inferiority. It seemed, in fact, that the more women's domestic duties shrank under the impact of industrialization, the more rigid became the assertion that "woman's place is in the home."[7]

Actually, woman's place had always been in the home, but during the pre-industrial era, the economy itself had been centered in the home and its surrounding farmland. While men had tilled the land (often aided by their wives), the women had been manufacturers, producing fabric, clothing, candles, soap and practically all the other family necessities. Women's place had indeed been in the home—but not simply because they bore and reared children or ministered to their husbands' needs. They had been productive workers within the home economy and their labor had been no less respected than their men's. When manufacturing moved out of the home and into the factory, the ideology of womanhood began to raise the wife and mother as ideals. As workers, women had at least enjoyed economic equality, but as wives, they were destined to become appendages to their men, servants to their husbands. As mothers, they would be defined as passive vehicles for the replenishment of human life. The situation of the white housewife was full of contradictions. There was bound to be resistance.[8]

The turbulent 1830s were years of intense resistance. Nat Turner's revolt, toward the beginning of the decade, unequivocally announced that Black men and women were profoundly dissatisfied with their lot as slaves and were determined, more than ever, to resist. In 1831, the year of Nat Turner's revolt, the organized abolitionist movement was born. The early thirties also brought "turn-outs" and strikes to the Northeastern textile factories, operated largely by young women and children. Around the same time, more prosperous white women began to fight for the right to education and for access to careers outside their homes.[9]

White women in the North—the middle-class housewife as well as the young "mill girl"—frequently invoked the metaphor of slavery as they sought to articulate their respective oppressions. Well-situated women began to denounce their unfulfilling domestic lives by defining marriage as a form of slavery. For working women, the economic oppression they suffered on the job bore a strong ressemblance to slavery. When the mill women in Lowell, Massachusetts, went out on strike in 1836, they marched through the town, singing:

Oh, I cannot be a slave,
I will not be a slave.
Oh, I'm so fond of liberty,
I will not be a slave.[10]

As between women who were workers and those who came from prosperous middle-class families, the former certainly had more legitimate grounds for comparing themselves to slaves. Although they were nominally free, their working conditions and low wages were so exploitative as to automatically invite the comparison with slavery. Yet it was the women of means who invoked the analogy of slavery most literally in their effort to express the oppressive nature of marriage.[11] During the first half of the nineteenth century the idea that the age-old, established institution of marriage could be oppressive was somewhat novel. The early feminists may well have described marriage as "slavery" of the same sort Black people suffered primarily for the shock value of the comparison—fearing that the seriousness of their protest might otherwise be missed. They seem to have ignored, however, the fact that their identification of the two institutions also implied that slavery was really no worse than marriage. But even so, the most important implication of this comparison was that white middle-class women felt a certain affinity with Black women and men, for whom slavery meant whips and chains.

During the 1830s white women—both housewives and workers —were actively drawn into the abolitionist movement. While mill women contributed money from their meager wages and organized bazaars to raise further funds, the middle-class women became agitators and organizers in the anti-slavery campaign.[12] By 1833, when the Philadelphia Female Anti-Slavery Society was born in the wake of the founding convention of the American Anti-Slavery Society, enough white women were manifesting their sympathetic attitudes toward the Black people's cause to have established the basis for a bond between the two oppressed groups.* In a widely publicized event that year, a young white woman emerged as a dramatic model of female courage and anti-racist militancy. Prudence Crandall was a teacher who defied her white townspeople in Canterbury, Connecticut, by accepting a Black girl into her school.[13] Her principled and unyielding stand throughout the entire controversy symbolized the possibility of forging a powerful alliance between the established struggle for Black Liberation and the embryonic battle for women's rights.

The parents of the white girls attending Prudence Crandall's school expressed their unanimous opposition to the Black pupil's presence by organizing a widely publicized boycott. But the Connecticut teacher refused to capitulate to their racist demands. Following the advice of Mrs. Charles Harris—a Black woman she employed—Crandall decided to recruit more Black girls, and if

*The first female anti-slavery society was formed by Black women in 1832 in Salem, Massachusetts.

necessary, to operate an all-Black school. A seasoned abolitionist,
Mrs. Harris introduced Crandall to William Lloyd Garrison, who
published announcements about the school in the *Liberator*, his
anti-slavery journal. The Canterbury townspeople countered by
passing a resolution in opposition to her plans which proclaimed
that "the government of the United States, the nation with all
its institutions of right belong to the white men who now possess
them."[14] No doubt they did mean white *men* quite literally, for
Prudence Crandall had not only violated their code of racial
segregation, she had also defied the traditional attitudes concerning the conduct of a *white lady*.

> Despite all threats, Prudence Crandall opened the school . . . The
> Negro students stood bravely by her side.
>   And then followed one of the most heroic—and most shameful
> —episodes in American history. The storekeepers refused to sell
> supplies to Miss Crandall. . . . The village doctor would not attend
> ailing students. The druggist refused to give medicine. On top of
> such fierce inhumanity, rowdies smashed the school windows,
> threw manure in the well and started several fires in the building.[15]

Where did this young Quaker woman find her extraordinary
strength and her astonishing ability to persevere in a dangerous
situation of daily siege? Probably through her bonds with the
Black people whose cause she so ardently defended. Her school
continued to function until Connecticut authorities ordered her
arrest.[16] By the time she was arrested, Prudence Crandall had
made such a mark on the epoch that even in apparent defeat, she
emerged as a symbol of victory.
   The Canterbury, Connecticut, events of 1833 erupted at the
beginning of a new era. Like Nat Turner's revolt, like the birth
of Garrison's *Liberator* and like the founding of the first national
anti-slavery organization, these events announced the advent of

an epoch of fierce social struggles. Prudence Crandall's unswerv-
ing defense of Black people's right to learn was a dramatic example—a more powerful example than ever could have been
imagined—for white women who were suffering the birth pangs
of political consciousness. Lucidly and eloquently, her actions
spoke of vast possibilities for liberation if white women en masse
would join hands with their Black sisters.

> Let Southern oppressors tremble—let their Northern apologists
> tremble—let all the enemies of the persecuted Blacks tremble
> . . . Urge me not to use moderation in a cause like the present. I
> am in earnest—I will not equivocate—I will not excuse—I will not
> retreat a single inch—and *I will be heard.* [17]

This uncompromising declaration was William Lloyd Garrison's
personal statement to readers of the first issue of the *Liberator.*
By 1833, two years later, this pioneering abolitionist journal had
developed a significant readership, which consisted of a large
group of Black subscribers and increasing numbers of whites.
Prudence Crandall and others like her were loyal supporters of the
paper. But white working women were also among those who
readily agreed with Garrison's militant anti-slavery position. Indeed, once the anti-slavery movement was organized, factory
women lent decisive support to the abolitionist cause. Yet the
most visible white female figures in the anti-slavery campaign
were women who were not compelled to work for wages. They
were the wives of doctors, lawyers, judges, merchants, factory
owners—in other words, women of the middle classes and the
rising bourgeoisie.

   In 1833 many of these middle-class women had probably begun
to realize that something had gone terribly awry in their lives. As
"housewives" in the new era of industrial capitalism, they had lost
their economic importance in the home, and their social status

as women had suffered a corresponding deterioration. In the process, however, they had acquired leisure time, which enabled them to become social reformers—active organizers of the abolitionist campaign. Abolitionism, in turn, conferred upon these women the opportunity to launch an implicit protest against their oppressive roles at home.

Only four women were invited to attend the 1833 founding convention of the American Anti-Slavery Society. The male organizers of this Philadelphia meeting stipulated, moreover, that they were to be "listeners and spectators"[18] rather than full-fledged participants. This did not deter Lucretia Mott—one of the four women—from audaciously addressing the men at the convention on at least two occasions. At the opening session, she confidently arose from her "listener and spectator" seat in the balcony and argued against a motion to postpone the gathering because of the absence of a prominent Philadelphia man:

> Right principles are stronger than names. If our principles are right, why should we be cowards? Why should we wait for those who never have had the courage to maintain the inalienable rights of the slave?[19]

A practicing Quaker minister, Lucretia Mott undoubtedly astounded the all-male audience, for in those days women never spoke out at public gatherings.[20] Although the convention applauded her and moved on to its business as she suggested, at the conclusion of the meeting neither she nor the other women were invited to sign the Declaration of Sentiments and Purposes. Whether the women's signatures were expressly disallowed or whether it simply did not occur to the male leaders that women should be asked to sign, the men were extremely short-sighted. Their sexist attitudes prevented them from grasping the vast potential of women's involvement in the anti-slavery movement.

Lucretia Mott, who was not so short-sighted, organized the founding meeting of the Philadelphia Female Anti-Slavery Society in the immediate aftermath of the men's convention.[21] She was destined to become a leading public figure in the anti-slavery movement, a woman who would be extensively admired for her overall courage and for her steadfastness in the face of raging racist mobs.

> In 1838, this frail-looking woman, dressed in the sober, starched garb of the Quakers, calmly faced the pro-slavery mob that burned down Pennsylvania Hall with the connivance of the mayor of Philadelphia.[22]

Mott's commitment to abolitionism involved other dangers, for her Philadelphia home was a well-traveled Underground Railroad station, where such renowned fugitives as Henry "Box" Brown stopped off during the northward journey. On one occasion, Lucretia Mott herself assisted a slave woman to escape in a carriage under armed guard.[23]

Like Lucretia Mott, many other white women with no previous political experience joined the abolitionist movement and literally received their baptism in fire. A pro-slavery mob burst into a meeting chaired by Maria Chapman Weston and dragged its speaker—William Lloyd Garrison—through the streets of Boston. A leader of the Boston Female Anti-Slavery Society, Weston realized that the white mob sought to isolate and perhaps violently attack the Black women in attendance, and thus insisted that each white woman leave the building with a Black woman at her side.[24] The Boston Female Anti-Slavery Society was one of the numerous women's groups that sprang up in New England immediately after Lucretia Mott founded the Philadelphia society. If the number of women who were subsequently assaulted by racist mobs or who otherwise risked their lives could actually be determined, the figures would no doubt be astoundingly large.

As they worked within the abolitionist movement, white women learned about the nature of human oppression—and in the process, also learned important lessons about their own subjugation. In asserting their right to oppose slavery, they protested —sometimes overtly, sometimes implicitly—their own exclusion from the political arena. If they did not yet know how to present their own grievances collectively, at least they could plead the cause of a people who were also oppressed.

The anti-slavery movement offered women of the middle class the opportunity to prove their worth according to standards that were not tied to their role as wives and mothers. In this sense, the abolitionist campaign was a home where they could be valued for their concrete *works*. Indeed, their political involvement in the battle against slavery may have been as intense, as passionate and as total as it was because they were experiencing an exciting alternative to their domestic lives. And they were resisting an oppression which bore a certain resemblance to their own. Furthermore, they learned how to challenge male supremacy within the anti-slavery movement. They discovered that sexism, which seemed unalterable inside their marriages, could be questioned and fought in the arena of political struggle. Yes, white women would be called upon to defend fiercely their rights *as women* in order to fight for the emancipation of Black people.

As Eleanor Flexner's outstanding study of the women's movement reveals, women abolitionists accumulated invaluable political experiences, without which they could not have effectively organized the campaign for women's rights more than a decade later.[25] Women developed fund-raising skills, they learned how to distribute literature, how to call meetings—and some of them even became strong public speakers. Most important of all, they became efficient in the use of the petition, which would become the central tactical weapon of the women's rights campaign. As they petitioned against slavery, women were compelled simultaneously to champion their own right to engage in political work. How else could they convince the government to accept the signatures of voteless women if not by aggressively disputing the validity of their traditional exile from political activity? And, as Flexner insists, it was necessary

> . . . for the average housewife, mother, or daughter to overstep the limits of decorum, disregard the frowns, or jeers, or outright commands of her menfolk and . . . take her first petition and walk down an unfamiliar street, knocking on doors and asking for signatures to an unpopular plea. Not only would she be going out unattended by husband or brother; but she usually encountered hostility, if not outright abuse for her unwomanly behavior.[26]

Of all the pioneering women abolitionists, it was the Grimke sisters from South Carolina—Sarah and Angelina—who most consistently linked the issue of slavery to the oppression of women. From the beginning of their tumultuous lecturing career, they were compelled to defend their rights as women to be public advocates of abolition—and by implication to defend the rights of all women to register publicly their opposition to slavery.

Born into a South Carolina slaveholding family, the Grimke sisters developed a passionate abhorrence of the "peculiar institution" and decided, as adults, to move North. Joining the abolitionist effort in 1836, they began to lecture in New England about their own lives and their daily encounters with the untold evils of slavery. Although the gatherings were sponsored by the female anti-slavery societies, increasing numbers of men began to attend. "Gentlemen, hearing of their eloquence and power, soon began timidly to slip into the back seats."[27] These assemblies were unprecedented, for no other women had ever addressed mixed audiences on such a regular basis without facing derogatory cries and disruptive jeers hurled by men who felt that public speaking should be an exclusively male activity.

While the men attending the Grimkes' meetings were undoubtedly eager to learn from the women's experiences, the sisters were vengefully attacked by other male forces. The most devastating attack came from religious quarters: on July 28, 1837, the Council of Congregationalist Ministers of Massachusetts issued a pastoral letter severely chastising them for engaging in activities which subverted women's divinely ordained role:

> The power of woman is her dependence, flowing from the consciousness of that weakness which God has given her for her protection . . .[28]

According to the ministers, the Grimkes' actions had created "dangers which at present threaten the female character with wide-spread and permanent injury."[29] Moreover,

> We appreciate the unostentatious prayers of woman in advancing the cause of religion. . . . But when she assumes the place and tone of man as a public reformer . . . , she yields the power which God has given her for her protection, and her character becomes unnatural. If the vine, whose strength and beauty is to lean on the trelliswork, and half conceal its cluster, thinks to assume the independence and overshadowing nature of the elm, it will not only cease to bear fruit, but fall in shame and dishonor into the dust.[30]

Framed by the largest Protestant denomination in Massachusetts, this pastoral letter had immense repercussions. If the ministers were correct, then Sarah and Angelina Grimke were committing the worst of all possible sins: they were challenging God's will. The echoes of this assault did not begin to fade until the Grimkes finally decided to terminate their lecturing career.

Neither Sarah nor Angelina had originally been concerned—
at least not expressly—about questioning the social inequality of
women. Their main priority had been to expose the inhuman and
immoral essence of the slave system and the special responsibility
women bore for its perpetuation. But once the male supremacist
attacks against them were unleashed, they realized that unless
they defended themselves as women—and the rights of women in general—they would be forever barred from the campaign to free the slaves. The more powerful orator of the two,
Angelina Grimke challenged this assault on women in her lectures. Sarah, who was the theoretical genius, began a series
of letters on *The Equality of the Sexes and the Condition
of Women.* [31]

Completed in 1838, Sarah Grimke's "Letters on the Equality
of the Sexes . . ." contain one of the first extensive analyses of the
status of women authored by a woman in the United States.
Setting down her ideas six years before the publication of Margaret Fuller's well-known treatise on women, Sarah disputed the
assumption that inequality between the sexes was commanded by
God. "Men and women were created equal: they are both moral
and accountable human beings."[32] She directly contested the
ministers' charge that women who seek to give leadership to social
reform movements were unnatural, insisting instead that "whatever is right for man is right for woman."[33]

The writings and lectures of these two outstanding sisters were
enthusiastically received by many of the women who were active in the female anti-slavery movement. But some of the
leading men in the abolitionist campaign claimed that
the issue of women's rights would confuse and alienate those
who were solely concerned about the defeat of slavery. Angelina's early response spelled out her (and her sister's) understanding of the strong threads tying women's rights to abolitionism:

We cannot push Abolitionism forward with all our might untill we take up the stumbling block out of the road. . . . (T)o meet this question may appear to be turning out of the road. . . . It is not: we must meet it and meet it now. . . . Why, my dear brothers, can you not see the deep laid scheme of the clergy against us as lecturers? . . . If we surrender the right to speak in public this year, we must surrender the right to petition next year and the right to write the year after, and so on. What then can woman do for the slave, when she herself is under the feet of man and shamed into silence?[34]

An entire decade before white women's mass opposition to the ideology of male supremacy received its organizational expression, the Grimke sisters urged women to resist the destiny of passivity and dependence which society had imposed upon them—in order to take their rightful place in the struggle for justice and human rights. Angelina's 1837 *Appeal to the Women of the Nominally Free States* forcefully argues this point:

It is related of Buonaparte, that he one day rebuked a French lady for busying herself with politics. "Sire," replied she, "in a country where *women* are put to death, it is very natural that *women* should wish to know the reason why." And, dear sisters, in a country where women are degraded and brutalized, and where their exposed persons bleed under the lash—where they are sold in the shambles of "negro brokers"—robbed of their heard earnings—torn from their husbands, and forcibly plundered of their virtue and their offspring; surely in *such* a country, it is very natural that *women* should wish to know "the reason *why*"—especially when these outrages of blood and nameless horror are practiced in violation of the principles of our Constitution. We do not, then, and cannot concede the position, that because this is a *political subject* women ought to fold their hands in idleness, and close their eyes and ears to the "horrible things" that are practiced in our land. The denial of our duty to

act is a bold denial of our right to act; and if we have no right to
act, then may *we* well be termed "the white slaves of the North"
—for like our brethren in bonds, we must seal our lips in silence
and despair.[35]

The above passage is also an illustration of the Grimke sisters'
insistence that white women in the North and South acknowledge the special bond linking them with Black women who suffered the pain of slavery. Again:

> They are our country women—*they are our sisters;* and to us, as
> women, they have a right to look for sympathy with their sorrows,
> and effort and prayer for their rescue.[36]

"The question of equality for women," as Eleanor Flexner put
it, was not "a matter of abstract justice" for the Grimkes, "but
of enabling women to join in an urgent task."[37] Since the abolition of slavery was the most pressing political necessity of the
times, they urged women to join in that struggle with the understanding that their own oppression was nurtured and perpetuated
by the continued existence of the slave system. Because the
Grimke sisters had such a profound consciousness of the insepara-
bility of the fight for Black Liberation and the fight for Women's
Liberation, they were never caught in the ideological snare of
insisting that one struggle was absolutely more important than the
other. They recognized the dialectical character of the relationship between the two causes.

More than any other women in the campaign against slavery,
the Grimkes urged the constant inclusion of the issue of women's
rights. At the same time they argued that women could never
achieve their freedom independently of Black people. "I want to
be identified with the Negro," said Angelina to a convention of
patriotic women supporting the Civil War effort in 1863. "Until

he gets his rights, we shall never have ours."[38] Prudence Crandall had risked her life in defense of Black children's right to education. If her stand contained a promise of a fruitful and powerful alliance, bringing Black people and women together in order to realize their common dream of liberation, then the analysis presented by Sarah and Angelina Grimke was the most profound and most moving theoretical expression of that promise of unity.

3 ～ Class and Race in the Early Women's Rights Campaign

As Lucretia Mott and Elizabeth Cady Stanton wended their way arm in arm down great Queen Street that night, reviewing the exciting scenes of the day, they agreed to hold a woman's rights convention on their return to America, as the men to whom they had just listened had manifested their great need of some education on that question. Thus the missionary work for the emancipation of woman in "the land of the free and the home of the brave" was then and there inaugurated.[1]

This conversation, which took place in London on the opening day of the 1840 World Anti-Slavery Convention, is frequently assumed to contain the real story behind the birth of the organized women's movement in the United States. As such, it has acquired a somewhat legendary significance. And like most legends, the truth it presumes to embody is far less unequivocal than it appears. This anecdote and its surrounding circumstances have been made the basis of a popular interpretation of the women's rights movement as having been primarily inspired—or rather provoked—by the insufferable male supremacy within the anti-slavery campaign.

No doubt the U.S. women who had expected to participate in the London conference were quite furious when they found themselves excluded by majority vote, "fenced off behind a bar and a curtain similar to those used in churches to screen the choir from public gaze."[2] Lucretia Mott, like the other women officially representing the American Anti-Slavery Society, had further cause for anger and indignation. For she had just recently emerged from a turbulent struggle around the issue of female abolitionists' right to participate on a basis of full equality in the work of the Anti-Slavery Society. Yet for a woman who had been excluded from membership in the Society some seven years previously, this was no new experience. If she was indeed inspired to fight for women's rights by the London events—by the fact that, as two contemporary feminist authors put it, "the leading male radicals, those most concerned with social inequalities . . . also discriminate against women"[3]—it was an inspiration that had struck her long before 1840.

Unlike Lucretia Mott, Elizabeth Cady Stanton was not an experienced political activist when the London convention took place. Accompanying her husband of only several weeks on what she called their "wedding journey",[4] she was attending her first anti-slavery meeting not as a delegate but, rather, as the wife of an abolitionist leader. Mrs. Stanton was thus somewhat handicapped, lacking the perspective forged by years of struggle in defense of women's right to contribute to the anti-slavery cause. When she wrote (along with Susan B. Anthony, in their *History of Woman Suffrage*) that during her conversation in 1840 with Lucretia Mott, "a missionary work for the emancipation of women . . . was then and there inaugurated,"[5] her remarks did not account for the accumulated lessons wrought by almost a decade during which abolitionist women had battled for their political emancipation as women.

Although they were defeated at the London convention, the abolitionist women did discover evidence that their past struggles had achieved a few positive results. For they were supported by some of the male anti-slavery leaders, who opposed the move to

exclude them. William Lloyd Garrison—"brave noble Garrison"[6]
—who arrived too late to participate in the debate, refused to take
his seat, remaining during the entire ten-day convention "a silent
spectator in the gallery."[7] According to Elizabeth Cady Stanton's
account, Nathaniel P. Rogers of Concord, New Hampshire, was
the only other male abolitionist who joined the women in the
gallery.[8] Why the Black abolitionist Charles Remond is not mentioned in Stanton's description of the events is rather puzzling.
He was also, as he himself wrote in an article published in the
Liberator, "a silent listener."[9]

Charles Remond wrote that he experienced one of the few
great disappointments of his life when he discovered, upon his
arrival, that the women had been excluded from the convention
floor. He had good reason to feel distressed, for his own travel
expenses had been paid by several women's groups.

> I was almost entirely indebted to the kind and generous members
> of the Bangor Female Anti-Slavery Society, the Portland Sewing
> Circle, and the Newport Young Ladies' Juvenile Anti-Slavery Soci-
> ety, for aid in visiting this country.[10]

Remond felt compelled to refuse his seat in the convention,
because he could not otherwise be the "honored representative of
the three female associations, at once most praiseworthy in their
object and efficient in this cooperation."[11] Not all of the men,
therefore, were the "bigoted Abolitionists"[12] to whom Stanton
refers in her historical account. At least some of them had learned
to detect and challenge the injustices of male supremacy.

Whereas Elizabeth Cady Stanton's interest in abolitionism was
quite recent, she had conducted a personal fight against sexism
throughout her youth. Encouraged by her father—a wealthy and
unabashedly conservative judge—she had defied orthodoxy in her
studies as well as in her leisure activities. She studied Greek and

mathematics and learned horseback riding, all of which were generally barred to girls. At age sixteen, Elizabeth was the only girl in her high school graduating class.[13] Before her marriage, the young Stanton passed much of her time with her father and had even begun to study the law seriously under his guidance.

By 1848 Stanton was a full-time housewife and mother. Living with her husband in Seneca Falls, New York, she was often unable to hire servants because they were so scarce in that area. Her own anticlimactic and frustrating life made her especially sensitive to the middle-class white woman's predicament. In explaining her decision to contact Lucretia Mott, whom she had not seen for eight years, she mentioned her domestic situation first among her several motives for issuing a call to a women's convention.

> The general discontent I felt with woman's portion as wife, mother, housekeeper, physician and spiritual guide . . . and the wearied, anxious look of the majority of women, impressed me with the strong feeling that some active measures should be taken to remedy the wrongs of society in general and of women in particular. My experiences at the World Anti-Slavery Convention, all I had read of the legal status of women, and the oppression I saw everywhere, together swept across my soul, intensified now by many personal experiences. It seemed as if all the elements had conspired to impel me to some onward step. I could not see what to do or where to begin—my only thought was a public meeting for protest and discussion.[14]

Elizabeth Cady Stanton's life exhibited all the basic elements, in their most contradictory form, of the middle-class woman's dilemma. Her diligent efforts to achieve excellence in her studies, the knowledge she had gained as a law student, and all the other ways she had cultivated her intellectual powers—all this had come to naught. Marriage and motherhood precluded the achievement of the goals she had set for herself as a single woman. Moreover, her involvement in the abolitionist movement during the years following the London convention had taught her that it was possible to organize a political challenge to oppression. Many of the women who would answer the call to attend the first women's rights convention in Seneca Falls were becoming conscious of similar contradictions in their lives and had likewise seen, from the example of the anti-slavery struggle, that it was possible to fight for equality.

As the Seneca Falls Convention was being planned, Elizabeth Cady Stanton proposed a resolution which appeared too radical even to her co-conventioner Lucretia Mott. Although Mrs. Mott's experiences in the anti-slavery movement had certainly persuaded her that women urgently needed to exercise political power, she opposed the introduction of a resolution on woman suffrage. Such a move would be interpreted as absurd and outrageous, she thought, and would consequently undermine the importance of the meeting. Stanton's husband also opposed the raising of the suffrage issue—and kept his promise to leave town if she insisted on presenting the resolution. Frederick Douglass was the only prominent figure who agreed that the convention should call for women's right to vote.

Several years before the Seneca Falls meeting, Elizabeth Cady Stanton had firmly convinced Frederick Douglass that the vote should be extended to women.

> I could not meet her arguments except with the shallow plea of "custom," "natural division of duties," "indelicacy of woman's taking part in politics," the common talk of "woman's sphere," and the like, all of which that able woman, who was then no less logical than now, brushed away by those arguments which she has so often and effectively used since and which no man has successfully

refuted. If intelligence is the only true and rational basis of government, it follows that that is the best government which draws its life and power from the largest sources of wisdom, energy and goodness at its command.[15]

Among the approximately three hundred women and men attending the Seneca Falls Convention, the issue of electoral power for women was the only major point of contention: the suffrage resolution alone was not unanimously endorsed. That the controversial proposal was presented at all, however, was due to Frederick Douglass' willingness to second Stanton's motion and to employ his oratorical abilities in defense of women's right to vote.[16]

During those early days when women's rights was not yet a legitimate cause, when woman suffrage was unfamiliar and unpopular as a demand, Frederick Douglass publicly agitated for the political equality of women. In the immediate aftermath of the Seneca Falls Convention, he published an editorial in his newspaper, the *North Star.* Entitled "The Rights of Women," its content was quite radical for the times:

> In respect to political rights, we hold woman to be justly entitled to all we claim for men. We go further, and express our conviction that all political rights which it is expedient for men to exercise, it is equally so for woman. All that distinguishes man as an intelligent and accountable being, is equally true of woman, and if that government only is just which governs by the free consent of the governed, there can be no reason in the world for denying to woman the exercise of the elective franchise, or a hand in making and administering the law of the land.[17]

Frederick Douglass was also responsible for officially introducing the issue of women's rights to the Black Liberation movement, where it was enthusiastically welcomed. As S. Jay Walker points

out, Douglass spoke out at the National Convention of Colored
Freedmen that was held in Cleveland, Ohio, around the time of
the Seneca Falls meeting:

> He succeeded in amending a resolution defining delegates so that
> it would be "understood 'to include *women,*'" an amendment that
> was carried "with three cheers for women's rights!"[18]

Elizabeth Cady Stanton devoted expressions of praise to
Douglass for his steadfast defense of the Seneca Falls Convention
in face of the widespread ridicule voiced in the press.

> So pronounced was the popular voice against us, in the parlor, press
> and pulpit, that most of the ladies who had attended the conven-
> tion and signed the declaration, one by one withdrew their names
> and influence and joined our persecutors. Our friends gave us the
> cold shoulder and felt themselves disgraced by the whole proceed-
> ing.[19]

The uproar did not dissuade Douglass, nor did it achieve its goal
of nipping the battle for women's rights in the bud. Parlor, press
and pulpit, try as they might, could not reverse this trend. Only
one month passed before another convention took place in
Rochester, New York—whose daring innovation and precedent
for future meetings was a female presiding officer.[20] Frederick
Douglass again manifested his loyalty to his sisters by arguing
once more for the suffrage resolution, which passed in Rochester
by a much larger margin than at Seneca Falls.[21]

The advocacy of women's rights could not be forbidden. Not
yet acceptable to the makers of public opinion, the issue of
women's equality, now embodied in an embryonic movement,
supported by Black people who were fighting for their own freedom, established itself as an indelible element of public life in the

United States. But what was it all about? How was the question of women's equality defined other than by the suffrage issue which had prompted the derogatory publicity about the Seneca Falls Convention? Were the grievances outlined in the Declaration of Sentiments and the demands put forth in the resolutions truly reflective of the problems and needs of the women of the United States?

The emphatic focus of the Seneca Falls Declaration was the institution of marriage and its many injurious effects on women: marriage robbed women of their property rights, making wives economically—as well as morally—dependent on their husbands. Demanding absolute obedience from wives, the institution of marriage gave husbands the right to punish their wives, and what is more, the laws of separation and divorce were almost entirely based on male supremacy.[22] As a result of women's inferior status within marriage, the Seneca Falls Declaration argued, they suffered inequalities in educational institutions as well as in the professions. "Profitable employments" and "all avenues to wealth and distinction" (such as medicine, law and theology) were absolutely inaccessible to women.[23] The Declaration concludes its list of grievances with an evocation of women's mental and psychological dependence, which has left them with little "confidence and self-respect."[24]

The inestimable importance of the Seneca Falls Declaration was its role as the *articulated consciousness of women's rights* at midcentury. It was the theoretical culmination of years of unsure, often silent, challenges aimed at a political, social, domestic and religious condition which was contradictory, frustrating and downright oppressive for women of the bourgeoisie and the rising middle classes. However, as a rigorous consummation of the consciousness of white middle-class women's dilemma, the Declaration all but ignored the predicament of white working-class women, as it ignored the condition of Black women in the South and North alike. In other words, the Seneca Falls Declaration proposed an analysis of the female condition which disregarded the circumstances of women outside the social class of the document's framers.

But what about those women who *worked* for a living—the white women, for example, who operated the textile mills in the Northeast? In 1831, when the textile industry was still the major focus of the new industrial revolution, women comprised the undisputed majority of industrial workers. In the textile mills, scattered throughout New England, there were 38,927 women workers as compared to 18,539 men.[25] The pioneering "mill girls" had been recruited from local farm families. The profit-seeking millowners represented life in the mills as an attractive and instructive prelude to married life. Both the Waltham and Lowell systems were portrayed as "surrogate families" where the young farm women would be rigorously supervised by matrons in an atmosphere akin to the finishing school. But what was the reality of mill life? Incredibly long hours—twelve, fourteen or even sixteen hours daily; atrocious working conditions; inhumanly crowded living quarters; and

> So little time was allowed for meals—one half hour at noon for dinner—that the women raced from the hot, humid weaving room several blocks to their boarding houses, gulped down their main meal of the day, and ran back to the mill in terror of being fined if they were late. In winter they dared not stop to button their coats and often ate without taking them off. This was pneumonia season. In summer, spoiled food and poor sanitation led to dysentery. Tuberculosis was with them in every season.[26]

The mill women fought back. Beginning in the late 1820s—long before the 1848 Seneca Falls Convention—working women staged "turn-outs" and strikes, militantly protesting the double oppression they suffered as women and as industrial workers. In Dover, New Hampshire, for example, the mill women walked off the job in 1828 to dramatize their opposition to newly instituted restrictions. They "shocked the community by parading with banners and flags, shooting off gunpowder."[27]

By the summer of 1848, when the Seneca Falls Convention took place, conditions in the mills—hardly ideal to begin with— had deteriorated to such an extent that the New England farmers' daughters were fast becoming a minority in the textile labor force. Replacing the women from "well-born," "Yankee" backgrounds were immigrant women who, like their fathers, brothers and husbands, were becoming the industrial proletariat of the nation. These women—unlike their predecessors, whose families owned land—had nothing to rely upon but their labor power. When they resisted, they were fighting for their right to survive. They fought so passionately that "in the 1840's, women workers were in the leadership of labor militancy in the United States."[28]

Campaigning for the ten-hour day, the Lowell Female Labor Reform Association presented petitions to the Massachusetts State Legislature in 1843 and 1844. When the Legislature agreed to hold public hearings, the Lowell women acquired the distinction of winning the very first investigation of labor conditions by a government body in the history of the United States.[29] This was clearly a blow for women's rights—and it predated, by four years, the official launching of the women's movement.

Judging from the struggles conducted by white working women —their relentless defense of their dignity as workers and as women, their conscious as well as implicit challenges to the sexist ideology of womanhood—they had more than earned the right to be lauded as pioneers of the women's movement. But their trailblazing role was all but ignored by the leading initiators of the new movement, who did not comprehend that women workers experienced and challenged male supremacy in their own special way. As if to drive this point home, history has imparted a final irony to the movement initiated in 1848: Of all the women attending the Seneca Falls Convention, the only one to live long enough to actually exercise her right to vote over seventy years later was a working woman by the name of Charlotte Woodward.[30]

Charlotte Woodward's motives for signing the Seneca Falls Declaration were hardly identical to those of the more prosperous women. Her purpose for attending the convention was to seek advice on improving her status as a worker. As a glovemaker, her occupation was not yet industrialized: she worked at home, receiving wages legally controlled by the men in her family. Describing the circumstances of her work, she expressed that spirit of rebellion which had brought her to Seneca Falls:

> We women work secretly in the seclusion of our bed chambers because all society was built on the theory that men, not women, earned money and that men alone supported the family . . . I do not believe that there was any community in which the souls of some women were not beating their wings in rebellion. For my own obscure self I can say that every fibre of my being rebelled, although silently, all the hours that I sat and sewed gloves for a miserable pittance which, as it was earned, could never be mine. I wanted to work, but I wanted to choose my task and I wanted to collect my wages. That was my form of rebellion against the life into which I was born.[31]

Charlotte Woodward and the several other working women present at the convention were serious—they were more serious about women's rights than about anything else in their lives.

At the last session of the convention, Lucretia Mott proposed a final resolution calling both for the overthrow of the pulpit and "for the securing to women *an equal participation with men in the various trades,* professions and commerce." [my emphasis][32] Was this a mere afterthought? A charitable gesture toward Charlotte Woodward and her working-class sisters? Or did the small contingent of working-class women protest the exclusion of their interests from the original resolutions, causing Lucretia Mott, the long-time anti-slavery activist, to stand up on their behalf? If Sarah Grimke had been present, she might have insisted, as she said on another occasion:

> There are in the poorer classes many strong honest hearts weary of being slaves and tools who are worthy of freedom and who will use it worthily.[33]

If the recognition accorded working women at the Seneca Falls meeting was all but negligible, there was not even a cursory mention of the rights of another group of women who also "rebelled against the lives into which they were born."[34] In the South they rebelled against slavery and in the North against a dubious condition of freedom called racism. While at least one Black man was present among the Seneca Falls conferees, there was not a single Black woman in attendance. Nor did the convention's documents make even a passing reference to Black women. In light of the organizers' abolitionist involvement, it would seem puzzling that slave women were entirely disregarded.

But this problem was not a new one. The Grimke sisters had previously criticized a number of female anti-slavery societies for ignoring the condition of Black women and for sometimes manifesting blatantly racist prejudices. During the preparations for the founding convention of the National Female Anti-Slavery Society, Angelina Grimke had to take the initiative to guarantee more than a token presence of Black women. Moreover, she suggested that a special address be delivered at that convention to the free Black people of the North. Since no one—not even Lucretia Mott

—would prepare the address, Angelina's sister Sarah had to deliver the speech.[35] As early as 1837 the Grimke sisters chastised the New York Female Anti-Slavery Society for failing to involve Black women in their work. "On account of their strong aristocratical feelings," Angelina regretfully said,

> . . . they were most exceedingly inefficient. . . . We have had serious thought of forming an Anti-Slavery Society among our colored sisters and getting them to invite their white friends to join them, in this way we think we could get the most efficient white females in the city to join them.[36]

The absence of Black women at the Seneca Falls Convention was all the more conspicuous in light of their previous contributions to the fight for women's rights. More than a decade before this meeting, Maria Stewart had responded to attacks on her right to deliver public lectures by emphatically asking, "What if I am a woman?"[37] This Black woman was the first native-born female lecturer who addressed audiences of both men and women.[38] And in 1827 *Freedom's Journal*—the first Black newspaper in this country—published a Black woman's letter on women's rights. "Matilda," as she identified herself, demanded education for Black women at a time when schooling for women was a controversial and quite unpopular issue. Her letter appeared in this pioneering New York journal the year before the Scottish-born Frances Wright began to lecture on equal education for women.

> I would address myself to all mothers, and say to them, that while it is necessary to possess a knowledge of pudding-making, something more is requisite. It is their bounden duty to store their daughters' minds with useful learning. They should be made to devote their leisure time to reading books, whence they would derive valuable information, which could never be taken from them.[39]

Long before the first women's convention, middle-class white women had struggled for the right to education. Matilda's comments—later confirmed by the ease with which Prudence Crandall recruited Black girls for her besieged school in Connecticut—demonstrated that white and Black women were indeed united in their desire for education. Unfortunately, this connection was not acknowledged during the convention at Seneca Falls.

The failure to recognize the potential for an integrated women's movement—particularly against sexism in education—was dramatically revealed in an episode occurring during the crucial summer of 1848. Ironically, it involved the daughter of Frederick Douglass. After her official admission to a girls' seminary in Rochester, New York, Douglass' daughter was formally prohibited from attending classes with the white girls. The principal who issued the order was an abolitionist woman! When Douglass and his wife protested this segregationist policy, the principal asked each white girl to vote on the issue, indicating that one objection would suffice to continue the exclusion. After the white girls voted in favor of integrating the classroom, the principal approached the girls' parents, using the one resulting objection as an excuse to exclude Douglass' daughter.[40]

That a white woman associated with the anti-slavery movement could assume a racist posture toward a Black girl in the North reflected a major weakness in the abolitionist campaign—its failure to promote a broad anti-racist consciousness. This serious shortcoming, abundantly criticized by the Grimke sisters and others, was unfortunately carried over into the organized movement for women's rights.

However oblivious the early women's rights activists may have been to the plight of their Black sisters, the echoes of the new women's movement were felt throughout the organized Black Liberation struggle. As mentioned above, the National Convention of Colored Freedmen passed a resolution on the equality of women in 1848.[41] Upon Frederick Douglass' initiative, this

Cleveland gathering had resolved that women should be elected delegates on an equal basis with men. Shortly thereafter, a convention of Negro people in Philadelphia not only invited Black women to participate, but in recognition of the new movement launched in Seneca Falls, also asked white women to join them. Lucretia Mott described her decision to attend in a letter to Elizabeth Cady Stanton:

> We are now in the midst of a convention of the colored people of the city. Douglass and Delany—Remond and Garnet are here—all taking an active part—and as they include women and *white* women too, I can do no less, with the interest I feel in the cause of the slave, as well as of woman, than be present and take a little part—So yesterday, in a pouring rain, Sarah Pugh and self walked down there and expect to do the same today.[42]

Two years after the Seneca Falls Convention, the first National Convention on Women's Rights was held in Worcester, Massachusetts. Whether she was actually invited or came on her own initiative, Sojourner Truth was among the participants. Her presence there and the speeches she delivered at subsequent women's rights meetings symbolized Black women's solidarity with the new cause. They aspired to be free not only from racist oppression but also from sexist domination. "Ain't I a Woman?"[43]—the refrain of the speech Sojourner Truth delivered at an 1851 women's convention in Akron, Ohio—remains one of the most frequently quoted slogans of the nineteenth-century women's movement.

Sojourner Truth single-handedly rescued the Akron women's meeting from the disruptive jeers of hostile men. Of all the women attending the gathering, she alone was able to answer aggressively the male supremacist arguments of the boisterous provocateurs. Possessing an undeniable charisma and powerful oratorical abilities, Sojourner Truth tore down the claims that female weakness was incompatible with suffrage—and she did this with irrefutable logic. The leader of the provocateurs had argued that it was ridiculous for women to desire the vote, since they could not even walk over a puddle or get into a carriage without the help of a man. Sojourner Truth pointed out with compelling simplicity that she herself had never been helped over mud puddles or into carriages. "And ain't I a woman?" With a voice like "rolling thunder,"[44] she said, "Look at me! Look at my arm," and rolled up her sleeve to reveal the "tremendous muscular power" of her arm.[45]

> I have ploughed, and planted, and gathered into barns and no man could head me! And ain't I a woman? I could work as much and eat as much as a man—when I could get it—and bear the lash as well! And ain't I a woman? I have borne thirteen children and seen them most all sold off to slavery, and when I cried out with my mother's grief, none but Jesus heard me! And ain't I a woman?[46]

As the only Black woman attending the Akron convention, Sojourner Truth had done what not one of her timid white sisters was capable of doing. According to the chairperson, "there were very few women in those days who dared to 'speak in meeting.' " Having powerfully pleaded the cause of her sex, having commanded the attention of the white women as well as their disruptive male adversaries, Sojourner Truth was spontaneously applauded as the hero of the day. She had not only dealt a crushing defeat to the men's "weaker sex" argument, but had also refuted their thesis that male supremacy was a Christian principle, since Christ himself was a man: *religion*

> That little man in black there, he says women can't have as much rights as men, because Christ wasn't a woman. Where did Christ come from?[47]

According to the presiding officer, "rolling thunder couldn't have stilled that crowd, as did those deep, wonderful tones, as she stood there with outstretched arms and eyes of fire."[48]

> Where did your Christ come from? From God and a woman! Man had nothing to do with him.[49]

As for the horrendous sin committed by Eve, this was hardly an argument against women's capabilities. On the contrary, it was an enormous plus:

> If the first woman God ever made was strong enough to turn the world upside down all alone, these women together ought to be able to get it right side up again! And now they are asking to do it, the men better let them.[50]

The men's belligerence was quieted and the women were bursting with pride, their "hearts beating with gratitude" and "more than one of us with streaming eyes."[51] Frances Dana Gage, the presiding officer of the Akron convention, continued her description of the impact of Sojourner Truth's speech:

> She had taken us up in her strong arms and carried us safely over the slough of difficulty, turning the whole tide in our favor. I have never in my life seen anything like the magical influence that subdued the mobbish spirit of the day, and turned the sneers and jeers of an excited crowd into notes of respect and admiration.[52]

Sojourner Truth's "Ain't I a Woman?" address had deeper implications, for it was also, it seems, a comment on the racist attitudes of the same white women who later praised their Black sister. Not a few of the Akron women had been initially opposed to a Black woman having a voice in their convention, and the anti-women's righters had tried to take advantage of this racism. In the words of Frances Dana Gage:

> The leaders of the movement trembled on seeing a tall, gaunt black woman in a gray dress and white turban, surmounted with an uncouth sunbonnet, march deliberately into the church, walk with the air of a queen up the aisle, and take her seat upon the pulpit steps. A buzz of disapprobation was heard all over the house, and there fell on the listening ear, "An abolition affair!" "I told you so!" "Go it, darkey!"[53]

On the second day of the convention, when Sojourner Truth rose to answer the male supremacist assault, leading white women attempted to persuade Gage to prevent her from speaking.

> "Don't let her speak!" gasped half a dozen in my ear. She moved slowly and solemnly to the front, laid her old bonnet at her feet, and turned her great speaking eyes to me. There was a hissing sound of disapprobation above and below. I rose and announced "Sojourner Truth," and begged the audience to keep silence for a few moments.[54]

Fortunately for the Ohio women, for the women's movement in general—for whom Sojourner Truth's speech established a militant fighting spirit—and for us today who still receive inspiration from her words, Frances Dana Gage did not succumb to these racist pressures of her comrades. When this Black woman did rise to speak, her answer to the male supremacists also contained a profound lesson for the white women. In repeating her question "Ain't I a woman?" no less than four times, she exposed the class-bias and racism of the new women's movement. All women were not white and all women did not enjoy the material comfort of the middle classes and the bourgeoisie. Sojourner

Truth herself was Black—she was an ex-slave—but she was no less a woman than any of her white sisters at the convention. That her race and her economic condition were different from theirs did not annul her womanhood. And as a Black woman, her claim to equal rights was no less legitimate than that of white middle-class women. At a national women's convention two years later, she was still fighting efforts to prevent her from speaking.

> I know that it feels a kind of hissing and tickling like to see a colored woman get up and tell you about things and Woman's Rights. We have all been thrown down so low that nobody thought we'd ever get up again; but we have been long enough trodden now; we will come up again, and now I am here.[55]

Throughout the 1850s local and national conventions attracted increasing numbers of women to the campaign for equality. It was never an unusual occurrence for Sojourner Truth to appear at these meetings, and despite inevitable hostility, to rise and have her say. In representing her Black sisters—both slave and "free" —she imparted a fighting spirit to the campaign for women's rights. This was Sojourner Truth's unique historical contribution. And in case white women tended to forget that Black women were no less women than they, her presence and her speeches served as a constant reminder. Black women were also going to get their rights.

Meanwhile, large numbers of Black women were manifesting their commitment to freedom and equality in ways that were less closely connected with the newly organized women's movement. The Underground Railroad claimed the energies of numerous Northern Black women. Jane Lewis, for example, a resident of New Lebanon, Ohio, regularly rowed her boat across the Ohio River, rescuing many a fugitive slave.[56] Frances E. W. Harper, a dedicated feminist and the most popular Black poet at midcentury, was one of the most active lecturers associated with the anti-slavery movement. Charlotte Forten, who became a leading Black educator during the post-Civil War period, was likewise an active abolitionist. Sarah Remond, who lectured against slavery in England, Ireland and Scotland, exercised a vast influence on public opinion, and according to one historian, "kept the Tories from intervening on the side of the Confederacy."[57]

Even the most radical white abolitionists, basing their opposition to slavery on moral and humanitarian grounds, failed to understand that the rapidly developing capitalism of the North was also an oppressive system. They viewed slavery as a detestable and inhuman institution, an archaic transgression of justice. But they did not recognize that the white worker in the North, his or her status as "free" laborer notwithstanding, was no different from the enslaved "worker" in the South: both were victims of economic exploitation. As militant as William Lloyd Garrison is supposed to have been, he was vehemently against wage laborers' right to organize. The inaugural issue of the *Liberator* included an article denouncing the efforts of Boston workers to form a political party:

> An attempt has been made—it is still in the making—we regret to say—to inflame the minds of our working classes against the more opulent, and to persuade men that they are condemned and oppressed by a wealthy aristocracy . . . It is in the highest degree criminal, therefore, to exasperate our mechanics to deeds of violence or to array them under a party banner.[58]

As a rule, white abolitionists either defended the industrial capitalists or expressed no conscious class loyalty at all. This unquestioning acceptance of the capitalist economic system was evident in the program of the women's rights movement as well. If most abolitionists viewed slavery as a nasty blemish which needed to be eliminated, most women's righters viewed male supremacy in a similar manner—as an immoral flaw in their otherwise acceptable society.

The leaders of the women's rights movement did not suspect that the enslavement of Black people in the South, the economic exploitation of Northern workers and the social oppression of women might be systematically related. Within the early women's movement, little was said about white working people —not even about white women workers. Though many of the women were supporters of the abolitionist campaign, they failed to integrate their anti-slavery consciousness into their analysis of women's oppression.

At the outbreak of the Civil War, the women's rights leaders were persuaded to redirect their energies toward a defense of the Union cause. But in suspending their agitation for sexual equality, they learned how deeply racism had planted itself in the soil of U.S. society. Elizabeth Cady Stanton, Lucretia Mott and Susan B. Anthony traveled throughout the state of New York delivering pro-Union lectures demanding "immediate and unconditional emancipation."[59]

> . . . and they received the roughest treatment of their lives at the hands of aroused mobs in every city where they stopped between Buffalo and Albany. In Syracuse the hall was invaded by a crowd of men brandishing knives and pistols.[60]

If they had not previously recognized that the South held no monopoly on racism, their experiences as agitators for the Union cause should have taught them that there was indeed racism in the North—and that it could be brutal.

When the military draft was instituted in the North, large-scale riots in major urban centers were fomented by pro-slavery forces.

They brought violence and death to the free Black population. In July, 1863, mobs in New York City

> . . . destroyed the recruiting stations, set fire to an armory, attacked the *Tribune* and prominent Republicans, burned a Negro orphan asylum, and generally created chaos throughout the city. The mobs directed their fury especially against the Negroes, assailing them wherever found. Many were murdered. . . . It is calculated that some 1,000 people were killed and wounded . . .[61]

If the degree to which the North itself was infected with racism had formerly gone unrecognized, the mob violence of 1863 demonstrated that anti-Black sentiment was deep and widespread and potentially murderous. If the South had a monopoly on slavery, it was certainly not alone in its sponsorship of racism.

Elizabeth Cady Stanton and Susan B. Anthony had agreed with the radical abolitionists that the Civil War could be hastily ended by emancipating the slaves and recruiting them into the Union Army. They attempted to rally masses of women to their position by issuing a call to organize a Women's Loyal League. At the founding meeting, hundreds of women agreed to promote the war effort by circulating petitions demanding the emancipation of the slaves. They were not so unanimous, however, in their response to Susan B. Anthony's resolution linking the rights of women to the liberation of Black people.

The proposed resolution stated that there can never be a true peace in this Republic until the "civil and political rights of all citizens of African descent and all women" are practically established.[62] Unfortunately, in light of the postwar developments, it appears that this resolution may have been motivated by the fear that (white) women might be left behind when the slaves emerged into the light of freedom. But Angelina Grimke proposed a principled defense of the unity between Black Liberation and Women's Liberation: "I want to be identified with the Negro," she insisted. "Until he gets his rights, we shall never have ours."[63]

> I rejoice exceedingly that the resolution should combine us with the Negro. I feel that we have been with him; that the iron has entered into our souls. True, we have not felt the slave-holder's lash! true we have not had our hands manacled, but our *hearts* have been crushed.[64]

At this founding convention of the Women's Loyal League—to which all the veterans of the abolitionist campaign and the women's rights movement were invited—Angelina Grimke characteristically proposed the most advanced interpretation of the war she described as "our second revolution."[65]

> The war is not, as the South falsely pretends, a war of races, nor of sections, nor of political parties, but a war of *Principles*, a war upon the working classes, whether white or black . . . In this war, the black man was the first victim, the workingman of whatever color the next; and now *all* who contend for the rights of labor, for free speech, free schools, free suffrage, and a free government . . . are driven to do battle in defense of these or to fall with them, victims of the same violence that for two centuries has held the black man a prisoner of war. While the South has waged this war against human rights, the North has stood by holding the garments of those who were stoning liberty to death . . .
>
> The nation is in a death-struggle. It must either become one vast slaveocracy of petty tyrants, or wholly the land of the free . . .[66]

Angelina Grimke's brilliant "Address to the Soldiers of Our Second Revolution" demonstrated that her political consciousness was far more advanced than most of her contemporaries. In her speech she proposed a radical theory and practice which *could have been realized* through an alliance embracing labor, Black people and women. If, as Karl Marx said, "labor in a white skin can never be free as long as labor in a black skin is branded," it was also true, as Angelina Grimke lucidly insisted, that the democratic struggles of the times—especially the fight for women's equality—could be most effectively waged in association with the struggle for Black Liberation.

4 ⌁ Racism in the Woman Suffrage Movement

Although this may remain a question for politicians to wrangle over for five or ten years, the black man is still, in a political point of view, far above the educated white women of the country. The representative women of the nation have done their uttermost for the last thirty years to secure freedom for the negro; and as long as he was lowest in the scale of being, we were willing to press his claims; but now, as the celestial gate to civil rights is slowly moving on its hinges, it becomes a serious question whether we had better stand aside and see "Sambo" walk into the kingdom first. As self-preservation is the first law of nature, would it not be wiser to keep our lamps trimmed and burning, and when the constitutional door is open, avail ourselves of the strong arm and blue uniform of the black soldier to walk in by his side, and thus make the gap so wide that no privileged class could ever again close it against the humblest citizen of the republic?

"This is the negro's hour." Are we sure that he, once entrenched in all his inalienable rights, may not be an added power to hold us at bay? Have not "black male citizens" been heard to say they doubted the wisdom of extending the right of suffrage to women? Why should the African prove more just and generous than his Saxon compeers? If the two millions of Southern black women are not to be secured the rights of person, property, wages and children, their emancipation is but another form of slavery. In fact, it is better to be the slave of an educated white man, than of a degraded, ignorant black one . . .[1]

This letter to the editor of the *New York Standard*, dated December 26, 1865, was authored by Elizabeth Cady Stanton. Its indisputably racist ideas indicate that Stanton's understanding of the relationship between the battle for Black Liberation and the struggle for women's rights was, at best, superficial. She was determined, it seems, to prevent further progress for Black people —for "Sambo" no less—if it meant that white women might not enjoy the immediate benefits of that progress.

The opportunistic and unfortunately racist line of reasoning in Stanton's letter to the *Standard* raises serious questions about the proposal to merge women's cause with the Black cause that was made at the first women's rights meeting since the eve of the Civil War. Held in New York City in May of 1866, the delegates to this women's rights convention decided to establish an Equal Rights Association incorporating the struggles for Black and woman suffrage into a single campaign. Many of the delegates no doubt understood the pressing need for unity—the kind of unity which would be mutually beneficial for Black people and women alike. Susan B. Anthony, for example, insisted that it was necessary ". . . to broaden our Woman's Rights platform and make it in *name* what it has always been in spirit—a Human Rights platform."[2] Yet the influence of racism in the convention's proceedings was unmistakable. In one of the major addresses to the gathering, the well-known abolitionist Henry Ward Beecher argued that white, native-born, educated women had far more compelling claims for suffrage than did Black people and immigrants, whom he portrayed in an obviously demeaning fashion:

> Now place this great army of refined and cultivated women on the one side, and on the other side the rising cloud of emancipated Africans, and in front of them the great emigrant band of the Emerald Isle, and is there force enough in our government to make it safe to give to the African and the Irishman the franchise? There

is. We shall give it to them. And will our force all fall, having done that? And shall we take the fairest and best part of our society, those to whom we owe it that we ourselves are civilized; our teachers; our companions; those to whom we go for counsel in trouble more than to any others; those to whom we trust everything that is dear to ourselves—our children's welfare, our household, our property, our name and reputation, and that which is deeper, our inward life itself, that no man may mention to more than one— shall we take them and say. "They are not, after all, fit to vote where the Irishman votes, and where the African votes?" . . .

. . . I say . . . *it is more important that women should vote* than that the black man should vote . . .[3]

Beecher's remarks reveal the deep ideological links between racism, class-bias and male supremacy, for the white women he praises are described in the language of the prevailing sexist stereotypes.

At the first annual meeting of the Equal Rights Association in May, 1867, Elizabeth Cady Stanton strongly echoed Henry Ward Beecher's argument that it was far more important for women (i.e., white Anglo-Saxon women) to receive the franchise than for Black men to win the vote.

With the black man, we have no new element in government, but with the education and elevation of women, we have a power that is to develop the Saxon race into a higher and nobler life and thus, by the law of attraction, to lift all races to a more even platform than can ever be reached in the political isolation of the sexes.[4]

The major issue at this convention was the impending enfranchisement of Black men—and whether the advocates of women's rights were willing to support Black suffrage even if women were unable to achieve the vote simultaneously. Elizabeth Cady Stanton and others who believed that because, in their eyes, emancipation had rendered Black people "equal" to white women, the vote would render Black men superior, were absolutely opposed to Black male suffrage. Yet there were those who understood that the abolition of slavery had not abolished the economic oppression of Black people, who therefore had a special and urgent need for political power. As Abby Kelly Foster disagreed with Stanton's logic, she asked this question:

> Have we any true sense of justice, are we not dead to the sentiment of humanity if we shall wish to postpone his security against present woes and future enslavement till woman shall obtain political rights?[5]

At the outbreak of the Civil War, Elizabeth Cady Stanton had urged her feminist colleagues to devote all their energies during the war years to the anti-slavery campaign. Later she argued that women's rights advocates had committed a strategic error in subordinating themselves to the cause of abolitionism. Alluding, in her *Reminiscences*, to the "six years (women) held their own claims in abeyance to those of the slaves in the South,"[6] she conceded that they were highly praised in Republican circles for their patriotic activism. "But when the slaves were emancipated," she lamented,

> . . . and these women asked that they should be recognized in the reconstruction as citizens of the Republic, equal before the law, all these transcendent virtues vanished like dew before the morning sun.[7]

According to Elizabeth Cady Stanton, the moral to be drawn from women's (i.e., white women's) Civil War experiences was that women should never "labor to second man's endeavors and exalt his sex above her own."[8]

There was a strong element of political naïveté in Stanton's analysis of the conditions prevailing at the war's end, which meant that she was more vulnerable than ever to racist ideology. As soon as the Union Army triumphed over their Confederate opponents, she and her co-workers insisted that the Republican party reward them for their wartime efforts. The reward they demanded was woman suffrage—as if a deal had been made; as if women's rights proponents had fought for the defeat of slavery with the understanding that their prize would be the vote.

Of course the Republicans did not lend their support to woman suffrage after the Union victory was won. But it was not so much because they were *men,* it was rather because, as politicians, they were beholden to the dominant economic interests of the period. Insofar as the military contest between the North and the South was a war to overthrow the Southern slaveholding class, it was a war which had been basically conducted in the interests of the Northern bourgeoisie, i.e., the young and enthusiastic industrial capitalists who found their political voice in the Republican party. The Northern capitalists sought economic control over the entire nation. Their struggle against the Southern slaveocracy did not therefore mean that they supported the liberation of Black men or women as human beings.

If woman suffrage was not to be included in the postwar agenda of the Republican party, neither were the innate political rights of Black people of any real concern to these triumphant politicians. That they conceded the necessity of extending the vote to newly emancipated Black men in the South did not imply that they favored Black males over white females. Black male suffrage —as spelled out in the Fourteenth and Fifteenth Constitutional Amendments proposed by the Republicans—was a tactical move designed to ensure the political hegemony of the Republican party in the chaotic postwar South. The Republican Senate leader Charles Sumner had been a passionate proponent of woman suffrage until the postwar period brought a sudden change in his attitude. The extension of the vote to women, he then insisted, was an "inopportune"[9] demand. In other words, ". . . the Republicans wanted nothing to interfere with winning two million black votes for their party."[10]

When the orthodox Republicans countered the postwar demand for woman suffrage with the slogan "This is the Negro's hour," they were actually saying under their breaths, "This is the hour of two million more votes for our party." Yet Elizabeth Cady Stanton and her followers seemed to believe that it was the "hour of the male" and that the Republicans were prepared to extend to Black men the full privileges of male supremacy. When she was asked by a Black delegate to the 1867 Equal Rights Convention whether she opposed the extension of the vote to Black men unless women were also enfranchised, she answered:

> . . . I say no; I would not trust him with my rights; degraded, oppressed, himself, he would be more despotic . . . than ever our Saxon rulers are . . . .[11]

The principle of unity underlying the creation of the Equal Rights Association was undoubtedly beyond reproach. That Frederick Douglass agreed to serve as co-vice-president with Elizabeth Cady Stanton (along with Lucretia Mott, who was elected president of the Association) symbolized the serious nature of this search for unity. It seems nonetheless that Stanton and some of her co-workers unfortunately perceived the organization as a means to ensure that Black men would not receive the franchise unless and until white women were also its recipients. When the Equal Rights Association resolved to agitate for the passage of the Fourteenth Amendment—which curtailed the apportionment of Congressional representatives in accordance with the number of *male* citizens denied the right to vote in federal elections—these white women felt fundamentally betrayed. After the Association voted to support the Fifteenth Amendment—which prohibited the use of race, color or previous condition of servitude as a basis for denying citizens the right to vote—the internal friction erupted into open and strident ideological struggle. As Eleanor Flexner put it:

> V (Stanton's) indignation and that of Miss Anthony knew no bounds. The latter made the pledge that "I will cut off this right arm of mine before I will ever work for or demand the ballot for the Negro and not the woman." Mrs. Stanton made derogatory references to "Sambo," and the enfranchisement of "Africans, Chinese, and all the ignorant foreigners the moment they touch our shores." She warned that the Republicans' advocacy of manhood suffrage "creates an antagonism between black men and all women that will culminate in fearful outrages on womanhood, especially in the Southern states."[12]

Whether the criticism of the Fourteenth and Fifteenth Amendments expressed by the leaders of the women's rights movement was justifiable or not is still being debated. But one thing seems clear: their defense of their own interests as white middle-class women—in a frequently egotistical and elitist fashion—exposed the tenuous and superficial nature of their relationship to the postwar campaign for Black equality. Granted, the two Amendments excluded women from the new process of enfranchisement and were thus interpreted by them as detrimental to their political aims. Granted, they felt they had as powerful a case for suffrage as Black men. Yet in articulating their opposition with arguments invoking the privileges of white supremacy, they revealed how defenseless they remained—even after years of involvement in progressive causes—to the pernicious ideological influence of racism.

Both Elizabeth Cady Stanton and Susan B. Anthony interpreted the Union victory as the *real* emancipation of the millions of Black people who had been the victims of the Southern slaveocracy. They assumed that the abolition of the slave system elevated Black people to a position in U.S. society that was comparable in almost every respect to that of middle-class white women.

> . . . (By) the act of emancipation and the Civil Rights Bill, the Negro and woman now had the same civil and political status, alike needing only the ballot.[13]

The assumption that emancipation had rendered the former slaves equal to white women—both groups equally requiring the vote for the completion of their social equality—ignored the utter precariousness of Black people's newly won "freedom" during the post-Civil War era. While the chains of slavery had been broken, Black people still suffered the pain of economic deprivation and they faced the terrorist violence of racist mobs in a form whose intensity was unmatched even by slavery.

In the opinion of Frederick Douglass, the abolition of slavery had been accomplished in name alone. The daily lives of Black people in the South still reeked of slavery. There was only one way, so Douglass argued, to consolidate and secure the new "free" status of Southern Blacks: "Slavery is not abolished until the black man has the ballot."[14] This was the basis for his insistence that the struggle for Black suffrage ought to take *strategic* priority, at that particular historical moment, over the effort to achieve the vote for women. Frederick Douglass viewed the franchise as an indispensable weapon which could complete the unfinished process of liquidating slavery. When he argued that woman suffrage was momentarily less urgent than the extension of the ballot to Black men, he was definitely not defending Black male superiority. Although Douglass was by no means entirely free of the

influence of male-supremacist ideology and while the polemical
formulations of his arguments often leave something to be
desired, the essence of his theory that Black suffrage was a strategic priority was not in the least anti-woman.

Frederick Douglass argued that without the vote, Black people
in the South would be unable to achieve any economic progress
at all.

> Without the elective franchise the Negro will still be practically a
> slave. Individual ownership has been abolished; but if we restore the
> Southern States without this measure (i.e., without the ballot), we
> shall establish an ownership of the blacks by the community among
> which they live. [15]

The need to defeat the continued economic oppression of the
postwar era was not the only reason for Black people's especially
urgent claim for the vote. Unabashed violence—perpetuated by
mobs encouraged by those who sought to profit from the labor of
the former slaves—would undoubtedly continue unless Black people achieved political power. In one of the first debates between
Frederick Douglass and the woman suffrage proponents inside the
Equal Rights Association, Douglass insisted that Black suffrage
took precedence because "with us disfranchisement means New
Orleans, it means Memphis, it means New York mobs." [16]

The Memphis and New Orleans riots took place in May and
July of 1866—less than a year before the debate between
Douglass and the white women took place. A U.S. Congressional
committee heard this testimony from a newly freed Black woman
who was a victim of the Memphis violence:

> I saw them kill my husband; . . . he was shot in the head while he
> was in bed, sick . . . there were between twenty and thirty men who
> came to the house . . . they made him get up and go out of doors

... they asked him if he had been a soldier;.... Then one stepped back, ... put the pistol to his head and shot him three times; ... when my husband fell he scuffled about a little, and looked as if he tried to get back into the house; then they told him if he did not make haste and die, they would shoot him again.[17]

In both Memphis and New Orleans, Black people and some white radicals had been killed and wounded. During both massacres the mobs who burned schools, churches and Black dwellings also raped, singly and in groups, the Black women whose paths they crossed. These two Southern riots had been foreshadowed by the New York violence of 1863, which had been instigated by pro-slavery, anti-draft forces in the North and had claimed the lives of some one thousand people.[18]

In light of the widespread violence and terror suffered by Black people in the South, Frederick Douglass' insistence that Black people's need for electoral power was more urgent than that of middle-class white women was logical and compelling. The former slave population was still locked in a struggle to defend their lives—and in Douglass' eyes, only the ballot could ensure their victory. By contrast, the white middle-class women, whose interests were represented by Elizabeth Cady Stanton and Susan B. Anthony, could not claim that their lives were in physical jeopardy. They were not, like Black men and women in the South, engaged in an actual war for liberation. And indeed, for Southern Blacks, the Union victory did not really mean that the violence of war had been entirely halted. As W. E. B. DuBois observed:

It is always difficult to stop war, and doubly difficult to stop civil war. Inevitably, when men have long been trained to violence and murder, the habit projects itself onto civil life, after peace, and there is crime and disorder and social upheaval.[19]

According to DuBois, many observers of the postwar situation felt that "Southern people seemed to have transferred their wrath at the Federal Government to the colored people."[20]

> In Alabama, Mississippi and Louisiana, it was said in 1866: "The life of a Negro is not worth much there. I have seen one who was shot in the leg while he was riding a mule because the ruffian thought it more trouble to ask him to get off the mule than to shoot him."[21]

As far as Black people in the postwar South were concerned, a state of emergency prevailed. Frederick Douglass' argument for Black suffrage was based on his insistence that the ballot was an emergency measure. However naïve he may have been about the potential power of the vote within the confines of the Republican party, he did not treat the issue of Black suffrage as a political game. For Douglass, the ballot was not a means of ensuring Republican party hegemony in the South. It was basically a survival measure—a means of guaranteeing the survival of the masses of his people.

The women's rights leaders of the post-Civil War era tended to view the vote as an end in itself. Already in 1866, it seemed that whoever furthered the cause of woman suffrage, however racist their motives, was a worthwhile recruit for the women's campaign. Even Susan B. Anthony detected no apparent contradiction in the advocacy of woman suffrage by a congressman who was a self-avowed white supremacist. To the great dismay of Frederick Douglass, Anthony publicly praised Congressman James Brooks, who was a former editor of a pro-slavery newspaper.[22] Although his support of woman suffrage was clearly a tactical move to counter the Republicans' sponsorship of Black suffrage, Brooks was enthusiastically lauded by Susan Anthony and her colleagues.

In representing the interests of the former slaveholding class, the Democratic party sought to prevent the enfranchisement of the Black male population in the South. Thus many Democratic leaders defended woman suffrage as a calculated measure against their Republican opponents. Expediency was the watchword of these Democrats, whose concern for women's equality was imbued with the same dishonesty as the Republicans' announced support for Black male suffrage. If Elizabeth Cady Stanton and Susan B. Anthony had more carefully analyzed the political situation of the post-Civil War period, they might have been less willing to associate their suffrage campaign with the notorious George Francis Train. "Woman first and Negro last is my program"[23] was the slogan of this unabashedly racist Democrat. When Stanton and Anthony met Train during their 1867 Kansas campaign, he offered to cover all the expenses of an extensive speaking tour for himself and the two women. "Most of our friends thought it a grave blunder," wrote Elizabeth Cady Stanton,

> ... but the result proved otherwise. Mr. Train was then in his prime —a gentleman in dress and manner, neither smoking, chewing, drinking, nor gormandizing. He was an effective speaker and actor . . .[24]

George Francis Train was also described as a "crack-brained harlequin and semi-lunatic,"[25] as Stanton acknowledges in her *Reminiscences.*

> He is as destitute of principle as he is of sense . . . He may be of use in drawing an audience, but so would a kangeroo, a gorilla, or a hippotamus.[26]

That was the opinion of William Lloyd Garrison, whose assessment of Train was shared by such figures as Lucy Stone and Henry Blackwell. But Stanton and Anthony were hurting for support, and since Train was willing to assist them, they welcomed him with open arms. With his financial backing, they founded a journal which—at his insistence—was called *Revolution*. The paper bore the motto—also at his insistence—"Men, their rights, and nothing more; women, their rights, and nothing less."27

By the time the Equal Rights Association held its 1869 convention, the Fourteenth Amendment—with its implication that only male citizens were unconditionally entitled to the ballot—had already been passed. The Fifteenth Amendment—prohibiting disfranchisement on the grounds of race, color or previous condition of servitude (but not sex!)—was on the verge of becoming law. On the agenda of this ERA convention was the endorsement of the Fifteenth Amendment. Since the leading proponents of woman suffrage passionately opposed this position, it was clear that an open schism was inevitable. Although the delegates recognized that this would probably be the Association's final meeting, Frederick Douglass made a last-minute appeal to his white sisters:

> When women, because they are women, are dragged from their homes and hung upon lamp-posts; when their children are torn from their arms and their brains dashed upon the pavement; when they are objects of insult and outrage at every turn; when they are in danger of having their homes burnt down over their heads; when their children are not allowed to enter schools; then they will have [the same] urgency to obtain the ballot.28

As blunt and polemical as this argument may have been, there was a lucidity about it that was unmistakable. Its vivid visual imagery demonstrated that the former Black slaves suffered an oppression that was qualitatively and brutally different from the predicament of white middle-class women.

As Frederick Douglass argued for the ERA's endorsement of
the Fifteenth Amendment, he did not counsel his suporters to
entirely dismiss the demand for woman suffrage. On the contrary,
the resolution he submitted called for the enthusiastic ratification
of "... the extension of suffrage to any class heretofore disenfran-
chised, as a cheering part of the triumph of our whole idea."[29]
Frederick Douglass envisioned the passage of the Fifteenth
Amendment as the "culmination of one-half of our demands"[30]
and the grounds for accelerating "our energy to secure the further
amendment guaranteeing the same sacred rights without limita-
tion to sex."[31]

Two years earlier Sojourner Truth might possibly have opposed
the position of Frederick Douglass. At the 1867 ERA convention,
she had opposed the ratification of the Fourteenth Amendment
because it effectively denied the franchise to *Black* women:

> There is a great stir about colored men getting their rights, but not
> a word about the colored women; and if colored men get their
> rights, and not colored women theirs, you see the colored men will
> be masters over the women, and it will be just as bad as it was
> before.[32]

By the final meeting of the Equal Rights Association in 1869,
Sojourner Truth had recognized the dangerous racism underlying
the feminists' opposition to Black male suffrage. In Frederick
Douglass' words, the position of Stanton's and Anthony's supporters was that "... no Negro shall be enfranchised while woman
is not."[33] When Sojourner Truth insisted that "if you bait the
suffrage-hook with a woman, you will certainly catch a black
man,"[34] she issued yet another profound warning about the
menacing influence of racist ideology.

Frederick Douglass' appeal for unity in respect to the ratification of the Fifteenth Amendment was also supported by Frances

E. W. Harper. This outstanding Black poet and leading advocate of woman suffrage insisted that the enfranchisement of Black men was far too vital to her entire people to risk losing it at such a critical moment. "When it was a question of race, she let the lesser question of sex go."[35] In her speech at the last convention of the Equal Rights Association, Harper appealed to her white sisters to support her people's struggle for liberation.

As women, Frances E. W. Harper and Sojourner Truth were outnumbered by those who were not persuaded by Frederick Douglass' appeal for unity. Elizabeth Cady Stanton and Susan B. Anthony were among those who successfully argued for the dissolution of the Equal Rights Association. Shortly thereafter they formed the National Woman Suffrage Association. As supporters within the ERA of the ratification of the Fifteenth Amendment, Lucy Stone and her husband were joined by Julia Ward Howe as founders of the American Woman Suffrage Association.

The dissolution of the Equal Rights Association brought to an end the tenuous, though potentially powerful, alliance between Black Liberation and Women's Liberation. In all fairness to such feminist leaders as Stanton and Anthony, it must be said that the former abolitionist men in the ERA were not always shining advocates of sexual equality. Indeed, some of the Association's male leaders were intransigent in their defense of male supremacist positions. The Black leader George Downing was really asking for a fight when he claimed that it was God's will, no less, that man should dominate woman.[36] While Downing's sexism was absolutely inexcusable, Elizabeth Cady Stanton's racist response was no less unjustifiable:

> When Mr. Downing puts the question to me: are you willing to have the colored man enfranchised before the women, I say no; I would not trust him with my rights; degraded, oppressed himself, he would be more despotic with the governing power than ever our

Saxon rulers are. If women are still to be represented by men, then I say let only the highest type of manhood stand at the helm of State.[37]

'despotic "

Although Black men in the ERA could not claim a spotless record as advocates of women's equality, such utterances as Downing's did not warrant the conclusion that Black men in general would be more "despotic" toward women than their white male counterparts. Moreover, the fact that Black men might also exhibit sexist attitudes was hardly a sound reason for arresting the progress of the overall struggle for Black Liberation.

Even Frederick Douglass was sometimes uncritical of the prevalent stereotypes and clichés associated with women. But his occasionally sexist remarks were never so oppressive as to depreciate the value of his contributions to the battle for women's rights in general. By any historian's estimate, Frederick Douglass remains the foremost male proponent of women's emancipation of the entire nineteenth century. If Douglass deserves any serious criticism for his conduct in the controversy surrounding the Fourteenth and Fifteenth Amendments, it is not so much for his support of Black male suffrage, but rather for his seemingly unquestioning faith in the power of the ballot within the confines of the Republican party.

Of course, Black people did need the vote—even if the prevailing political climate prevented women (Black and white alike) from simultaneously winning the franchise. And the decade of Radical Reconstruction in the South, which was based on the new Black vote, was an era of unparalleled progress—for the former slaves and poor white people as well. Yet the Republican party was basically opposed to the revolutionary demands of the Black population in the South. Once the Northern capitalists had established their hegemony in the South, the Republican party—which represented the capitalists' interests—participated in the systematic disfranchisement of Black people in the South. Although Frederick Douglass was the nineteenth-century's most brilliant proponent of Black Liberation, he did not fully understand the capitalist loyalties of the Republican party, for whom racism became no less expedient than the initial push for Black suffrage. The real tragedy of the controversy surrounding Black suffrage within the Equal Rights Association is that Douglass' vision of the franchise as a quasi-panacea for Black people may have encouraged the racist rigidity of the feminists' stand on woman suffrage.

Sufferage

Black vote (man)
 — puts man above women. (sexist?)

— white womans vote
 — white above black (racist?)

5 ∾ The Meaning of Emancipation According to Black Women

"Cursed be Cannan!" cried the Hebrew priests. "A servant of servants shall he be unto his brethren." . . . Are not Negroes servants? *Ergo!* Upon such spiritual myths was the anachronism of American slavery built, and this was the degradation that once made menial servants the aristocrats among colored folk. . . .

. . . When emancipation came . . . the lure of house service for the Negro was gone. The path of salvation for the emancipated host of black folk no longer lay through the kitchen door, with its wide hall and pillared yards beyond. It lay, as every Negro soon knew and knows, in escape from menial serfdom.[1]

After a quarter of a century of "freedom," vast numbers of Black women were still working in the fields. Those who had made it into the "big house" found the door toward new opportunities sealed shut—unless they preferred, for example, to wash clothes at home for a medley of white families as opposed to performing a medley of household jobs for a single white family. Only an infinitesimal number of Black women had managed to escape from the fields, from the kitchen or from the washroom. According to the 1890 census, there were 2.7 million Black girls and women over the age of ten. More than a million of them worked for wages: 38.7 percent in agriculture; 30.8 percent in household domestic service; 15.6 percent in laundry work; and a negligible 2.8 percent in manufacturing.[2] The few who found jobs in industry usually performed the dirtiest and lowest-paid work. And they had not really made a significant breakthrough, for their slave mothers had also worked in the Southern cotton mills, in the sugar refineries and even in the mines. For Black women in 1890, freedom must have appeared to be even more remote in the future than it had been at the end of the Civil War.

As during slavery, Black women who worked in agriculture— as sharecroppers, tenant farmers or farmworkers—were no less oppressed than the men alongside whom they labored the day long. They were often compelled to sign "contracts" with landowners who wanted to reduplicate the antebellum conditions. The contract's expiration date was frequently a mere formality, since landlords could claim that workers owed them more than the equivalent of the prescribed labor period. In the aftermath of emancipation the masses of Black people—men and women alike —found themselves in an indefinite state of peonage. Sharecroppers, who ostensibly owned the products of their labor, were no better off than the outright peons. Those who "rented" land immediately after emancipation rarely possessed money to meet the rent payments, or to purchase other necessities before they harvested their first crop. Demanding as much as 30 percent in interest, landowners and merchants alike held mortgages on the crops.

> Of course the farmers could pay no such interest and the end of the first year found them in debt—the second year they tried again, but there was the old debt and the new interest to pay, and in this way, the "mortgage system" has gotten a hold on everything that it seems impossible to shake off.[3]

Through the convict lease system, Black people were forced to play the same old roles carved out for them by slavery. Men and women alike were arrested and imprisoned at the slightest pretext —in order to be leased out by the authorities as convict laborers. Whereas the slaveholders had recognized limits to the cruelty with which they exploited their "valuable" human property, no such cautions were necessary for the postwar planters who rented Black convicts for relatively short terms. "In many cases sick convicts are made to toil until they drop dead in their tracks."[4]

Using slavery as its model, the convict lease system did not discriminate between male and female labor. Men and women were frequently housed together in the same stockade and were yoked together during the workday. In a resolution passed by the 1883 Texas State Convention of Negroes, "the practice of yoking or chaining male and female convicts together" was "strongly condemned."[5] Likewise, at the Founding Convention of the Afro-American League in 1890, one of the seven reasons motivating the creation of this organization was "(t)he odious and demoralizing penitentiary system of the South, its chain gangs, convict leases and indiscriminate mixing of males and females."[6]

As W. E. B. DuBois observed, the profit potential of the convict lease system persuaded many Southern planters to rely exclusively on convict labor—some employing a labor force of hundreds of Black prisoners.[7] As a result, both employers and state authorities acquired a compelling economic interest in increasing the prison population. "Since 1876," DuBois points out, "Negroes have been arrested on the slightest provocation and given long sentences or fines which they were compelled to work out."[8]

This perversion of the criminal justice system was oppressive to the ex-slave population as a whole. But the women were especially susceptible to the brutal assaults of the judicial system. The sexual abuse they had routinely suffered during the era of slavery was not arrested by the advent of emancipation. As a matter of fact, it was still true that "colored women were looked upon as the legitimate prey of white men . . ."[9]—and if they resisted white men's sexual attacks, they were frequently thrown into prison to be further victimized by a system which was a "return to another form of slavery."[10]

During the post-slavery period, most Black women workers who did not toil in the fields were compelled to become domestic servants. Their predicament, no less than that of their sisters who were sharecroppers or convict laborers, bore the familiar stamp of slavery. Indeed, slavery itself had been euphemistically called the "domestic institution" and slaves had been designated as innocuous "domestic servants." In the eyes of the former slaveholders, "domestic service" must have been a courteous term for a contemptible occupation not a half-step away from slavery. While Black women worked as cooks, nursemaids, chambermaids and all-purpose domestics, white women in the South unanimously rejected this line of work. Outside the South, white women who worked as domestics were generally European immigrants who, like their ex-slave sisters, were compelled to take whatever employment they could find.

The occupational equation of Black women with domestic service was not, however, a simple vestige of slavery destined to disappear with the passage of time. For almost a century they would be unable to escape domestic work in any significant numbers. A Georgia domestic worker's story, recorded by a New York journalist in 1912,[11] reflected Black women's economic predicament of previous decades as well as for many years to come. More than two-thirds of the Black women in her town were forced to hire themselves out as cooks, nursemaids, washerwomen, chambermaids, hucksters and janitresses, and were caught up in conditions ". . . just as bad as, if not worse than, it was during slavery."[12]

For more than thirty years this Black woman had involuntarily lived in all the households where she was employed. Working as many as fourteen hours a day, she was generally allowed an afternoon visit with her own family only once every two weeks. She was, in her own words, "the slave, body and soul"[13] of her white employers. She was always called by her first name—never Mrs. . . .—and was not infrequently referred to as their "nigger," in other words, their slave.[14]

One of the most humiliating aspects of domestic service in the South—another affirmation of its affinity with slavery—was the temporary revocation of Jim Crow laws as long as the Black servant was in the presence of a white person.

> . . . I have gone on the streetcars or the railroad trains with the white children, and . . . I could sit anywhere I desired, front or back. If a white man happened to ask some other white man, "What is that nigger doing in here?" and was told, "Oh, she's the nurse of those white children in front of her" immediately there was the hush of peace. Everything was all right, as long as I was in the white man's part of the streetcar or in the white man's coach as a servant —a slave—but as soon as I did not present myself as a menial . . . by my not having the white children with me, I would be forthwith assigned to the "nigger" seats or the "colored people's coach."[15]

From Reconstruction to the present, Black women household workers have considered sexual abuse perpetrated by the "man of the house" as one of their major occupational hazards. Time after time they have been victims of extortion on the job, compelled to choose between sexual submission and absolute poverty for themselves and their families. The Georgia woman lost one of her live-in jobs because "I refused to let the madam's husband kiss me."[16]

... (S)oon after I was installed as cook, he walked up to me, threw his arms around me, and was in the act of kissing me, when I demanded to know what he meant, and shoved him away. I was young then, and newly married, and didn't know then what has been a burden to my mind and heart ever since: that a colored woman's virtue in this part of the country has no protection.[17]

As during slavery times, the Black man who protested such treatment of his sister, daughter or wife could always expect to be punished for his efforts.

When my husband went to the man who had insulted me, the man cursed him, and slapped him, and—had him arrested! The police fined my husband $25.[18]

After she testified under oath in court, "(t)he old judge looked up and said: 'This court will never take the word of a nigger against the word of a white man.' "[19]

In 1919, when the Southern leaders of the National Association of Colored Women drew up their grievances, the conditions of domestic service were first on their list. It was with good reason that they protested what they politely termed, "exposure to moral temptations"[20] on the job. Undoubtedly, the domestic worker from Georgia would have expressed unqualified agreement with the Association's protests. In her words,

I believe nearly all white men take, and expect to take, undue liberties with their colored female servants—not only the fathers, but in many cases the sons also. Those servants who rebel against such familiarity must either leave or expect a mighty hard time, if they stay.[21]

Since slavery, the vulnerable condition of the household worker has continued to nourish many of the lingering myths about the "immorality" of Black women. In this classic "catch-22" situation, household work is considered degrading because it has been disproportionately performed by Black women, who in turn are viewed as "inept" and "promiscuous." But their ostensible ineptness and promiscuity are myths which are repeatedly confirmed by the degrading work they are compelled to do. As W. E. B. DuBois said, any white man of "decency" would certainly cut his daughter's throat before he permitted her to accept domestic employment.[22]

When Black people began to migrate northward, men and women alike discovered that their white employers outside the South were not fundamentally different from their former owners in their attitudes about the occupational potentials of the newly freed slaves. They also believed, it seemed, that *"Negroes are servants, servants are Negroes."*[23] According to the 1890 census, Delaware was the only state outside the South where the majority of Black people were farmworkers and sharecroppers as opposed to domestic servants.[24] In thirty-two out of forty-eight states, domestic service was the dominant occupation for men and women alike. In seven out of ten of these states, there were more Black people working as domestics than in all the other occupations combined.[25] The census report was proof that *Negroes are servants, servants are Negroes.*

Isabel Eaton's companion essay on domestic service, published in DuBois' 1899 study *The Philadelphia Negro,* reveals that 60 percent of all Black workers in the state of Pennsylvania were engaged in some form of domestic work.[26] The predicament of women was even worse, for all but nine percent—14,297 out of 15,704—of Black women workers were employed as domestics.[27] When they had traveled North seeking to escape the old slavery, they had discovered that there were simply no other occupations open to them. In researching her study, Eaton interviewed several women who had previously taught school, but had been fired because of "prejudice."[28] Expelled from the classroom, they were compelled to work in the washroom and the kitchen.

Of the fifty-five employers interviewed by Eaton, only one preferred white servants over Black ones.[29] In the words of one woman,

> I think the colored people are much maligned in regard to honesty, cleanliness and trustworthiness; my experience of them is that they are immaculate in every way, and they are perfectly honest; indeed I can't say enough about them.[30]

Racism works in convoluted ways. The employers who thought they were complimenting Black people by stating their preference for them over whites were arguing, in reality, that menial servants —slaves, to be frank—were what Black people were destined to be. Another employer described her cook as ". . . very industrious and careful—painstaking. She is a good, faithful creature, and very grateful."[31] Of course, the "good" servant is always faithful, trustworthy and grateful. U.S. literature and the popular media in this country furnish numerous stereotypes of the Black woman as faithful, enduring servant. The Dilseys (à la Faulkner), the Berenices (of *Member of the Wedding*) and the Aunt Jemimas of commercial fame have become stock characters of U.S. culture. Thus the one woman interviewed by Eaton who did prefer white servants confessed that she actually employed Black help ". . . because they look more like servants."[32] The tautological definition of Black people as servants is indeed one of the essential props of racist ideology.

Racism and sexism frequently converge—and the condition of white women workers is often tied to the oppressive predicament of women of color. Thus the wages received by white women domestics have always been fixed by the racist criteria used to calculate the wages of Black women servants. Immigrant women compelled to accept household employment earned little more than their Black counterparts. As far as their wage-earning potential was concerned, they were closer, by far, to their Black sisters than to their white brothers who worked for a living.[33]

If white women never resorted to domestic work unless they were certain of finding nothing better, Black women were trapped in these occupations until the advent of World War II. Even in the 1940s, there were street-corner markets in New York and other large cities—modern versions of slavery's auction block— inviting white women to take their pick from the crowds of Black women seeking work.

> Every morning, rain or shine, groups of women with brown paper bags or cheap suitcases stand on streetcorners in the Bronx and Brooklyn waiting for a chance to get some work. . . . Once hired on the "slave market," the women often find after a day's back-breaking toil, that they worked longer than was arranged, got less than was promised, were forced to accept clothing instead of cash and were exploited beyond human endurance. Only the urgent need for money makes them submit to this routine daily.[34]

New York could claim about two hundred of these "slave markets," many of them located in the Bronx, where "almost any corner above 167th Street" was a gathering point for Black women seeking work.[35] In a 1938 article published in *The Nation,* "Our Feudal Housewives," as the piece was entitled, were said to work some seventy-two hours a week, receiving the lowest wages of all occupations.[36]

The least fulfilling of all employment, domestic work has also been the most difficult to unionize. As early as 1881, domestic workers were among the women who joined the locals of the Knights of Labor when it rescinded its ban on female membership.[37] But many decades later, union organizers seeking to unite domestic workers confronted the very same obstacles as their predecessors. Dora Jones founded and led the New York Domestic Workers Union during the 1930s.[38] By 1939—five years after the union was founded—only 350 out of 100,000 domestics in the state had been recruited. Given the enormous difficulties of organizing domestics, however, this was hardly a small accomplishment.

White women—feminists included—have revealed a historical reluctance to acknowledge the struggles of household workers. They have rarely been involved in the Sisyphean task of ameliorating the conditions of domestic service. The convenient omission of household workers' problems from the programs of "middle-class" feminists past and present has often turned out to be a veiled justification—at least on the part of the affluent women—of their own exploitative treatment of their maids. In 1902 the author of an article entitled "A Nine-Hour Day for Domestic Servants" described a conversation with a feminist friend who had asked her to sign a petition urging employers to furnish seats for women clerks.

> "The girls," she said, "have to stand on their feet ten hours a day and it makes my heart ache to see their tired faces."
> "Mrs. Jones," said I, "how many hours a day does your maid stand upon her feet?"
> "Why, I don't know," she gasped, "five or six I suppose."
> "At what time does she rise?"
> "At six."
> "And at what hour does she finish at night?"
> "Oh, about eight, I think, generally."
> "That makes fourteen hours . . ."
> ". . . (S)he can often sit down at her work."
> "At what work? Washing? Ironing? Sweeping? Making beds? Cooking? Washing dishes? . . . Perhaps she sits for two hours at

her meals and preparing vegetables, and four days in the week she has an hour in the afternoon. According to that, your maid is on her feet at least eleven hours a day with a score of stair-climbings included. It seems to me that her case is more pitiable than that of the store clerk."

My caller rose with red cheeks and flashing eyes. "My maid always has Sunday after dinner," she said.

"Yes, but the clerk has all day Sunday. Please don't go until I have signed that petition. No one would be more thankful than I to see the clerks have a chance to sit . . ."[39]

This feminist activist was perpetrating the very oppression she protested. Yet her contradictory behavior and her inordinate insensitivity are not without explanation, for people who work as servants are generally viewed as less than human beings. Inherent in the dynamic of the master-servant (or mistress-maid) relationship, said the philosopher Hegel, is the constant striving to annihilate the consciousness of the servant. The clerk referred to in the conversation was a wage laborer—a human being possessing at least a modicum of independence from her employer and her work. The servant, on the other hand, labored solely for the purpose of satisfying her mistress' needs. Probably viewing her servant as a mere extension of herself, the feminist could hardly be conscious of her own active role as an oppressor.

As Angelina Grimke had declared in her *Appeal to the Christian Women of the South,* white women who did not challenge the institution of slavery bore a heavy responsibility for its inhumanity. In the same vein, the Domestic Workers Union exposed the role of middle-class housewives in the oppression of Black domestic workers.

The housewife stands condemned as the worst employer in the country . . .

> The housewives of the United States make their million and a
> half employees work an average of seventy-two hours a week and
> pay them . . . whatever they can squeeze out of their budget after
> the grocer, the butcher . . . (etc.) have been paid.[40]

Black women's desperate economic situation—they perform
the worst of all jobs and are ignored to boot—did not show signs
of change until the outbreak of World War II. On the eve of the
war, according to the 1940 census, 59.5 percent of employed
Black women were domestic workers and another 10.4 percent
worked in non-domestic service occupations.[41] Since approximately 16 percent still worked in the fields, scarcely one out of
ten Black women workers had really begun to escape the old grip
of slavery. Even those who managed to enter industry and profes-
sional work had little to boast about, for they were consigned, as
a rule, to the worst-paid jobs in these occupations. When the
United States stepped into World War II and female labor kept
the war economy rolling, more than four hundred thousand Black
women said goodbye to their domestic jobs. At the war's peak,
they had more than doubled their numbers in industry. But even
so—and this qualification is inevitable—as late as 1960 at least
one-third of Black women workers remained chained to the same
old household jobs and an additional one-fifth were non-domestic
service workers.[42]

In a fiercely critical essay entitled "The Servant in the House,"
W. E. B. DuBois argued that as long as domestic service was the
rule for Black people, emancipation would always remain a con-
ceptual abstraction. ". . . (T)he Negro," DuBois insisted, "will not
approach freedom until this hateful badge of slavery and medie-
valism has been reduced to less than ten percent."[43] The changes
prompted by the Second World War provided only a hint of
progress. After eight long decades of "emancipation," the signs
of freedom were shadows so vague and so distant that one strained
and squinted to get a glimpse of them.

6 ~ Education and Liberation: Black Women's Perspective

Millions of Black people—and especially the women—were convinced that emancipation was "the coming of the Lord."[1]

> This was the fulfillment of prophecy and legend. It was the Golden Dawn, after chains of a thousand years. It was everything miraculous and perfect and promising.[2]

> There was joy in the South. It rose like perfume—like a prayer. Men stood quivering. Slim, dark girls, wild and beautiful with wrinkled hair, wept silently; young women, black, tawny, white and golden, lifted shivering hands, and old and broken mothers, black and gray, raised great voices and shouted to God across the fields and up to the rocks and the mountains.[3]

> A great song arose, the loveliest thing born this side of the seas. It was a new song . . . and its deep and plaintive beauty, its great cadences and wild appeal wailed, throbbed and thundered on the world's ears with a message seldom voiced by man. It swelled and blossomed like incense, improvised and born anew out of an age long past and weaving into its texture the old and new melodies in word and in thought.[4]

Black people were hardly celebrating the abstract principles of freedom when they hailed the advent of emancipation. As that

". . . great human sob shrieked in the wind and tossed its tears upon the sea—free, free, free,"[5] Black people were not giving vent to religious frenzy. They knew exactly what they wanted: the women and the men alike wanted land, they wanted the ballot and ". . . they were consumed with desire for schools."[6]

Like the young slave child Frederick Douglass, many of the four million people who celebrated emancipation had long since realized that "knowledge unfits a child to be a slave."[7] And like Douglass' master, the former slaveholders realized that ". . . if you give a nigger an inch, he will take an ell. Learning will spoil the best nigger in the world."[8] Master Hugh's proscription notwithstanding, Frederick Douglass secretly continued his pursuit of knowledge. Soon he could write all the words from *Webster's Spelling-Book*, further perfecting his skill by examining the family Bible and other books in the clandestinity of the night. Of course, Frederick Douglass was an exceptional human being who became a brilliant thinker, writer and orator. But his desire for knowledge was by no means exceptional among Black people, who had always manifested a deep-seated urge to acquire knowledge. Great numbers of slaves also wanted to be "unfit" for the harrowing existence they led. A former slave interviewed during the 1930s, Jenny Proctor recalled the *Webster's Spelling-Book* which she and her friends had surreptitiously studied.

> None of us was 'lowed to see a book or try to learn. They say we git smarter than they was if we learn anything, but we slips around and gits hold of that Webster's old blue-back speller and we hides it till 'way in the night and then we lights a little pine torch, and studies that spelling book. We learn it too. I can read some now and write a little too.[9]

Black people learned that emancipation's "forty acres and a mule" was a malicious rumor. They would have to fight for land;

they would have to fight for political power. And after centuries of educational deprivation, they would zealously assert their right to satisfy their profound craving for learning. Thus, like their sisters and brothers all over the South, the newly liberated Black people of Memphis assembled and resolved that education was their first priority. On the first anniversary of the Emancipation Proclamation, they urged the Northern teachers to make haste and

> ... to bring their tents with them, ready for erection in the field, by the roadside, or in the fort, and not to wait for magnificent houses to be erected in time of war . . .[10]

The mystifying powers of racism often emanate from its irrational, topsy-turvy logic. According to the prevailing ideology, Black people were allegedly incapable of intellectual advancement. After all, they had been chattel, naturally inferior as compared to the white epitomes of humankind. But if they really were biologically inferior, they would have manifested neither the desire nor the capability to acquire knowledge. Ergo, no prohibition of learning would have been necessary. In reality, of course, Black people had always exhibited a furious impatience as regards the acquisition of education.

The yearning for knowledge had always been there. As early as 1787, Black people petitioned the state of Massachusetts for the right to attend Boston's free schools.[11] After the petition was rejected, Prince Hall, who was the leader of this initiative, established a school in his own home.[12] Perhaps the most stunning illustration of this early demand for education was the work of an African-born woman who was a former slave. In 1793 Lucy Terry Prince boldly demanded an audience before the trustees of the newly established Williams College for Men, who had refused to admit her son into the school. Unfortunately, the racist prejudices were so strong that Lucy Prince's logic and eloquence could not sway the trustees of this Vermont institution. Yet she aggressively defended her people's desire for—and right to—education. Two years later Lucy Terry Prince successfully defended a land claim before the highest court of the land, and according to surviving records, she remains the first woman to have addressed the Supreme Court of the United States.[13]

Seventeen ninety-three was also the year an ex-slave woman, who had purchased her freedom, established a school in the city of New York which was known as Katy Ferguson's School for the Poor. Her pupils, whom she recruited from the poorhouse, were both Black and white (twenty-eight and twenty respectively)[14] and were quite possibly both boys and girls. Forty years later the young white teacher Prudence Crandall steadfastly defended Black girls' right to attend her Canterbury, Connecticut, school. Crandall persistently taught her Black pupils until she was dragged off to jail for refusing to shut down her school.[15] Margaret Douglass was another white woman who was imprisoned in Norfolk, Virginia, for operating a school for Black children.[16]

The most outstanding examples of white women's sisterly solidarity with Black women are associated with Black people's historical struggle for education. Like Prudence Crandall and Margaret Douglass, Myrtilla Miner literally risked her life as she sought to impart knowledge to young Black women.[17] In 1851, when she initiated her project to establish a Black teachers' college in Washington, D.C., she had already instructed Black children in Mississippi, a state where education for Blacks was a criminal offense. After Myrtilla Miner's death, Frederick Douglass described his own incredulousness when she first announced her plans to him. During their first meeting he wondered about her seriousness in the beginning, but then he realized that

. . . the fire of enthusiasm lighted in her eye and that the true
martyr spirit flamed in her soul. My feelings were those of min-
gled joy and sadness. Here I thought is another enterprise—wild,
dangerous, desperate and impracticable, and destined only to
bring failure and suffering. Yet I was deeply moved with admiration by the heroic purpose of the delicate and fragile person who
stood or rather moved to and fro before me.[18]

It was not long before Douglass recognized that none of the
warnings he issued to her—and not even the stories of the attacks
on Prudence Crandall and Margaret Douglass—could shake her
determination to found a college for Black women teachers.

To me the proposition was reckless almost to the point of madness. In my fancy I saw this fragile little woman harassed by the
law, insulted in the street, a victim of slaveholding malice and
possibly beaten down by the mob.[19]

In Frederick Douglass' opinion, relatively few white people
outside the anti-slavery activists would sympathize with Myrtilla
Miner's cause and support her against the mob. This was a period,
he argued, of diminishing solidarity with Black people. Moreover,

. . . the District of Columbia (was) the very citadel of slavery, the
place most watched and guarded by the slave power and where
humane tendencies were more speedily detected and sternly opposed.[20]

In retrospect, however, Douglass confessed that he did not really
understand the depth of this white woman's individual courage.
Despite the grave risks, Myrtilla Miner opened her school in the
fall of 1851, and within a few months her initial six students had
grown to forty. She taught her Black students passionately over
the next eight years, simultaneously raising money and urging

congressmen to support her efforts. She even acted as a mother to the orphan girls whom she brought into her home so that they might attend the school.[21]

As Myrtilla Miner struggled to teach and as her pupils struggled to learn, they all fought evictions, arson attempts and the other misdeeds of racist stone-throwing mobs. They were supported by the young women's families and abolitionists such as Harriet Beecher Stowe, who donated a portion of the royalties she received from the sale of *Uncle Tom's Cabin.* [22] Myrtilla Miner may have been "frail," as Frederick Douglass observed, but she was definitely formidable, and was always able, at lesson time, to discover the eye of that racist storm. Early one morning, however, she was abruptly awakened by the odor of smoke and raging flames, which soon consumed her schoolhouse. Although her school was destroyed, the inspiration she provided lived on, and eventually Miner's Teachers College became a part of the District of Columbia public educational system.[23] "I never pass the Miner Normal School for colored girls," so Frederick Douglass confessed in 1883,

> . . . without a feeling of self reproach that I could have said ought to quench the zeal, shake the faith, and quail the courage of the Noble woman by whom it was founded and whose name it bears.[24]

Sisterhood between Black and white women was indeed possible, and as long as it stood on a firm foundation—as with this remarkable woman and her friends and students—it could give birth to earthshaking accomplishments. Myrtilla Miner kept the candle burning that others before her, like the Grimke sisters and Prudence Crandall, had left as a powerful legacy. It could not have been a mere historical coincidence that so many of the white women who defended their Black sisters in the most dangerous of situations were involved in the struggle for education. They must have understood how urgently Black women needed to acquire knowledge—a lamp unto their people's feet and a light unto the path toward freedom.

Black people who did receive academic instruction inevitably associated their knowledge with their people's collective battle for freedom. As the first year of Black schooling in Cincinnati drew to a close, pupils who were asked "What do you think *most* about?" furnished these answers:

> 1st. We are going . . . to be good boys and when we get a man to get the poor slaves from bondage. And I am sorrow to hear that the boat of Tiskilwa went down with two hundred poor slaves . . . it grieves my heart so that I could faint in one minute. (seven years old)

> 2nd. . . . What we are studying for is to try to get the yoke of slavery broke and the chains parted asunder and slave holding cease for ever. . . . (twelve year old)

> 3rd. . . . Bless the cause of abolition . . . My mother and step-father, my sister and myself were all born in slavery. The Lord did let the oppressed go free. Roll on the happy period that all nations shall know the Lord. We thank him for his many blessings. (eleven year old)

> 4th. . . . This is to inform you that I have two cousins in slavery who are entitled to their freedom. They have done everything that the will requires and now they won't let them go. They talk of selling them down the river. If this was your case what would you do? . . . (ten year old)[25]

The last surviving answer came from a sixteen-year-old attending this new Cincinnati school. It is an extremely fascinating example of the way the students gleaned a contemporary meaning from world history that was as close to home as the desire to be free.

5th. Let us look back and see the state in which the Britons and Saxons and Germans lived. They had no learning and had not a knowledge of letters. But not look, some of them are our first men. Look at King Alfred and see what a great man he was. He at one time did not know his a,b,c, but before his death he commanded armies and nations. He was never discouraged but always looked forward and studied the harder. I think if the colored people study like King Alfred they will soon do away the evil of slavery. I can't see how the Americans can call this a land of freedom where so much slavery is.[26]

As far as Black people's faith in knowledge was concerned, this sixteen-year-old child said it all.

This unquenchable thirst for knowledge was as powerful among the slaves in the South as among their "free" sisters and brothers in the North. Needless to say, the anti-literacy restrictions of the slave states were far more rigid than in the North. After the Nat Turner Revolt in 1831, legislation prohibiting the education of slaves was strengthened throughout the South. In the words of one slave code, ". . . teaching slaves to read and write tends to dissatisfaction in their minds, and to produce insurrection and rebellion."[27] With the exception of Maryland and Kentucky, every Southern state absolutely prohibited the education of slaves.[28] Throughout the South, slaveholders resorted to the lash and the whipping post in order to counter their slaves' irrepressible will to learn. Black people wanted to be educated.

The poignancy of the slaves' struggle for learning appeared everywhere. Frederika Bremer found a young woman desperately trying to read the Bible. "Oh, this book," she cried out to Miss Bremer. "I turn and turn over its leaves and I wish I understood what is on them. I try and try; I should be so happy if I could read, but I cannot.[29]

Susie King Taylor was a nurse and teacher in the first Black regiment of the Civil War. In her autobiography she described her persistent efforts to educate herself during slavery. White children, sympathetic adults, as well as her grandmother, assisted her to acquire the skills of reading and writing.[30] Like Susie King's grandmother, numerous slave women ran great risks as they imparted to their sisters and brothers the academic skills they had secretly procured. Even when they were compelled to convene their schools during the late hours of the night, women who had managed to acquire some knowledge attempted to share it with their people.[31]

These were some of the early signs—in the North and South alike—of that post-emancipation phenomenon which DuBois called "a frenzy for schools."[32] Another historian described the ex-slaves' thirst for learning in these words:

> With a yearning born of centuries of denial, ex-slaves worshipped the sight and sound of the printed word. Old men and women on the edge of the grave could be seen in the dark of the night, poring over the Scripture by the light of a pine knot, painfully spelling out the sacred words.[33]

According to yet another historian,

> (M)any educators reported that they found a keener desire to learn among the Negro children of the Reconstruction South than among white children in the North.[34]

About half of the volunteer teachers who joined the massive educational campaign organized by the Freedman's Bureau were women. Northern white women went South during Reconstruction to assist their Black sisters who were absolutely determined to wipe out illiteracy among the millions of former slaves. The dimensions of this task were herculean: according to DuBois, the prevailing illiteracy rate was 95 percent.[35] In the histories chronicling the Reconstruction Era and in the historical accounts of the Women's Rights Movement, the experiences of Black and white women working together in the struggle for education have received sparse attention. Judging, however, from the articles in the *Freedman's Record*, these teachers undoubtedly inspired each other and were themselves inspired by their students. Almost universally mentioned in the white teachers' observations was the former slaves' unyielding commitment to knowledge. In the words of a teacher working in Raleigh, North Carolina, "[i]t is surprising to me to see the amount of suffering which many of the people endure for the sake of sending their children to school."[36] Material comfort was unhesitatingly sacrificed for the furtherance of educational progress:

> A pile of books is seen in almost every cabin, though there be no furniture except a poor bed, a table and two or three broken chairs.[37]

As teachers, the Black and white women seem to have developed a profound and intense mutual appreciation. A white woman working in Virginia, for example, was immensely impressed by the work of a Black woman teacher who had just emerged from slavery. It ". . . seems almost a miracle," this white woman exclaimed, that ". . . a colored woman, who had been a slave up to the time of the Surrender, would succeed in a vocation to her so novel . . ."[38] In the reports she authored, the Black woman in question expressed sincere—though by no means servile—gratitude for the work of her "friends from the North."[39]

By the time of the Hayes Betrayal and the overthrow of Radical Reconstruction, the accomplishments in education had become one of the most powerful proofs of progress during that potentially revolutionary era. Fisk University, Hampton Institute and several other Black colleges and universities had been established in the post-Civil War South.[40] Some 247,333 pupils were attending 4,329 schools—and these were the building blocks for the South's first public school system, which would benefit Black and white children alike. Although the post-Reconstruction period and the attendant rise of Jim Crow education drastically diminished Black people's educational opportunities, the impact of the Reconstruction experience could not be entirely obliterated. The dream of land was shattered for the time being and the hope for political equality waned. But the beacon of knowledge was not easily extinguished—and this was the guarantee that the fight for land and for political power would unrelentingly go on.

> Had it not been for the Negro school and college, the Negro would, to all intents and purposes, have been driven back to slavery. . . . His reconstruction leadership had come from Negroes educated in the North, and white politicians, capitalists and philanthropic teachers. The counter-revolution of 1876 drove most of these, save the teachers, away. But already, through establishing public schools and private colleges, and by organizing the Negro church, the Negro had acquired enough leadership and knowledge to thwart the worst designs of the new slave drivers.[41]

Aided by their white sister allies, Black women played an indispensable role in creating this new fortress. The history of women's struggle for education in the United States reached a true peak when Black and white women together led the post-Civil War battle against illiteracy in the South. Their unity and solidarity preserved and confirmed one of our history's most fruitful promises.

7 ☞ Woman Suffrage at the Turn of the Century: The Rising Influence of Racism

One morning (Susan B. Anthony) had engagements in the city which would prevent her from using the stenographer whom she had engaged. She remarked at the breakfast table that I could use the stenographer to help me with my correspondence, since she had to be away all the morning and that she would tell her when she went upstairs to come in and let me dictate some letters to her.

When I went upstairs to my room, I waited for her to come in; when she did not do so, I concluded she didn't find it convenient, and went on writing my letters in longhand. When Miss Anthony returned she came to my room and found me busily engaged. "You didn't care to use my secretary, I suppose. I told her to come to your room when you came upstairs. Didn't she come?" I said no. She said no more, but turned and went into her office. Within ten minutes she was back again in my room. The door being open, she walked in and said, "Well, she's gone." And I said, "Who?" She said, "The stenographer." I said, "Gone where?" "Why," she said, "I went into the office and said to her, 'You didn't tell Miss Wells what I said about writing some letters for her?" The girl said, "No, I didn't." "Well, why not?" Then the girl said, "It is all right for you, Miss Anthony, to treat Negroes as equals, but I refuse to take dictation from a colored woman." "Indeed!" said Miss Anthony. "Then," she said, "you needn't take any more dictation from me.

Miss Wells is my guest and any insult to her is an insult to me. So if that is the way you feel about it, you needn't stay any longer."[1]

This interchange between Susan B. Anthony and Ida B. Wells, who later founded the first Black women's suffrage club, occurred during those ". . . precious days in which I [Wells] sat at the feet of this pioneer and veteran in the work of women's suffrage."[2] Wells' admiration for Anthony's individual stance against racism was undeniable and her respect for the suffragist's contributions to the women's rights campaign was profound. But she unhesitatingly criticized her white sister for failing to make her personal fight against racism a public issue of the suffrage movement.

Susan B. Anthony was never lacking in praises for Frederick Douglass, consistently reminding people that he was the first man to publicly advocate the enfranchisement of women. She considered him a lifetime honorary member of her suffrage organization. Yet, as Anthony explained to Wells, she pushed Douglass aside for the sake of recruiting white Southern women into the movement for woman suffrage.

> In our conventions . . . he was the honored guest who sat on our platform and spoke at our gatherings. But when the . . . Suffrage Association went to Atlanta, Georgia, knowing the feeling of the South with regard to Negro participation on equality with whites, I myself asked Mr. Douglass not to come. I did not want to subject him to humiliation, and *I did not want anything to get in the way of bringing the southern white women into our suffrage association.* [my emphasis][3]

In this particular conversation with Ida B. Wells, Anthony went on to explain that she had also refused to support the efforts of several Black women who wanted to form a branch of the suffrage association. She did not want to awaken the anti-Black hostility of her white Southern members, who might withdraw from the organization if Black women were admitted.

> "And you think I was wrong in so doing?" she asked. I answered uncompromisingly yes, for I felt that although she may have made gains for suffrage, she had also confirmed white women in their attitude of segregation.[4]

This conversation between Ida B. Wells and Susan B. Anthony took place in 1894. Anthony's self-avowed capitulation to racism "on the ground of expediency"[5] characterized her public stance on this issue until she resigned in 1900 from the presidency of the National American Woman Suffrage Association. When Wells admonished Anthony for legitimizing the Southern white women's commitment to segregation, the underlying question was far more consequential than Anthony's individual attitude. Racism was objectively on the rise during this period and the rights and lives of Black people were at stake. By 1894 the disfranchisement of Black people in the South, the legal system of segregation and the reign of lynch law were already well established. More than at any other time since the Civil War, this was an era demanding consistent and principled protests against racism. The increasingly influential "expediency" argument proposed by Anthony and her colleagues was a feeble justification for the suffragists' indifference to the pressing requirements of the times.

In 1888 Mississippi enacted a series of statutes legalizing racial segregation, and by 1890 that state had ratified a new constitution which robbed Black people of the vote.[6] Following Mississippi's example, other Southern states framed new constitutions which guaranteed the disfranchisement of Black men. South Carolina's constitution was adopted in 1898, followed by North Carolina and Alabama in 1901 and Virginia, Georgia and Oaklahoma in 1902, 1908 and 1918, respectively.[7]

Ida B. Wells' uncompromising criticism of Susan B. Anthony's public indifference toward racism was certainly justified by the prevailing social conditions, but something far deeper than historical evidence was involved. Just two years before the two women's debate on suffrage and racism, Wells had suffered a traumatic firsthand encounter with racist mob violence. The three victims of Memphis' first lynching since the riots of 1866 were personal friends of hers. The horrible incident itself inspired Wells to investigate and expose the accelerating pattern of mob murders throughout the Southern states. Traveling in England in 1893, seeking support for her crusade against lynching, she vigorously decried the silence with which hundreds and thousands of mob murders had been received.

> In the past ten years over a thousand black men and women and children have met this violent death at the hands of a white mob. And the rest of America has remained silent. . . . The pulpit and press of our country remains silent on these continued outrages and the voice of my race thus tortured and outraged is stifled or ignored wherever it is lifted in America in a demand for justice.[8]

Given the uncamouflaged violence visited upon Black people during the 1890s, how could white suffragists argue in good faith that "for the sake of expediency" they should "stoop to conquer on this color question"?[9] The ostensibly "neutral" stance assumed by the leadership of the NAWSA with respect to the "color question" actually encouraged the proliferation of undisguised racist ideas within the ranks of the suffrage campaign. At the Association's 1895 convention, appropriately held in Atlanta, Georgia, one of the most prominent figures in the campaign for the vote ". . . urged the South to adopt woman suffrage as one solution to the negro problem."[10] This "negro problem" could be simply solved, so Henry Blackwell proclaimed, by attaching a literacy qualification to the right to vote.

In the development of our complex political society, we have today two great bodies of illiterate citizens: in the North, people of foreign birth; in the South, people of the African race and a considerable portion of the white population. Against foreigners and Negroes, as such, we would not discriminate. But in every state save one, there are more educated white women than all the illiterate voters, white and black, native and foreign.[11]

Ironically, this argument, designed to persuade white Southerners that woman suffrage held great advantages for white supremacy, was initially proposed by Henry Blackwell when he announced his support for the Fourteenth and Fifteenth Amendments. Already in 1867 he had addressed an appeal to "the legislatures of the Southern States" urging them to take note of the fact that female enfranchisement could potentially eliminate the Black population's impending political power.

Consider the result from the Southern standpoint. Your 4,000,000 of Southern white women will counterbalance your 4,000,000 of negro men and women, and thus the political supremacy of your white race will remain unchanged.[12]

This renowned abolitionist assured the Southern politicians at that time that woman suffrage could reconcile the North and the South. "Capital and population would flow, like the Mississippi, toward the Gulf"—and, as for Black people, they "would gravitate, by the law of nature toward the tropics."[13]

The very element which has destroyed slavery would side with the victorious South, and "out of the nettle danger you would pluck the flower safety."[14]

Blackwell and his wife, Lucy Stone, assisted Elizabeth Cady Stanton and Susan B. Anthony during their 1867 Kansas campaign. That Stanton and Anthony welcomed at this time the support of a notorious Democrat, whose program was "woman first, the negro last," was an indication that they implicitly assented to Blackwell's racist logic. Moreover, they uncritically described, in their *History of Woman Suffrage,* the Kansas politicians' fear of Black suffrage.

> The men of Kansas in their speeches would say, ". . . if negro suffrage passes, we will be flooded with ignorant, impoverished blacks from every State of the Union. If woman suffrage passes, we invite to our borders people of character and position, of wealth and education. . . . Who can hesitate to decide, when the question lies between educated women and ignorant negroes?"[15]

However racist these early postures of the women's movement may seem, it was not until the last decade of the nineteenth century that the woman suffrage campaign began to definitively accept the fatal embrace of white supremacy. The two factions: Stanton-Anthony and Blackwell-Stone—which had split on the issue of the Fourteenth and Fifteenth Amendments—were reunited in 1890. In 1892 Elizabeth Cady Stanton had grown disillusioned about the ballot's potential power to liberate women and ceded the presidency of the National American Woman Suffrage Association to her colleague Susan B. Anthony. During the second year of Anthony's term the NAWSA passed a resolution which was a variation of Blackwell's racist and class-biased argument of more than a century earlier.

> *Resolved.* That without expressing any opinion on the proper qualifications for voting, we call attention to the significant facts that in every State there are more women who can read and write than the whole number of illiterate male voters; more white women who can read and write than all negro voters; more American women

who can read and write than all foreign voters; so that the enfranchisement of such women would settle the vexed question of rule by illiteracy, whether of home-grown or foreign-born production.[16]

This resolution cavalierly dismissed the rights of Black and immigrant *women* along with the rights of their male relations. Moreover, it pointed to a fundamental betrayal of democracy that could no longer be justified by the old expediency argument. Implied in the logic of this resolution was an attack on the working class as a whole and a willingness—whether conscious or not —to make common cause with the new monopoly capitalists whose indiscriminate search for profits knew no human bounds.

In passing the 1893 resolution, the suffragists might as well have announced that if they, as white women of the middle classes and bourgeoisie, were given the power of the vote, they would rapidly subdue the three main elements of the U.S. working class: Black people, immigrants and the uneducated native white workers. It was these three groups of people whose labor was exploited and whose lives were sacrificed by the Morgans, Rockefellers, Mellons, Vanderbilts—by the new class of monopoly capitalists who were ruthlessly establishing their industrial empires. They controlled the immigrant workers in the North as well as the former slaves and poor white laborers who were operating the new railroad, mining and steel industries in the South.

Terror and violence compelled Black workers in the South to accept slavelike wages and working conditions that were frequently worse than slavery. This was the logic behind the rising waves of lynchings and the pattern of legal disfranchisement in the South. In 1893—the year of that fatal NAWSA resolution— the Supreme Court reversed the Civil Rights Act of 1875. With this decision, Jim Crow and lynch law—a new mode of racist enslavement—received judicial sanction. Indeed, three years later the *Plessy* v. *Ferguson* decision announced the "separate but equal" doctrine, which consolidated the South's new system of racial segregation.

The last decade of the nineteenth century was a critical moment in the development of modern racism—its major institutional supports as well as its attendant ideological justifications. This was also the period of imperialist expansion into the Philippines, Hawaii, Cuba and Puerto Rico. The same forces that sought to subjugate the peoples of these countries were responsible for the worsening plight of Black people and the entire U.S. working class. Racism nourished those imperialist ventures and was likewise conditioned by imperialism's strategies and apologetics.

On November 12, 1898, the *New York Herald* ran stories about the U.S. presence in Cuba, the "race riot" in Phoenix, South Carolina, and the massacre of Black people in Wilmington, North Carolina. The Wilmington Massacre was the most murderous of an entire series of organized mob attacks on Black people during that period. According to a Black minister at that time, Wilmington was "Cuba's kindergarten of ethics and good government,"[17] as it was also proof of the profound hypocrisy of U.S. foreign policy in the Philippines.

In 1899 the suffragists were quick to furnish evidence of their consistent loyalty to the avaricious monopoly capitalists. As the dictates of racism and chauvinism had shaped the NAWSA's policy toward the domestic working class, they accepted without question the new feats of U.S. Imperialism. At their convention that year Anna Garlin Spencer delivered an address entitled "Duty to the Women of Our New Possessions."[18] *Our new possessions?* During the discussion Susan B. Anthony did not attempt to conceal her anger—but, as it turned out, she was not angry about the seizures themselves. She had been

> . . . overflowing with wrath ever since the proposal was made to engraft our half-barbaric form of government on Hawaii and our other new possessions.[19]

Anthony consequently advanced the demand with all the force of her wrath ". . . that the ballot be given to the women of our new possessions upon the same terms as to the men."[20] As if women in Hawaii and Puerto Rico should demand the right to be victimized by U.S. Imperialism on an equal basis with their men.

During this 1899 convention of the NAWSA a revealing contradiction emerged. While the suffragists invoked their "duty to the women of our possessions," a Black woman's appeal for a resolution against Jim Crow went entirely unheeded. The Black suffragist—Lottie Wilson Jackson—was admitted to the convention because the host state was Michigan, one of the few chapters welcoming Black women into the suffrage association. During her train trip to the convention Lottie Jackson had suffered the indignities of the railroads' segregationist policies. Her resolution was very simple: "That colored women ought not to be compelled to ride in smoking cars, and that suitable accommodations should be provided for them."[21]

As the convention's presiding officer, Susan B. Anthony brought the discussion on the Black woman's resolution to a close. Her comments assured the overwhelming defeat of the resolution:

> We women are a helpless disfranchised class. Our hands are tied. While we are in this condition, it is not for us to go passing resolutions against railroad corporations or anybody else.[22]

The meaning of this incident was far deeper than the issue of whether or not to send an official letter protesting a railroad company's racist policies. In refusing to defend their Black sister, the NAWSA symbolically abandoned the entire Black people at the moment of their most intense suffering since emancipation. This gesture definitively established the suffrage association as a potentially reactionary political force which would cater to the demands of white supremacy.

The NAWSA's evasion of the issue of racism posed by Lottie Jackson's resolution would indeed encourage the expression of anti-Black prejudices within the organization. Objectively, an open invitation had been extended to Southern women who were not about to relinquish their commitment to white supremacy. At best, this noncommittal posture on the struggle for Black equality constituted an acquiescence to racism, and at worst, it was a deliberate incentive, on the part of an influential mass organization, for the violence and devastation spawned by the white supremacist forces of the times.

Susan B. Anthony should not, of course, be held personally responsible for the suffrage movement's racist errors. But she was the movement's most outstanding leader at the turn of the century—and her presumably "neutral" public posture toward the fight for Black equality did indeed bolster the influence of racism within the NAWSA. Had Anthony seriously reflected on the findings of her friend Ida B. Wells, she might have realized that a noncommittal stand on racism implied that lynchings and mass murders by the thousands could be considered a neutral issue. By 1899 Wells had completed an enormous amount of research on lynchings and had published her tragically astounding results. Over the previous ten years, between one and two hundred officially recorded lynchings had occurred on an annual basis.[23] In 1898 Wells created something of a public stir by directly demanding that President McKinley order federal intervention in the lynching case of a South Carolina postmaster.[24]

In 1899, when Susan B. Anthony urged the defeat of the anti-Jim Crow resolution, Black people massively denounced President McKinley's encouragement of white supremacy. The Massachusetts branch of the Colored National League charged that McKinley had been apologetically silent during the reign of terror in Phoenix, South Carolina, and that he failed to intervene when Black people were massacred in Wilmington, North Carolina. During his trip South, they told McKinley,

> . . . you preached patience, industry, moderation to your long-suffering black fellow citizens, and patriotism, jingoism and imperialism to your white ones.[25]

While McKinley was in Georgia, a mob broke into a prison, seized five Black men and

> . . . almost in your hearing, before your eyes . . . they were atrociously murdered. Did you speak? Did you open your lips to express horror of the awful crime . . . which outbarbarized barbarism and stained through and through with indelible infamy before the world your country's justice, honor and humanity.[26]

And not a presidential word was uttered about one of the period's most notorious lynchings—the burning that year of Sam Hose in Georgia.

> (He) was taken one quiet Sunday morning from his captors and burned to death with indescribable and hellish cruelty in the presence of cheering thousands of the so-called best people of Georgia —men, women and children, who had gone forth on a Christian Sabbath to the burning of a human being as to a country festival and holiday of innocent enjoyment and amusement.[27]

Countless historical documents confirm the atmosphere of racist aggression as well as the powerful challenges emanating from Black people during the year 1899. An especially symbolic document is the call issued by the National Afro-American Council urging Black people to observe June 2 as a day of fasting and prayer. Published in the *New York Tribune*, this proclamation denounced the unjustified and indiscriminate arrests which leave men and women easy prey for mobs of "ignorant, vicious, whisky-besotted men" who "torture, hang, shoot, butcher, dismember and burn."[28]

It was thus not even a question of reading the handwriting on the wall. The reign of terror had already descended upon Black people. How could Susan B. Anthony claim to believe in human rights and political equality and at the same time counsel the members of her organization to remain silent on the issue of racism? Bourgeois ideology—and particularly its racist ingredients—must really possess the power of dissolving real images of terror into obscurity and insignificance, and of fading horrible cries of suffering human beings into barely audible murmurings and then silence.

When the new century rolled around, a serious ideological marriage had linked racism and sexism in a new way. White supremacy and male supremacy, which had always had an easy courtship, openly embraced and consolidated the affair. During the first years of the twentieth century the influence of racist ideas was stronger than ever. The intellectual climate—even in progressive circles—seemed to be fatally infected with irrational notions about the superiority of the Anglo-Saxon race. This escalated promotion of racist propaganda was accompanied by a similarly accelerated promotion of ideas implying female inferiority. If people of color—at home and abroad—were portrayed as incompetent barbarians, women—white women, that is—were more rigorously depicted as mother-figures, whose fundamental raison d'être was the nurturing of the male of the species. White women were learning that as mothers, they bore a very special responsibility in the struggle to safeguard white supremacy. After all, they were the "mothers of the race." Although the term *race* allegedly referred to the "human race," in practice—especially as the eugenics movement grew in popularity—little distinction was made between "the race" and "the Anglo-Saxon race."

As racism developed more durable roots within white women's organizations, so too did the sexist cult of motherhood creep into the very movement whose announced aim was the elimination of male supremacy. The coupling of sexism and racism was mutually strengthening. Having opened its doors to the prevailing racist ideology more widely than ever before, the suffrage movement had opted for an obstacle course which placed its own goal of woman suffrage in continuous jeopardy. The 1901 convention of the NAWSA was the first in many years at which Susan B. Anthony was not the presiding officer. Having retired the preceding year, she was nonetheless in attendance and was introduced by the new president, Carrie Chapman Catt, to deliver the welcoming message. Anthony's remarks reflected the influence of the rejuvenated eugenics campaign. While women, she argued, had been corrupted in the past by "man's appetites and passions,"[29] it was time for them to fulfill their purpose of becoming saviors of "the Race."[30] It would be through women's

> . . . intelligent emancipation that (the race) shall be purified . . . It is through woman (that) the race is to be redeemed. For this reason I ask for her immediate and unconditional emancipation from all political, industrial and religious subjection.[31]

The main address, delivered by Carrie Chapman Catt, pointed to three "great obstacles" to woman suffrage: militarism, prostitution and

> . . . the inertia in the growth of democracy which has come as a reaction following the aggressive movements that with possibly ill advised haste enfranchised the foreigner, the negro and the indian. Perilous conditions seeming to follow from the introduction into the body politic vast numbers of irresponsible citizens, have made the nation timid.[32]

By 1903 the NAWSA witnessed such an outburst of racist argumentation that it appeared that the upholders of white supremacy were determined to seize control over the organization. Significantly, the 1903 convention was held in the Southern city of New Orleans. It was hardly a coincidence that the racist arguments heard by the delegates were complemented by numerous defenses of the motherhood cult. If Edward Merrick, son of the Louisana Supreme Court Chief Justice, spoke about "the crime of enfranchising 'a horde of ignorant negro men,' "[33] Mary Chase, a delegate from New Hampshire, claimed that women should be enfranchised "as the natural guardians and protectors of the home."[34]

At the 1903 convention it was Belle Kearney from Mississippi whose remarks most blatantly confirmed the dangerous alliance between racism and sexism. Bluntly referring to the Southern Black population as the "4,500,000 ex-slaves, illiterate and semi-barbarous,"[35] she histrionically evoked their enfranchisement as a "death-weight," under which the South had struggled "for nearly forty years, bravely and magnanimously."[36] However inadequate Booker T. Washington's theory of vocational education for Black people may have been in reality, Kearney insisted that Tuskegee and similar schools were ". . . only fitting (the negro) for power, and when the black man becomes necessary to a community by reason of his skill and acquired wealth,"[37] something of a race war will result.

> [T]he poor white man, embittered by his poverty and humiliated by his inferiority, finds no place for himself and his children, then will come the grapple between the races.[38]

Of course, no such struggle between white workers and Black workers was inevitable. The apologists of the new monopoly capitalist class were, however, determined to provoke these rac-

racial conflict ?

ist divisions. Around the same time that Kearney spoke before the New Orleans convention, an identical alarm was issued to the U.S. Senate. On February 24, 1903, Senator Ben Tillman from South Carolina warned that the colleges and schools for Black people in the South would lead inexorably to racial conflict. Designed to equip "these people" who, in his eyes, were "the nearest to the missing link with the monkey" to "compete with their white neighbors," these schools would

> ... create an antagonism between the poorer classes of our citizens and these people upon whose level they are in the labor market.[39]

Moreover,

> There has been no contribution to elevate the white people in the South, to aid and assist the Anglo-Saxon Americans, the men who are descended from the people who fought with Marion and Dumter. They are allowed to struggle in poverty and in ignorance and to do everything they can to get along, and they see Northern people pouring in thousands and thousands to help build up an African domination.[40]

Contrary to Kearney's and Tillman's logic, racial conflict did not emerge spontaneously, but rather was consciously planned by the representatives of the economically ascendant class. They needed to impede working-class unity so as to facilitate their own exploitative designs. The forthcoming "race riots"—Atlanta; Brownsville, Texas; Springfield, Ohio—like the 1898 massacres in Wilmington and Phoenix, South Carolina, were orchestrated precisely in order to heighten the tensions and antagonism within the multiracial working class.

Belle Kearney informed her sisters at the New Orleans convention that she had discovered a sure way of containing the racial antagonisms within manageable limits. She claimed she knew exactly how to prevent the otherwise inevitable race war.

> To avoid this unspeakable culmination, the enfranchisement of women will have to be effected, and an educational and property qualification for the ballot be made to apply . . .
> The enfranchisement of women would insure immediate and durable white supremacy, honestly attained; for, upon unquestionable authority, it is stated that "in every Southern State but one, there are more educated women than all the illiterate voters, white and black, native and foreign, combined."[41]

The utterly horrifying tone of Kearney's address should not conceal the fact that she invoked theories which had become quite familiar within the woman suffrage movement. The statistical argument and the call for a literacy requirement had been heard many times before by delegates to previous NAWSA conventions. In proposing a property qualification for the vote, Kearney reflected the anti-working-class ideas which had unfortunately gained a stronghold in the suffrage movement.

There was an ironical twist to the words Belle Kearney delivered to the convened membership of the National American Woman Suffrage Association. For years and years, leading suffragists had justified the Association's indifference to the cause of racial equality by invoking the catch-all argument of *expediency*. Now woman suffrage was represented as the most expedient means to achieve racial supremacy. The NAWSA had unwittingly caught itself in its own trap—in the trap of expediency which was supposed to catch the vote. Once the pattern of capitulation to racism had taken hold—and especially at that historical juncture when the new and ruthless monopolist expansion required more intense forms of racism—it was inevitable that the suffragists would eventually be hurt by its backfire. The delegate from Mississippi confidently declared:

> Some day the North will be compelled to look to the South for redemption . . . on account of the purity of its Anglo-Saxon blood, the simplicity of its social and economic structure . . . and the maintenance of the sanctity of its faith, which has been kept inviolate.[42]

Not an ounce of sisterly solidarity could be detected here, and there was not a word about the defeat of male supremacy or about women eventually coming into their own. It was not women's rights or women's political equality but, rather, the reigning racial superiority of white people which had to be preserved at all cost.

> Just as surely as the North will be forced to turn to the South for the nation's salvation, just so surely will the South be compelled to look to its Anglo-Saxon women as the medium through which to retain the supremacy of the white race over the African. . . .[43]

"Thank God the black man was freed!" she exclaimed with deliberately racist arrogance.

> I wish for him all possible happiness and all possible progress, but not in encroachments upon the holy of holies of the Anglo-Saxon race . . .[44]

8 ~ Black Women and the Club Movement

The General Federation of Women's Clubs could have celebrated its tenth birthday in 1900 by taking a stand against racism
within its ranks. Unfortunately, its stance was unequivocally pro-
racist: the convention's credentials committee decided to exclude
the Black delegate sent by Boston's Women's Era Club. Among
the scores of clubs represented in the Federation, the one club
deemed inadmissible carried a mark of distinction which could be
claimed by no more than two of the white women's groups. If
Sorosis and the New England Women's Club were pioneer organizations among white clubwomen, the Women's Era Club, then
five years old, was the fruit of Black women's first organizing
efforts within the club movement. Its representative, Josephine
St. Pierre Ruffin, was known in white club circles in Boston as a
"cultured" woman. She was the wife of a Harvard graduate, who
became the first Black judge in the state of Massachusetts. As the
credentials committee informed her, she would be welcomed in
the convention as a delegate from the white club to which she also
belonged. In this case, of course, she would have been the necessary exception proving the rule of racial segregation within the
GFWC. But since Ruffin insisted on representing the Black
women's club (which, incidentally, had already received a certifi-
cate of GFWC membership), she was refused entrance into the
convention hall. Moreover, ". . . to enforce this ruling an attempt
was made to snatch from her breast the badge which had been
handed her . . ."[1]

Shortly after the "Ruffin incident," the Federation's newsletter carried a fictitious story designed to frighten those white women who had protested the racism manifested within their organization. According to Ida B. Wells' account, the article was entitled "The Rushing in of Fools"[2] and it described the pitfalls of integrated club life in a certain unnamed city. The president of the unidentified club had invited a Black woman, whom she had befriended, to become a member of her group. But alas, the white woman's daughter fell in love and married the Black woman's son, who, like his mother, was so light-complexioned as to be hardly recognizable as Black. Yet, the article confided, he had that "invisible drop" of black blood, and when the young white wife gave birth to a "jet black baby . . . the shock was so great that (she) turned her face to the wall and died."[3] While any Black person would realize that the story was contrived, the newspapers picked it up and widely disseminated the message that integrated women's clubs would result in the defilement of white womanhood.

The first national convention called by Black women had taken place five years after the 1890 founding meeting of the General Federation of Women's Clubs. Black women's organizational experiences could be traced back to the pre-Civil War era, and like their white sisters, they had participated in literary societies and benevolent organizations. Their main efforts during that period were associated with the anti-slavery cause. Unlike white women, however, who had also flocked into the abolitionist campaign, Black women had been motivated less by considerations of charity or by general moral principles than by the palpable demands of their people's survival. The 1890s were the most difficult years for Black people since the abolition of slavery, and women naturally felt obligated to join their people's resistance struggle. It was in response to the unchecked wave of lynchings and the indiscriminate sexual abuse of Black women that the first Black women's club was organized.

According to the accepted interpretations, the origins of the white women's General Federation go back to the immediate postwar period, when the exclusion of women from the New York Press Club resulted in the organization of a women's club in 1868.[4] After the founding of Sorosis in New York, Boston women established the New England Women's Clubs. Thus the trend was set for such a proliferation of clubs in the two leading cities of the Northeast that by 1890 a national federation could be founded.[5] In the brief span of two years, the General Federation of Women's Clubs had acquired 190 affiliates and over 20,000 members.[6] One student of feminist history explains in this way the seemingly magnetic attraction these clubs held for white women:

> Subjectively, clubs met the need of middle class, middle aged women for leisure activities outside of, but related to, their traditional sphere. There were, it soon became clear, literally millions of women whose lives were not filled up by domestic and religious pursuits. Poorly educated for the most part, unwilling or unable to secure paid employment, they found in club life a solution to their personal dilemma.[7]

Black women, North and South, worked outside their homes to a far greater extent than their white counterparts. In 1890, of the four million women in the labor force, almost one million were Black.[8] Not nearly as many Black women were confronted with the domestic void which plagued their white middle-class sisters. Even so, the leadership of the Black club movement did not come from the masses of working women. Josephine St. Pierre Ruffin, for example, was the wife of a Massachusetts judge. What set such women apart from the white club leaders was their consciousness of the need to challenge racism. Indeed, their own familiarity with the routine racism of U.S. society linked them far more intimately to their working-class sisters than did the experience of sexism for white women of the middle classes. Prior to the emergence of the club movement, the first large meeting independently organized by Black women was prompted by the racist assaults on the newspaperwoman Ida B. Wells. After her newspaper offices in Memphis were destroyed by a mob of racists who opposed her anti-lynching work, Wells decided to take up permanent residence in New York. As she relates in her autobiography, two women were deeply moved upon reading her articles in the *New York Age* about the lynching of three of her friends and the destruction of her paper.

> . . . (T)wo colored women remarked on my revelations during a visit with each other and said they thought that the women of New York and Brooklyn should do something to show appreciation of my work and to protest the treatment which I had received.[9]

Victoria Matthews and Maritcha Lyons initiated a series of meetings among the women they knew, and eventually a committee of 250 women was charged with "stir(ring) up sentiment throughout the two cities."[10] Within several months they had organized an immense meeting, which took place in October, 1892, at New York's Lyric Hall. At that rally, Ida B. Wells made a moving presentation on lynching.

> The hall was crowded . . . The leading colored women of Boston and Philadelphia had been invited to join in this demonstration, and they came, a brilliant array. Mrs. Gertrude Mossell of Philadelphia, Mrs. Josephine St. Pierre Ruffin of Boston, Mrs. Sarah Garnett, widow of one of our great men, a teacher in the public schools of New York City, Dr. Susan McKinner of Brooklyn, the leading woman physician of our race, were all there on the platform, a solid array behind a lonely, homesick girl who was an exile because she had tried to defend the manhood of her race.[11]

Ida B. Wells received a good sum of money toward the establishment of another newspaper and—a sign of the relative affluence of the campaign's leaders—a gold brooch in the shape of a pen.[12]

In the aftermath of this inspiring rally, the women who had organized it created permanent organizations in Brooklyn and New York, which they called the Women's Loyal Union. According to Ida B. Wells, these were the first clubs created and exclusively led by Black women. "(I)t was the real beginning of the club movement among the colored women in this country."[13] Boston's Women's Era Club—subsequently banned by the GFWC —was an outgrowth of a meeting called by Josephine St. Pierre Ruffin on the occasion of Ida B. Wells' visit to Boston.[14] Similar meetings addressed by Wells led to permanent clubs in New Bedford, Providence and Newport, and later in New Haven.[15] In 1893 an anti-lynching speech delivered by Wells in Washington occasioned one of the first public appearances of Mary Church Terrell, who later became the founding president of the National Association of Colored Women's Clubs.[16]

Ida B. Wells was much more than a drawing card for Black women who were recruited into the club movement. She was also an active organizer, initiating and serving as president of the first Black women's club in Chicago. After her first anti-lynching tour abroad, she assisted Frederick Douglass in organizing a protest against the 1893 World's Fair. Due to her efforts, a women's committee was organized to raise money for the publication of a brochure to be distributed at the fair entitled "The Reason Why the Colored American is not in the World's Columbian Exposition."[17] In the aftermath of the Chicago World's Fair, Wells persuaded the women to create a permanent club as Black women in the northeastern cities had done.[18]

Some of the women recruited by Wells came from Chicago's most affluent Black families. Mrs. John Jones, for example, was the wife of "the wealthiest colored man in Chicago at that time."[19] It should be noted, however, that this successful businessman had formerly worked on the Underground Railroad and had led the movement to repeal Illinois' Black Laws. Aside from the women representing the incipient "Black Bourgeoisie" and "the most prominent women in church and secret society,"[20] there were "school teachers and housewives and high-school girls"[21] among the almost three hundred members of the Chicago Women's Club. In one of their earliest activist endeavors, they raised funds to prosecute a policeman who had killed a Black man. The Black clubwomen in Chicago were manifestly committed to the struggle for Black Liberation.

The pioneering Women's Era Club in Boston continued the strenuous defense of Black people, which Ida B. Wells had urged at their first meeting. When the National Conference of the Unitarian Church refused to pass an anti-lynching resolution, New Era members issued a strong protest in an open letter to one of the leading women of the church.

> We, the members of the Women's Era Club, believe we speak for the colored women of America. . . . As colored women we have suffered and do suffer too much to be blind to the suffering of others, but naturally we are more keenly alive to our own suffering than to others. We therefore feel that we should be false to ourselves, to our opportunities and to our race should we keep silent in a case like this.
>
> We have endured much and we believe with patience; we have seen our world broken down, our men made fugitives and wanderers or their youth and strength spent in bondage. We ourselves are daily hindered and oppressed in the race of life; we know that every opportunity for advancement, for peace and happiness will be denied us; . . . Christian men and women absolutely refuse . . . to open their churches to us; . . . our children . . . are considered legitimate prey for insult; . . . our young girls can at any time be thrust into foul and filthy cars, and, no matter their needs, be refused food and shelter.[22]

After referring to the educational and cultural deprivation suffered by Black women, the protest letter called for a massive
outcry against lynching.

> . . . (I)n the interest of justice, for the good name of our country,
> we solemnly raise our voice against the horrible crimes of lynch law.
> . . . And we call upon Christians everywhere to do the same or be
> branded as sympathizers with the murderers.[23]

When the First National Conference of Colored Women convened in Boston in 1895, the Black clubwomen were not simply
emulating their white counterparts, who had federated the club
movement five years earlier. They had come together to decide
upon a strategy of resistance to the current propagandistic assaults
on Black women and the continued reign of lynch law. Responding to an attack on Ida B. Wells by the pro-lynching president
of the Missouri Press Association, the conference delegates protested that "insult to Negro womanhood"[24] and sent out ". . . to
the country a unanimous endorsement of the course (Wells) had
pursued in (her) agitation against lynching."[25]

Fannie Barrier Williams, whom white women in Chicago had
excluded from their club, summed up the difference between the
white club movement and the club movement among her people.
Black women, she said, had come to realize that

> . . . progress includes a great deal more than what is generally meant
> by the terms culture, education and contact.
>   The club movement among colored women reaches into
> the sub-condition of the entire race. . . . (T)he club movement is
> only one of the many means for the social uplift of a race . . .
>   The club movement is well purposed. . . . It is not a fad . . . It
> is rather the force of a new intelligence against the old ignorance.
> The struggle of an enlightened conscience against the whole brood
> of social miseries, born out of the stress and pain of a hated past.[26]

While the Black women's club movement was emphatically committed to the struggle for Black Liberation, its middle-class leaders were sometimes unfortunately elitist in their attitudes toward the masses of their people. Fannie Barrier Williams, for example, envisioned the clubwomen as "the new intelligence, the enlightened conscience"[27] of the race.

> Among white women, clubs mean the forward movement of the best women in the interest of the best womanhood. Among colored women the club is the effort of the few competent in behalf of the many incompetent.[28]

Prior to the definitive establishment of a national Black women's club organization, there was apparently some unfortunate competition among leading clubwomen. Based on the 1895 Boston conference called by Josephine St. Pierre Ruffin, the National Federation of Afro-American Women was founded the same year, electing Margaret Murray Washington as its president.[29] It brought together over thirty clubs, which were active in twelve states. In 1896 the National League of Colored Women was founded in Washington, D.C., with Mary Church Terrell as its president. The competing organizations soon merged, however, forming the National Association of Colored Women's Clubs, which elected Terrell to its highest office. Over the next several years Mary Church Terrell and Ida B. Wells would express a mutual hostility within the national Black club movement. In her autobiography, Wells claims that Terrell was personally responsible for her exclusion from the 1899 convention of the National Association of Colored Women's Clubs that was held in Chicago.[30] According to Wells, Terrell's fears about her own re-election as president caused her to exclude the former newspaperwoman and to minimize, during the convention, the struggle against lynching which her rival had come to personify.[31]

Mary Church Terrell was the daughter of a slave who had received, after the emancipation, a considerable inheritance from his slavemaster father. Because of her family's wealth, she enjoyed unique educational opportunities. After four years at Oberlin College, Terrell became the third Black woman college graduate in the country[32]—and she went on to study at several institutions of higher learning abroad. A high school teacher and later a university professor, Mary Church Terrell became the first Black woman appointed to the Board of Education in the District of Columbia. Had she sought personal wealth and fulfillment through a political or academic career, she would undoubtedly have succeeded. But her concern for the collective liberation of her people led her to devote her entire adult life to the struggle for Black liberation. More than anyone else, Mary Church Terrell was the driving force that molded the Black women's club movement into a powerful political group. While Ida B. Wells was one of Terrell's severest critics, she acknowledged the importance of her role in the club movement. As she pointed out, "Mrs. Terrell was by all odds the best educated woman among us . . ."[33]

Like Mary Church Terrell, Ida B. Wells was born into a family of ex-slaves. When an epidemic of yellow fever claimed the lives of her parents, Wells was still a teenager, with five younger sisters and brothers to support. She embarked upon a teaching career as a direct response to this enormous burden. But her personal hardships were not so overwhelming as to prevent her from pursuing a path of anti-racist activism. At the young age of twenty-two, she challenged the racial discrimination she suffered as a railroad traveler by filing suit against the railroad in court. Ten years later Ida B. Wells was publishing her own newspaper in Memphis, Tennessee, and after three of her friends were murdered by a racist mob, turned the paper into a powerful weapon against lynching. Forced into exile when the racists threatened her life and destroyed her newspaper offices, Wells launched her astoundingly effective crusade against lynching. Calling upon Black and white alike to massively oppose the reign of lynch law, she traveled from city to city and town to town all over the United States. Her tours abroad encouraged Europeans to organize solidarity campaigns against the lynching of Black people in the United States. Two decades later, at the age of fifty-seven, Ida B. Wells rushed to the scene of the East Saint Louis Riot. When she was sixty-three years old she conducted an investigation into a mob attack by racists in Arkansas. And on the eve of her death she was as militant as ever, leading a Black women's demonstration against the segregationist policies of a major Chicago hotel.

In her protracted crusade against lynching, Ida B. Wells had become an expert at agitation-confrontation tactics. But few could equal Mary Church Terrell as an advocate of Black Liberation through the written and spoken word. She sought freedom for her people through logic and persuasion. An eloquent writer, a powerful orator and a master at the art of debate, Terrell waged persistent and principled defenses of Black equality and woman suffrage, as well as the rights of working people. Like Ida B. Wells, she was active up to the year of her death—at the age of ninety. In one of her last defiant gestures against racism, she marched in a Washington, D.C., picket line when she was eighty-nine years old.

Ida B. Wells and Mary Church Terrell were unquestionably the two outstanding Black women of their era. Their personal feud, which spanned several decades, was a tragic thread within the history of the Black women's club movement. While their separate accomplishments were monumental, their united efforts could have really moved mountains for their sisters and for their people as a whole.

9 ᴐ Working Women, Black Women and the History of the Suffrage Movement

In January, 1868, when Susan B. Anthony published the first issue of *Revolution,* working women, whose ranks in the labor force had recently expanded, had begun to defend their rights conspicuously. During the Civil War more white women than ever before had gone to work outside their homes. In 1870, while 70 percent of women workers were domestics, one-fourth of all non-farm workers in general were female.[1] Within the garment industry, they had already become the majority. At this time the labor movement was a rapidly expanding economic force, comprising no less than thirty nationally organized unions.[2]

Inside the labor movement, however, the influence of male supremacy was so powerful that only the Cigarmakers and Printers had opened their doors to women. But some women workers had attempted to organize themselves. During the Civil War and in its immediate aftermath, the sewing women constituted the largest group of women working outside their homes. When they began to organize, the spirit of unionization spread from New York to Boston and Philadelphia and to all the major cities where the garment industry flourished. When the National Labor Union was founded in 1866, its delegates were compelled to acknowledge the sewing women's efforts. At the initiative of

William Sylvis, the convention resolved to support not only the "daughters of toil in the land"[3]—as the sewing women were called—but the general unionization of women and their full equality with respect to wages.[4] When the National Labor Union reconvened in 1868, electing Sylvis as their president, the presence of several women among the delegates, including Elizabeth Cady Stanton and Susan B. Anthony, compelled the convention to pass stronger resolutions and generally treat the cause of working women's rights with greater seriousness than before.

Women were welcomed at the 1869 founding convention of the National Colored Labor Union. As the Black workers explained in one resolution, they did not want to commit "the mistakes heretofore made by our white fellow citizens in omitting women."[5] This Black labor organization, created because of the exclusionary policies of white labor groups, proved by its practice to be more seriously committed to working women's rights than its white counterpart and predecessor. While the NLU had simply passed resolutions supporting women's equality, the NCLU actually elected a woman—Mary S. Carey[6]—to serve on the organization's policymaking executive committee. Susan B. Anthony and Elizabeth Cady Stanton did not record any acknowledgment of the Black labor organization's anti-sexist accomplishments. They were probably too absorbed in the suffrage battle to take note of that important development.

In the first issue of Anthony's *Revolution*, the newspaper financed by the racist Democrat George Francis Train, the overall message was that women should seek the ballot. Once the reality of woman suffrage was established, so the paper seemed to say, it would be the millennium for women—and the final triumph of morality for the nation as a whole.

We shall show that the ballot will secure for woman equal place and equal wages in the world of work; that it will open to her the schools, colleges, professions and all the opportunities and advantages of life; that in her hand it will be a moral power to stay the tide of crime and misery on every side.[7]

Though its vision was often too narrowly focused on the ballot, *Revolution* played an important role in the struggles of working women during the two years it was published. The demand for the eight-hour day was repeatedly raised within the pages of the paper, as was the anti-sexist slogan "equal pay for equal work." From 1868 to 1870 working women—especially in New York—could rely upon *Revolution* to publicize their grievances as well as their strikes, their strategies and their goals.

Anthony's involvement in women's labor struggles of the postwar period was not restricted to journalistic solidarity. During the first year of her paper's publication she and Stanton used the *Revolution*'s offices to organize printers into the Working Women's Association. Shortly thereafter the National Typographers became the second union to admit women, and in the *Revolution*'s offices, the Women's Typographical Union, Local #1, was established.[8] Thanks to Susan B. Anthony's initiative, a second Working Women's Association was later organized among the sewing women.

Although Susan B. Anthony, Elizabeth Cady Stanton and their colleagues on the paper made important contributions to the cause of working women, they never really accepted the principle of trade unionism. As they had been previously unwilling to concede that Black Liberation might claim momentary priority over their own interests as white women, they did not fully embrace the fundamental principles of unity and class solidarity, without which the labor movement would remain powerless. In the eyes of the suffragists, "woman" was the ultimate test—if the cause of woman could be furthered, it was not wrong for women to function as scabs when male workers in their trade were on strike. Susan B. Anthony was excluded from the 1869 convention of the National Labor Union because she had urged women printers to go to work as scabs.[9] In defending herself at this convention, Anthony proclaimed that

> . . . men have great wrongs in the world between the existence of labor and capital, but these wrongs as compared to the wrongs of women, in whose faces the doors of the trades and vocations are slammed shut, are not as a grain of sand on the sea shore.[10]

Anthony's and Stanton's postures during this episode were astonishingly similar to the suffragists' anti-Black position within the Equal Rights Association. As Anthony and Stanton attacked Black men when they realized that the ex-slaves might receive the vote before white women, so they lashed out in a parallel fashion against the men of the working class. Stanton insisted that the exclusion from the NLU proved ". . . what the *Revolution* has said again and again, that the worst enemies of Woman Suffrage will ever be the laboring classes of men."[11]

"Woman" was the test, but not every woman seemed to qualify. Black women, of course, were virtually invisible within the protracted campaign for woman suffrage. As for white working-class women, the suffrage leaders were probably impressed at first by the organizing efforts and militancy of their working-class sisters. But as it turned out, the working women themselves did not enthusiastically embrace the cause of woman suffrage. Although Susan B. Anthony and Elizabeth Cady Stanton persuaded several female labor leaders to protest the disfranchisement of women, the masses of working women were far too concerned about their immediate problems—wages, hours, working conditions—to fight for a cause that seemed terribly abstract. According to Anthony,

The great distinctive advantage possessed by the workingmen of this republic is that the son of the humblest citizen, black or white, has equal chances with the son of the richest in the land.[12]

Susan B. Anthony would never have made such a statement if she had familiarized herself with the realities of working-class families. As working women knew all too well, their fathers, brothers, husbands and sons who exercised the right to vote continued to be miserably exploited by their wealthy employers. Political equality did not open the door to economic equality.

"Woman Wants Bread, Not the Ballot"[13] was the title of a speech Susan B. Anthony frequently delivered as she sought to recruit more working women into the fight for suffrage. As the title indicates, she was critical of the working women's tendency to focus on their immediate needs. But they naturally sought tangible solutions to their immediate economic problems. And they were seldom moved by the suffragists' promise that the vote would permit them to become equal to their men—their exploited, suffering men. Even the members of the Working Women's Association, organized by Anthony in the offices of her newspaper, elected to refrain from fighting for suffrage. "Mrs. Stanton was anxious to have a workingwomen's suffrage association," explained the first vice-president of the Working Women's Association.

> It was left to a vote, and ruled out. The society at one time comprised over one hundred working women, but, as there was nothing practical done to ameliorate their condition, they gradually withdrew.[14]

Early in her career as a women's rights leader, Susan B. Anthony concluded that the ballot contained the real secret of women's emancipation, and that sexism itself was far more oppressive than class inequality and racism. In Anthony's eyes, "(T)he most odious oligarchy ever established on the face of the globe"[15] was the rule of men over women.

> An oligarchy of wealth, where the rich govern the poor; an oligarchy of learning, where the educated govern the ignorant; or even an oligarchy of race, where the Saxon rules the African, might be endured; but this oligarchy of sex which makes father, brothers, husband, sons, the oligarchs over the mother and sisters, the wife and daughters of every household; which ordains all men sovereigns, all women subjects—carries discord and rebellion into every home of the nation.[16]

Anthony's staunchly feminist position was also a staunch reflection of bourgeois ideology. And it was probably because of the ideology's blinding powers that she failed to realize that working-class women and Black women alike were fundamentally linked to their men by the class exploitation and racist oppression which did not discriminate between the sexes. While their men's sexist behavior definitely needed to be challenged, the real enemy—their common enemy—was the boss, the capitalist, or whoever was responsible for the miserable wages and unbearable working conditions and for racist and sexist discrimination on the job.

Working women did not raise the banner of suffrage en masse until the early twentieth century, when their own struggles forged special reasons for demanding the right to vote. When women struck the New York garment industry in the renowned "Uprising of the 20,000" during the winter of 1909–1910, the ballot began to acquire a special relevance to working women's struggles. As women labor leaders began to argue, working women could use the vote to demand better wages and improved conditions on the job. Woman suffrage could serve as a powerful weapon of class struggle. After the tragic fire at the New York Triangle Shirtwaist Company claimed the lives of 146 women, the need for legislation prohibiting the hazardous conditions of women's work became dramatically obvious. In other words, working women needed the ballot in order to guarantee their very survival.

The Women's Trade Union League urged the creation of Wage Earners' Suffrage Leagues. A leading member of the New York Suffrage League, Leonora O'Reilly, developed a powerful working-class defense of women's right to vote. Aiming her argument at the anti-suffrage politicians, she also questioned the legitimacy of the prevailing cult of motherhood.

> You may tell us that our place is in the home. There are 8,000,000 of us in these United States who must go out of it to earn our daily bread and we come to tell you that while we are working in the mills, the mines, the factories and the mercantile houses we have not the protection that we should have. You have been making laws for us and the laws you have made have not been good for us. Year after year working women have gone to the Legislature in every state and have tried to tell the story of their need . . .[17]

Now, so Leonora O'Reilly and her working-class sisters proclaimed, they were going to fight for the ballot—and indeed they would use it as a weapon to remove all those legislators from office whose loyalties were with big business. Working-class women demanded the right to suffrage as an arm to assist them in the ongoing class struggle. This new perspective within the campaign for woman suffrage bore witness to the rising influence of the socialist movement. Indeed, women socialists brought a new energy into the suffrage movement and defended the vision of struggle born of the experiences of their working-class sisters.

Of the eight million women in the labor force during the first decade of the twentieth century, more than two million were

Black. As women who suffered the combined disabilities of sex, class and race, they possessed a powerful argument for the right to vote. But racism ran so deep within the woman suffrage movement that the doors were never really opened to Black women. The exclusionary policies of the NAWSA did not entirely deter Black women from raising the demand for the vote. Ida B. Wells, Mary Church Terrell and Mary McCleod Bethune were among the most well-known Black suffragists.

Margaret Murray Washington, who was a leading figure of the National Association of Colored Women, confessed that ". . . personally, woman suffrage has never kept me awake at night . . ."[18] This casual indifference may well have been a reaction to the racist stance of the National American Woman Suffrage Association, for Washington also argued that

> (c)olored women, quite as much as colored men, realize that if there is ever to be equal justice and fair play in the protection in the courts everywhere for all races, then there must be an equal chance for women as well as men to express their preference through their votes.[19]

As Washington points out, the National Association of Colored Women's Clubs established a Suffrage Department to impart to its members knowledge about governmental affairs, ". . . so that women may be prepared to handle the vote intelligently and wisely . . ."[20] The entire Black women's club movement was imbued with the spirit of woman suffrage—and despite the rejection they received from the NAWSA, they continued to defend women's right to vote. When the Black Northeastern Federation of Clubs applied for membership in the NAWSA as late as 1919— just one year before victory—the leadership's response was a repeat of Susan B. Anthony's rejection of Black women suffragists a quarter century earlier. Informing the Federation that its application could not be considered, the NAWSA leader explained that

... if the news is flashed throughout the Southern States at this most critical moment that the National American Association has just admitted an organization of 6,000 colored women, the enemies can cease from further effort—the defeat of the amendment will be assured.[21]

Still, Black women supported the battle for suffrage until the very end.

Unlike their white sisters, Black women suffragists enjoyed the support of many of their men. Just as a Black man—Frederick Douglass—had been the most outstanding male advocate of women's equality during the nineteenth century, so W. E. B. DuBois emerged as the leading male advocate of woman suffrage in the twentieth century. In a satirical article on the 1913 suffrage parade in Washington, DuBois described the white men who hurled jeers as well as physical blows—and over one hundred people were injured—as the upholders of "the glorious traditions of Anglo-Saxon manhood."[22]

> Wasn't it glorious? Does it not make you burn with shame to be a mere black man when such mighty deeds are done by the Leaders of Civilization? Does it not make you "ashamed of your race"? Does it not make you "want to be white."[23]

Concluding the article on a serious note, DuBois quotes one of the white women marchers, who said that Black men had been unanimously respectful. Of the thousands watching the parade, "... not one of them was boisterous or rude ... The difference between them and those insolent, bold white men was remarkable."[24]

This parade, whose most sympathetic male spectators were Black, was rigidly segregated by its white women organizers. They even instructed Ida B. Wells to leave the Illinois contingent and to march with the segregated Black group—in deference to the white women from the South.

The request was made publicly during the rehearsal of the Illinois contingent, and while Mrs. Barnett (Ida Wells) glanced about the room, looking for support, the ladies debated the question of principle versus expediency, most of them evidently feeling that they must not prejudice Southerners against suffrage.[25]

Ida B. Wells was not one to follow racist instructions, however, and, at parade time, she slipped into the Illinois section.

As a male advocate of woman suffrage, W. E. B. DuBois was peerless among Black and white men alike. His militancy, his eloquence and the principled character of his numerous appeals caused many of his contemporaries to view him as the most outstanding male defender of women's political equality of his time. DuBois' appeals were impressive not only for their lucidity and persuasiveness, but also for their relative lack of male-supremacist undertones. In his speeches and writings, he welcomed the expanding leadership roles played by Black women, who ". . . are moving quietly but forcibly toward the intellectual leadership of the race."[26] While some men would have interpreted this rising power of women as a definite cause for alarm, W. E. B. DuBois argued that, on the contrary, this situation created a special urgency for extending the ballot to Black women. "The enfranchisement of these women will not be a mere doubling of our vote and voice in the nation," but will lead to a "stronger and more normal political life."[27]

In 1915 an article entitled "Votes for Women: A Symposium by Leading Thinkers in Colored America" was published by DuBois in *The Crisis.*[28] It was the transcript of a forum, whose participants included judges, ministers, university professors, elected officials, church leaders and educators. Charles W. Chesnutt, Reverend Francis J. Grimke, Benjamin Brawley and the Honorable Robert H. Terrell were some of the many male advocates of woman suffrage who spoke during this symposium. The women included Mary Church Terrell, Anna Jones and Josephine St. Pierre Ruffin.

The vast majority of the women who participated in the forum on woman suffrage were affiliated with the National Association of Colored Women. In their statements, there were surprisingly few invocations of the popular argument among white suffragists that women's "special nature," their domesticity and their innate morality gave them a special claim to the vote. There was one glaring exception, however. Nannie H. Burroughs—educator and church leader—carried the womanly morality thesis so far as to imply the absolute superiority of Black women over their men. Women needed the vote, Burroughs insisted, because their men had "bartered and sold" this valuable weapon.

> The Negro woman . . . needs the ballot to get back, by the wise *use* of it, what the Negro man has lost by the *misuse* of it. She needs it to ransom her race. . . . A comparison with the men of her race, in moral issues, is odious. She carries the burdens of the Church, and of the school and bears a great deal more than her economic share in the home.[29]

Of the dozen or so women participants, Burroughs alone assumed a position which rested on the convoluted argument that women were morally superior (implying, of course, that they were inferior to men in most other respects). Mary Church Terrell spoke on "Woman Suffrage and the Fifteenth Amendment," Anna Jones on "Woman Suffrage and Social Reform" and Josephine St. Pierre Ruffin described her own historical experiences in the woman suffrage campaign. Others focused their remarks on working women, education, children and club life. In concluding her remarks on "Women and Colored Women," Mary Talbert summed up the admiration for Black women expressed throughout the symposium.

> By her peculiar position, the colored woman has gained clear powers of observation and judgment—exactly the sort of powers which are today peculiarly necessary to the building of an ideal country.[30]

Black women had been more than willing to contribute those "clear powers of observation and judgement" toward the creation of a multi-racial movement for women's political rights. But at every turn, they were betrayed, spurned and rejected by the leaders of the lily-white woman suffrage movement. For suffragists and clubwomen alike, Black women were simply expendable entities when it came time to woo Southern support with a white complexion. As for the woman suffrage campaign, it appears that all those concessions to Southern women made very little difference in the end. When the votes on the Nineteenth Amendment were tallied, the Southern states were still lined up in the opposition camp—and, in fact, almost managed to defeat the amendment.

After the long-awaited victory of woman suffrage, Black women in the South were violently prevented from exercising their newly acquired right. The eruption of Ku Klux Klan violence in places like Orange County, Florida, brought injury and death to Black women and their children. In other places, they were more peacefully prohibited from exercising their new right. In Americus, Georgia, for instance,

> . . . more than 250 colored women went to the polls to vote but were turned down or their ballots refused to be taken by the election manager . . .[31]

In the ranks of the movement which had so fervently fought for the enfranchisement of women, there was hardly a cry of protest to be heard.

10 ᵒ Communist Women

In 1848, the year Karl Marx and Frederick Engels published their *Communist Manifesto,* Europe was the scene of countless revolutionary uprisings. One of the participants in the Revolution of 1848—an artillery officer, and close co-worker of Marx and Engels, named Joseph Weydemeyer—immigrated to the United States and founded the first Marxist organization in the country's history.[1] When Weydemeyer established the Proletarian League in 1852, no women appear to have been associated with the group. If indeed there were any women involved, they have long since faded into historical anonymity. Over the next few decades women continued to be active in their own labor associations, in the anti-slavery movement and in the developing campaign for their own rights. But, to all intents and purposes, they appear to have been absent from the ranks of the Marxist socialist movement. Like the Proletarian League, the Workingmen's National Association and the Communist Club were utterly dominated by men. Even the Socialist Labor party was also predominantly male.[2]

By the time the Socialist party was founded in 1900, the composition of the socialist movement had begun to change. As the general demand for women's equality grew stronger, women were increasingly attracted to the struggle for social change. They began to assert their right to participate in this new challenge to the oppressive structures of their society. From 1900 on, to a greater or lesser extent, the Marxist Left would feel the influence of its female adherents.

As the main champion of Marxism for almost two decades, the Socialist party supported the battle for women's equality. For many years, in fact, it was the only political party to advocate woman suffrage.[3] Thanks to such socialist women as Pauline Newman and Rose Schneiderman, a working-class suffrage movement was forged, breaking the decade-long stronghold of middle-class women on the mass campaign for the vote.[4] By 1908 the Socialist party had created a national women's commission. On March 8 of that year women Socialists active on New York's Lower East Side organized a mass demonstration in support of equal suffrage, whose anniversary continues to be observed all over the world as International Women's Day.[5] When the Communist party was founded in 1919 (actually, two Communist parties, which later united, were established), former Socialist party women were among its earliest leaders and activists: "Mother" Ella Reeve Bloor, Anita Whitney, Margaret Prevey, Kate Sadler Greenhalgh, Rose Pastor Stokes and Jeanette Pearl were all Communists who had been associated with the left wing of the Socialist party.[6]

Although the International Workers of the World was not a political party—and, in fact, opposed the organization of political parties—it was the second major influence on the formation of the Communist party. The IWW, popularly known as the "Wobblies," was founded in June of 1905. Defining itself as an industrial union, the IWW proclaimed that there could never be a harmonious relationship between the capitalist class and the workers it employed. The Wobblies' ultimate goal was socialism, and their strategy was unrelenting class struggle. When "Big Bill" Haywood convened that first meeting, two of the leading labor organizers who sat on the platform were women—"Mother" Mary Jones and Lucy Parsons.

While both the Socialist party and the IWW admitted women to their ranks and encouraged them to become leaders and agita-

tors, only the IWW embraced a complementary policy of forthright struggle against racism. Under the leadership of Daniel
DeLeon, the Socialist party did not acknowledge the unique oppression of Black people. Although the majority of Black people
were agricultural workers—sharecroppers, tenant farmers and
farm laborers—the Socialists argued that only the proletarians
were relevant to their movement. Even the outstanding leader
Eugene Debs argued that Black people required no overall defense of their rights to be equal and free as a group. Since the
Socialists' overriding concern was the struggle between capital
and labor, so Debs maintained, "we have nothing special to offer
the Negro."[7] As for the International Workers of the World,
their main goal was to organize the wage-earning class and to
develop revolutionary, socialist class consciousness. Unlike the
Socialist party, however, the IWW focused explicit attention on
the special problems of Black people. According to Mary White
Ovington,

> (t)here are two organizations in this country that have shown they
> do care about full rights for the Negro. The first is the National
> Association for the Advancement of Colored People. . . . The
> second organization that attacks Negro segregation is the Industrial
> Workers of the World. . . . The IWW has stood with the Negro.[8]

Helen Holman was a Black Socialist, a leading spokesperson in
the campaign to defend her imprisoned party leader, Kate Rich-
ards O'Hare. As a Black woman, however, Helen Holman was a
rarity within the ranks of the Socialist party. Prior to World War
II, the numbers of Black women working in industry were negligible. As a consequence, they were all but ignored by Socialist party
recruiters. The Socialists' posture of negligence vis-à-vis Black
women was one of the unfortunate legacies the Communist party
would have to overcome.

Socialists: not including blacks

According to the Communist leader and historian, William Z. Foster, "during the early 1920's, the Party . . . was neglectful of the particular demands of Negro women in industry."[9] Over the next decade, however, Communists came to recognize the centrality of racism in U.S. society. They developed a serious theory of Black Liberation and forged a consistent activist record in the overall struggle against racism.

LUCY PARSONS

Lucy Parsons remains one of those few Black women whose name has occasionally appeared in the chronicles of the U.S. labor movement. Almost universally, however, she is simplistically identified as the "devoted wife" of the Haymarket martyr Albert Parsons. To be sure, Lucy Parsons was one of her husband's most militant defenders, but she was far more than a faithful wife and angry widow who wanted to defend and avenge her husband. As Carolyn Asbaugh's recent biography[10] confirms, her journalistic and agitational defense of the working class as a whole spanned a period of more than sixty years. Lucy Parsons' involvement in labor struggles began almost a decade before the Haymarket Massacre and continued for another fifty-five years afterward. Her political development ranged from her youthful advocacy of anarchism to her membership in the Communist party during her mature years.

Born in 1853, Lucy Parsons became active in the Socialist Labor party as early as 1877. Over the years to come, this anarchist organization's newspaper, the *Socialist,* would publish her articles and poems, and Parsons would also become an active organizer for the Chicago Working Women's Union.[11] Following the police-instigated riot on May 1, 1886, in Chicago's Haymarket Square, her husband was one of the eight radical labor leaders arrested by the authorities. Lucy Parsons immediately initiated a militant campaign to free the Haymarket Defendants. As she traveled throughout the country, she became known as a prominent labor leader and a leading advocate of anarchism. Her reputation caused her to become an all-too-frequent target of repression. In Columbus, Ohio, for example, the mayor banned a speech she was scheduled to deliver during the month of March—and her refusal to respect this banning order led the police to throw her in jail.[12] In city after city,

> (h)alls were closed to her at the last moment, detectives stood in every corner of the meeting halls, police kept her under constant surveillance.[13]

Even as her husband was being executed, Lucy Parsons and her two children were arrested by Chicago police, one of whom made the comment: "(t)hat woman is more to be feared than a thousand rioters."[14]

Although she was Black—a fact miscegenation laws often caused her to conceal—and although she was a woman, Lucy Parsons argued that racism and sexism were overshadowed by the capitalists' overall exploitation of the working class. Since they were victims of capitalist exploitation, said Parsons, Black people and women, no less than white people and men, should devote all their energies to the class struggle. In her eyes, Black people and women did not suffer special forms of oppression and there was no real need for mass movements to oppose racism and sexism explicitly. Sex and race, according to Lucy Parsons' theory, were facts of existence manipulated by employers who sought to justify their greater exploitation of women and people of color. If Black people suffered the brutality of lynch law, it was because their poverty as a group made them the most vulnerable workers of all. "Are there any so stupid," Parsons asked in 1886, "as to believe

these outrages have been . . . heaped upon the Negro because he
is black?"[15]

*not because of
color status
→ status*

> Not at all. It is because he is *poor.* It is because he is dependent.
> Because he is poorer as a class than his white wage-slave brother
> of the North.[16]

Lucy Parsons and "Mother" Mary Jones were the first two
women to join the radical labor organization known as the International Workers of the World. Highly respected in the labor
movement, both were invited to sit in the presidium alongside
Eugene Debs and Big Bill Haywood during the 1905 founding
convention of the IWW. In the speech Lucy Parsons delivered
to the convention delegates, she revealed her special sensitivity to
the oppression of working women who, in her view, were manipulated by the capitalists as they sought to reduce the wages of the
entire working class.

> We, the women of this country, have no ballot even if we wished
> to use it . . . but we have our labor. . . . Wherever wages are to be
> reduced, the capitalist class uses women to reduce them.[17]

Moreover, during this era when the plight of prostitutes was
virtually ignored, Parsons told the IWW convention that she also
spoke for "my sisters whom I can see in the night when I go out
in Chicago."[18]

During the 1920s Lucy Parsons began to associate herself with
the struggles of the young Communist party. One of the many
people who was deeply impressed by the 1917 workers' revolution
in Russia, she became confident that eventually the working class
could triumph in the United States of America. When Communists and other progressive forces founded the International
Labor Defense in 1925, Parsons became an active worker for the
new group. She fought for the freedom of Tom Mooney in Cali-

fornia, for the Scottsboro Nine in Alabama and for the young Black Communist Angelo Herndon, whom Georgia authorities had imprisoned.[19] It was in 1939, according to her biographer's research, that Lucy Parsons formally joined the Communist party.[20] When she died in 1942, a tribute in the *Daily Worker* described her as

> . . . a link between the labor movement of the present and the great historic events of the 1880's . . .
>
> She was one of America's truly great women, fearless, and devoted to the working class.[21]

ELLA REEVE BLOOR

Born in 1862, the remarkable labor organizer and agitator for women's rights, Black equality, peace and socialism, who was popularly known as "Mother" Bloor, became a member of the Socialist party soon after it was founded. She went on to become a Socialist leader and a living legend for the working class across the country. Hitchhiking from one end of the United States to the other, she became the heart and soul of untold numbers of strikes. Streetcar operators in Philadelphia heard her first strike speeches. In other parts of the country, miners, textile workers and sharecroppers were among the workers who benefited from her astounding oratorical talents and her powerful skills as an organizer. At the age of sixty-two Mother Bloor was still thumbing rides from one state to another.[22]

When she was seventy-eight Mother Bloor published the story of her life as a labor organizer, from her pre-Socialist days through the period of her Communist party membership. As a Socialist, her working-class consciousness did not include an explicit awareness of Black people's special oppression. As a Communist, however, Mother Bloor fought numerous manifestations of racism and urged others to follow her example. In 1929, for example, when the International Labor Defense held its convention in Pittsburgh, Pennsylvania,

> (w)e had engaged rooms for all the delegates in the Monogahala Hotel. When we arrived late at night with twenty-five Negro delegates, the manager of the hotel said that while they could stay there that night, they must all get out immediately the next morning.
>
> Next morning, we voted that the whole convention should adjourn to the hotel in an orderly fashion. We marched to the hotel carrying banners emphasizing "no discrimination." We filed into the lobby, which by that time was filled with newspapermen, policemen, and curious crowds . . .[23]

During the early 1930s Mother Bloor addressed a meeting in Loup City, Nebraska, in support of women who had struck against their poultry-farm employers. The strike assembly was violently assaulted by a racist mob opposed to the presence of Black people at the meeting. When the police arrived, Mother Bloor was arrested, together with a Black woman and her husband. The Black woman, Mrs. Floyd Booth, was a leading member of the local Anti-War Committee and her husband was an activist in the town's Unemployed Council. When the local farmers raised sufficient bail money to obtain Mother Bloor's release, she refused their aid, insisting that she would not leave until the Booths could accompany her.[24]

> I felt I could not accept the bail and leave the two Negro comrades in jail, in an atmosphere so dangerously charged with bitter hate of Negroes.[25]

During this period Mother Bloor organized a U.S. delegation to attend an International Women's Conference in Paris. Four of the women included in the delegation were Black:

Capitola Tasker, Alabama sharecropper, tall and graceful, the life of the whole delegation; Lulia Jackson, elected by the Pennsylvania miners; a woman who represented the mothers of the Scottsboro Boys; and Mabel Byrd, a brilliant young honor graduate of the University of Washington, who had had a position with the International Labor Office in Geneva.[26]

At the 1934 Paris conference, Capitola Tasker was one of three U.S. women elected to serve as a member of the assembly's executive committee—along with Mother Bloor and the woman representing the Socialist party. Mabel Byrd, the Black college graduate, was elected as one of the conference secretaries.[27]

Lulia Jackson, the Black representative of Pennsylvania miners, emerged as one of the Paris Women's Conference's leading personalities. In her persuasive response to the pacifist faction attending the gathering, she argued that support for the war against fascism was the sole means of guaranteeing a meaningful peace. During the course of the women's deliberations, a committed pacifist had complained:

> I think there is too much about fighting in that (anti-war) manifesto. It says fight against war, fight for peace—fight, fight, fight . . . We are women, we are mothers—we don't want to fight. We know that even when our children are bad, we are nice to them, and we win them by love, not by fighting them.[28]

Lulia Jackson's counterargument was forthright and lucid:

> Ladies, it has just been said that we must not fight, that we must be gentle and kind to our enemies, to those who are for war. I can't agree with that. Everyone knows the cause of war—it is capitalism. We can't just give those bad capitalists their supper and put them to bed the way we do with our children. We must fight them.[29]

As Mother Bloor relates in her autobiography, "everyone laughed, and applauded, even the pacifist,"[30] and the anti-war manifesto was consequently approved by the entire body.

When the conference was addressed by Capitola Tasker—the Black sharecropper from Alabama—they heard her compare the current European fascism with the racist terror suffered by Black people in the United States. Having vividly described the Southern and mob murders, she acquainted the Paris delegates with the violent repression aimed at sharecroppers who were attempting to organize in Alabama. Her own opposition to fascism ran deep, so Capitola Tasker explained, for she herself had already been victimized by its terrible ravages. She concluded her speech with the "sharecroppers' song," which she adapted to fit the occasion:

> Like a tree that's standing by the water,
> We shall not be moved—
> We're against war and fascism
> We shall not be moved.[31]

As the U.S. delegation returned home by boat, Mother Bloor recorded Capitola Tasker's moving testimony about her Paris experiences:

"Mother, when I get back to Alabama and go out to that cotton patch back of our little old shack, I'll stand there thinking to myself, 'Capitola, did you really go over there to Paris and see all those wonderful women and hear all those great talks, or was it just a dream that you were over there?' And if it turns out that it really wasn't a dream, why Mother, I'm just going to broadcast all over Alabama all that I've learned over here, and tell them how women from all over the world are fighting to stop the kind of terror we have in the South, and to stop war."[32]

As Mother Bloor and her Communist party comrades concluded, the working class cannot assume its historical role as a revolutionary force if workers do not struggle relentlessly against the social poison of racism. The long list of stunning accomplishments associated with the name of Ella Reeve Bloor reveals that this white Communist woman was a deeply principled ally of the Black Liberation movement.

ANITA WHITNEY

When Anita Whitney was born in 1867 to a wealthy San Francisco family, no one would have suspected that she would eventually be the chairperson of the California Communist party. Perhaps she was destined to become a political activist, for as a fresh graduate of Wellesley—the prestigious New England women's college—she did volunteer charity and settlement-house work and soon became an active champion of woman suffrage. Upon her return to California, Anita Whitney joined the Equal Suffrage League and was elected president in time to see her state become the sixth in the nation to extend the vote to women.[33]

In 1914 Anita Whitney joined the Socialist party. Despite her party's posture of relative indifference toward Black people's struggles, she readily supported anti-racist causes. When the San Francisco Bay Area chapter of the National Association for the Advancement of Colored People was founded, Whitney enthusiastically agreed to serve as a member of its executive committee.[34] Having identified with the positions of left-wing members of the Socialist party, she joined those who established the Communist Labor party in 1919.[35] Shortly thereafter, this group merged with the Communist Party, U.S.A.

Nineteen-nineteen was the year of the infamous anti-Communist raids initiated by Attorney General A. Mitchell Palmer. Anita was destined to become one of the many victims of the Palmer raids. She was informed that a speech she was scheduled to deliver before clubwomen associated with the Oakland Center of the California Civic League had been banned by the authorities. But despite the official prohibition, she spoke on November 28, 1919, about "The Negro Problem In the United States."[36] Her remarks were sharply focused on the issue of lynching.

> Since 1890, when our statistics have their beginning, there have occurred in these United States 3,228 lynchings, 2,500 of colored men and 50 of colored women. I would that I could leave the subject with these bare facts recording numbers, but I feel that we must face all the barbarity of the situation in order to do our part in blotting this disgrace from our country's record.[37]

She went on to pose a question to the audience of white clubwomen: Did they know that "a colored man once said that if he owned Hell and Texas, he would prefer to rent out Texas and live in Hell . . ."?[38] His reasoning, she explained in a serious vein, was based on the fact that Texas could claim the third largest number of racist mob murders committed throughout the Southern states. (Only Georgia and Mississippi could boast of more.)

In 1919 it was still something of a rarity for a white person to appeal to others of her race to stand up against the scourge of lynching. The generalized racist propaganda, and the repeated evocation of the mythical Black rapist in particular, had resulted in the desired division and alienation. Even in progressive circles, white people were often hesitant to speak out against lynchings, since they were justified as unfortunate reactions to Black sexual attacks against white womanhood in the South. Anita Whitney was one of those white people whose vision remained clear despite the power of the prevailing racist propaganda. And she was willing to risk the consequences of her anti-racist stance. Although it was clear that she would be arrested, she chose to speak about lynching to the white Oakland clubwomen. Sure enough, she was taken into custody at the conclusion of her speech and charged by the authorities with criminal syndicalism. Whitney was later convicted and sentenced to San Quentin Prison, where she spent several weeks before her release on appeal bond. It was not until 1927 that Anita Whitney was pardoned by the governor of California.[39]

As a twentieth-century white woman, Anita Whitney was indeed a pioneer in the struggle against racism. Together with her Black comrades, she and others like her would forge the Communist party's strategy for working-class emancipation. In this strategy, the fight for Black Liberation would be a central ingredient. In 1936 Anita Whitney became the state chairperson of the Communist party of California, and was elected soon thereafter to serve on the party's National Committee.

> Once she was asked, "Anita, how do you regard the Communist Party? What has it come to mean to you?"
> "Why," she smiled incredulously, a bit taken aback by such an amazing question. "Why . . . it has given purpose to my life. The Communist Party is the hope of the World."[40]

ELIZABETH GURLEY FLYNN

When Elizabeth Gurley Flynn died in 1964 at the age of seventy-four, she had been active in Socialist and Communist causes for almost sixty years. Raised by parents who were members of the Socialist party, she discovered, at an early age, her own affinity with the Socialists' challenge to the capitalist class. The young Elizabeth was not yet sixteen when she delivered her first public lecture in defense of socialism. Based on her readings of

Mary Wollstonecraft's *Vindication of the Rights of Women* and August Bebel's *Women and Socialism,* she delivered a speech in 1906, at the Harlem Socialist Club, entitled "What Socialism Will Do for Women."[41] Although her somewhat "male-supremacist" father had been reluctant to allow Elizabeth to speak in public, the enthusiastic reception in Harlem caused him to change his mind. Accompanying her father, she became familiar with street speaking, which was a typical radical tactic of the period. Elizabeth Gurley Flynn experienced her first arrest soon thereafter—charged with "speaking without a permit," she was carted off to jail with her father.[42]

By the time Elizabeth Gurley Flynn was sixteen, her career as an agitator for the rights of the working class had been launched. Her first task was the defense of Big Bill Haywood, whose frame-up on criminal charges had been instigated by the copper trusts. During her westward travels on behalf of Haywood, she joined the IWW's struggles in Montana and Washington.[43] After two years as a Socialist party member, Elizabeth Gurley Flynn became a leading IWW organizer. She resigned from the Socialist party, "convinced that it was sterile and sectarian compared with this grass-roots movement that was sweeping the country."[44]

With an abundance of strike experiences behind her, including numerous clashes with the police, Elizabeth Gurley Flynn headed for Lawrence, Massachusetts, in 1912 when the textile workers went out on strike. The grievances of the Lawrence workers were simple and compelling. In the words of Mary Heaton Vorse,

> Wages in Lawrence were so low that thirty-five percent of the people made under seven dollars a week. Less than a fifth got more than twelve dollars a week. They were divided by nationality. They spoke over forty languages and dialects, but they were united by meager living and the fact that their children died. For every five

children under one year of age, one died. . . . Only a few other towns in America had higher death rates. These were all mill towns.[45]

Of all the speakers addressing the strike meeting, said Vorse, who was covering these events for *Harper's Weekly,* Elizabeth Gurley Flynn was the workers' most powerful inspiration. It was her words which encouraged them to perservere.

> When Elizabeth Gurley Flynn spoke, the excitement of the crowd became a visible thing. She stood there, young, with her Irish blue eyes, her face magnolia white and her cloud of black hair, the picture of a youthful revolutionary girl leader. She stirred them, lifted them up in her appeal for solidarity. . . . It was as though a spurt of flame had gone through this audience, something stirring and powerful, a feeling which had made the liberation of people possible.[46]

As a traveling strike agitator for the IWW, Elizabeth Gurley Flynn sometimes worked alongside the well-known Native American Indian leader, Frank Little. In 1916, for example, they both represented the Wobblies during the Mesabi iron range strike in Minnesota. It was barely a year later when Elizabeth learned that Frank Little had been lynched in Butte, Montana. He had been attacked by a mob after making agitational speeches to the miners on strike in the area.

> . . . (S)ix masked men came to the hotel at night, broke down the door, dragged Frank from his bed, took him to a railroad trestle on the outskirts of town and there hanged him.[47]

A month following Frank Little's death, a federal indictment charged that 168 people had conspired with him "to hinder the execution of certain laws of the United States . . ."[48] Elizabeth Gurley Flynn was the only woman among the accused, and Ben

Fletcher, a Philadelphia longshoreman and leader of the IWW, was the only Black person named in the indictment.[49]

Judging from Elizabeth Gurley Flynn's autobiographical reflections, she was aware, from the very beginning of her political career, of the special oppression suffered by Black people. Her consciousness of the importance of anti-racist struggles was doubtlessly intensified by her involvement in the IWW. The Wobblies publicly proclaimed that

> (t)here is only *one* labor organization in the United States that admits the colored worker on a footing of absolute equality with the white—the Industrial Workers of the World. . . . In the IWW the colored worker, man or woman, is on an equal footing with every other worker.[50]

But the IWW was a syndicalist organization concentrating on industrial workers, who—thanks to racist discrimination—were still overwhelmingly white. The tiny minority of Black industrial workers included practically no women, who remained absolutely banned from industrial occupations. Indeed, most Black workers, male and female alike, still worked in agriculture or domestic service. As a result, only a fraction of the Black population could be reached through an industrial union—unless the union strenuously fought for Black people's admission into industry.

Elizabeth Gurley Flynn became active in the Communist party in 1937[51] and emerged soon afterward as one of the organization's major leaders. Working on an intimate basis with such Black Communists as Benjamin Davis and Claudia Jones, she developed a new understanding of the central role of Black Liberation within the overall battle for the emancipation of the working class. In 1948 Flynn published an article in *Political Affairs*, the party's theoretical journal, on the meaning of International Women's Day. As she argued in this article, (t)he right to work, to training, upgrading, and equal seniority; safeguards for health and safety; adequate child care facilities—these remain the urgent demands of organized workingwomen, and are needed by all who toil, especially Negro women . . .[52]

Criticizing the inequality between women war veterans and men war veterans, she reminded her readers that Black women veterans suffered to an even greater degree than their white sisters. Indeed, Black women were generally caught in a threefold bond of oppression.

Every inequality and disability inflicted on American white women is aggravated a thousandfold among Negro women, who are triply exploited—as Negroes, as workers, and as women.[53]

This same "triple jeopardy" analysis, incidentally, was later proposed by Black women who sought to influence the early stages of the contemporary Women's Liberation movement.

While Elizabeth Gurley Flynn's first autobiography, *I Speak My Own Piece* (or *The Rebel Girl*), provides fascinating glimpses into her experiences as an IWW agitator, her second book, *The Alderson Story* (or *My Life as a Political Prisoner*), reveals a new political maturity and a more profound consciousness of racism. During the McCarthy Era assault on the Communist party, Flynn was arrested in New York, along with three other women, and charged with "teaching and advocating the violent overthrow of the government."[54] The other women were Marian Bachrach, Betty Gannet and Claudia Jones, a Black woman from Trinidad who had immigrated to the United States as a young girl. In June, 1951, the four Communist women were taken by the police to the New York Women's House of Detention. The "one pleasant episode" which "lighted up our stay here" involved the birthday party which Elizabeth, Betty and Claudia organized for one of the prisoners. "Discouraged and lonely," a nineteen-year-old Black woman had "happened to mention that the next day would be her birthday."[55] The three women managed to obtain a cake from the commissary.

> We made candles of tissue paper for the cake, covered the table as nicely as possible with paper napkins, and sang "Happy Birthday." We made speeches to her and she cried with surprise and happiness. The next day we received a note from her as follows: (exact spelling)
> Dear Claudia, Betty and Elizabeth. I am very glad for what you did for me for my birthday. I really don't know how to thank you. . . . Yesterday was one of the best years of my life. I think even thou you all are Communist people that you are the best people I have ever met. The reason I put Communists in this letter is because some people don't like Communists for the simple reason they think Communist people is against the American people but I don't think so. I think that you are some of the nicest people I ever met in my hol 19 teen years of living and I will never forget you all no matter where I be. . . . I hope you all will get out of this trouble and never have to come back to a place like this.[56]

After the three women's Smith Act trial (Marian Bachrach's health problems led to the severance of her case), they were convicted and sentenced to serve time in the Federal Reformatory for Women in Alderson, Virginia. Shortly before they arrived, the prison had been placed under court order to desegregate its facilities. Another Smith Act victim—Dorothy Rose Blumenberg from Baltimore—had already served a portion of her three-year sentence as one of the first white prisoners to be housed with Black women. "We felt both amused and flattered that Communists were called upon to help integrate prison houses."[57] Yet, as Elizabeth Gurley Flynn pointed out, the legal desegregation of the prison's cottages did not have the result of ending racial discrimination. The Black women continued to be assigned to the hardest jobs—"on the farm, in the cannery, in maintenance and at the piggery until it was abolished."[58]

As a leader of the Communist party, Elizabeth Gurley Flynn had developed a deep commitment to the Black Liberation struggle and had come to realize that Black people's resistance is not always consciously political. She observed that among the prisoners in Alderson,

> (t)here was greater solidarity among Negro women, undoubtedly a result of life outside, especially in the South. It seemed to me that they were of better character, by and large, stronger and more dependable, with less inclination to tattle or be a stool pigeon, than the white inmates.[59]

She made friends more easily among the Black women in prison than she did among the white inmates. "Frankly, I trusted the Negro women more than I did the whites. They were more controlled, less hysterical, less spoiled, more mature."[60] And the Black women, in turn, were more receptive to Elizabeth. Perhaps they sensed in this white woman Communist an instinctive kinship in struggle.

CLAUDIA JONES

Born in Trinidad when it was still the British West Indies, Claudia Jones immigrated to the United States with her parents when she was still quite young. She later became one of the countless Black people throughout the country who joined the movement to free the Scottsboro Nine. It was through her work in the Scottsboro Defense Committee that she became acquainted with members of the Communist party, whose organization she enthusiastically joined.[61] As a young woman in her twenties, Claudia Jones assumed responsibility for the party's Women's Commission and became a leader and symbol of struggle for Communist women throughout the country.

Among the many articles Claudia Jones published in the journal *Political Affairs,* one of the most outstanding was the June 1949 piece entitled "An End to the Neglect of the Problems of Negro Women."[62] Her vision of Black women in this essay was meant to refute the usual male-supremacist stereotypes regarding the nature of women's role. Black women's leadership, as Jones pointed out, had always been indispensable to their people's fight for freedom. Seldom mentioned in the orthodox histories, for example, was the fact that "the sharecroppers' strikes of the 1930's were sparked by Negro women."[63] Moreover,

> Negro women played a magnificent part in the pre-CIO days in strikes and other struggles, both as workers and as wives of workers, to win recognition of the principle of industrial unionism, in such industries as auto, packing, steel, etc. More recently, the militancy of Negro women unionists is shown in the strike of the packinghouse workers, and even more so in the tobacco workers' strike, in which such leaders as Moranda Smith and Velma Hopkins emerged as outstanding trade unionists.[64]

Claudia Jones chided progressives—and especially trade unionists—for failing to acknowledge Black domestic workers' efforts to organize themselves. Because the majority of Black women workers were still employed in domestic service, she argued, the paternalistic attitudes toward maids influenced the prevailing social definition of Black women as a group:

> The continued relegation of Negro women to domestic work has helped to perpetuate and intensify chauvinism directed against all Negro Women.[65]

Jones was not afraid to remind her own white friends and comrades that "(t)oo many progressives, and even some Communists, are still guilty of exploiting Negro domestic workers."[66] And they are sometimes guilty of ". . . participating in the vilification of 'maids' when speaking to their bourgeois neighbors and their own families."[67] Claudia Jones was very much a Communist—a dedicated Communist who believed that socialism held the only promise of liberation for Black women, for Black people as a whole and indeed for the multi-racial working class. Thus, her criticism was motivated by the constructive desire to urge her white co-workers and comrades to purge themselves of racist and sexist attitudes. As for the party itself,

> in our . . . clubs, we must conduct an intense discussion of the role of Negro women, so as to equip our Party membership with a clear understanding for undertaking the necessary struggles in the shops and communities.[68]

As many Black women had argued before her, Claudia Jones claimed that white women in the progressive movement—and especially white women Communists—bore a special responsibility toward Black women.

> The very economic relationship of Negro women to white women, which perpetuates "madam-maid" relationships, feeds chauvinist attitudes and makes it incumbent on white women progressives, and especially Communists, to fight consciously against all manifestations of white chauvinism, open and subtle.[69]

When Claudia Jones' Smith Act conviction led to her imprisonment in Alderson Federal Reformatory for Women, she discovered a veritable microcosm of the racist society she already knew so well. Although the prison was under court order to desegregate its facilities, Claudia was assigned to a "colored cottage," which isolated her from her two white comrades, Elizabeth Gurley Flynn and Betty Gannet. Elizabeth Gurley Flynn especially suffered from this separation, for she and Claudia Jones were close friends as well as comrades. When Claudia was released from prison in October of 1955—ten months after the Communist women had arrived at Alderson—Elizabeth was happy for her friend yet aware of the pain she would suffer in Claudia's absence.

> My window faced the roadway, and I was able to see her leave. She turned to wave—tall, slender, beautiful, dressed in golden brown, and then she was gone. This was the hardest day I spent in prison. I felt so alone.[70]

On the day Claudia Jones left Alderson, Elizabeth Gurley Flynn wrote a poem entitled "Farewell to Claudia":

> Nearer and nearer drew this day, dear comrade,
> When I from you must sadly part,
> Day after day, a dark foreboding sorrow,
> Crept through my anxious heart.
>
> No more to see you striding down the pathway,
> No more to see your smiling eyes and radiant face.
> No more to hear your gay and pealing laughter,
> No more encircled by your love, in this sad place.
>
> How I will miss you, words will fail to utter,
> I am alone, my thoughts unshared, these weary days,
> I feel bereft and empty, on this gray and dreary morning,
> Facing my lonely future, hemmed in by prison ways.
>
> Sometimes I feel you've never been in Alderson,
> So full of life, so detached from here you seem.

So proud of walk, of talk, of work, of being,
Your presence here is like a fading fevered dream.

Yet as the sun shines now, through fog and darkness,
I feel a sudden joy that you are gone,
That once again you walk the streets of Harlem,
That today for you at least is Freedom's dawn.

I will be strong in our common faith, dear comrade,
I will be self-sufficient, to our ideals firm and true,
I will be strong to keep my mind and soul outside a prison,
Encouraged and inspired by ever loving memories of you.[71]

Soon after Claudia Jones was released from Alderson, the pressures of McCarthyism resulted in her deportation to England. She continued her political work for a while, editing a journal called the *West Indian Gazette.* But her failing health continued to deteriorate and she soon fell ill with a disease which claimed her life.

11 ~ Rape, Racism and the Myth of the Black Rapist

Some of the most flagrant symptoms of social deterioration are acknowledged as serious problems only when they have assumed such epidemic proportions that they appear to defy solution. Rape is a case in point. In the United States today, it is one of the fastest-growing violent crimes.[1] After ages of silence, suffering and misplaced guilt, sexual assault is explosively emerging as one of the telling dysfunctions of present-day capitalist society. The rising public concern about rape in the United States has inspired countless numbers of women to divulge their past encounters with actual or would-be assailants. As a result, an awesome fact has come to light: appallingly few women can claim that they have not been victims, at one time in their lives, of either attempted or accomplished sexual attacks.

In the United States and other capitalist countries, rape laws as a rule were framed originally for the protection of men of the upper classes, whose daughters and wives might be assaulted. What happens to working-class women has usually been of little concern to the courts; as a result, remarkably few white men have been prosecuted for the sexual violence they have inflicted on these women. While the rapists have seldom been brought to justice, the rape charge has been indiscriminately aimed at Black men, the guilty and innocent alike. Thus, of the 455 men executed between 1930 and 1967 on the basis of rape convictions, 405 of them were Black.[2]

In the history of the United States, the fraudulent rape charge stands out as one of the most formidable artifices invented by racism. The myth of the Black rapist has been methodically conjured up whenever recurrent waves of violence and terror against the Black community have required convincing justifications. If Black women have been conspicuously absent from the ranks of the contemporary anti-rape movement, it may be due, in part, to that movement's indifferent posture toward the frame-up rape charge as an incitement to racist aggression. Too many innocents have been offered sacrificially to gas chambers and lifer's cells for Black women to join those who often seek relief from policemen and judges. Moreover, as rape victims themselves, they have found little if any sympathy from these men in uniforms and robes. And stories about police assaults on Black women—rape victims sometimes suffering a second rape—are heard too frequently to be dismissed as aberrations. "Even at the strongest time of the civil rights movement in Birmingham," for example,

> young activists often stated that nothing could protect Black women from being raped by Birmingham police. As recently as December, 1974, in Chicago, a 17-year old Black woman reported that she was gang-raped by 10 policemen. Some of the men were suspended, but ultimately the whole thing was swept under the rug.[3]

During the early stages of the contemporary anti-rape movement, few feminist theorists seriously analyzed the special circumstances surrounding the Black woman as rape victim. The historical knot binding Black women—systematically abused and violated by white men—to Black men—maimed and murdered because of the racist manipulation of the rape charge—has just begun to be acknowledged to any significant extent. Whenever Black women have challenged rape, they usually and simultaneously expose the use of the frame-up rape charge as a deadly racist weapon against their men. As one extremely perceptive writer put it:

> The myth of the black rapist of white women is the twin of the myth of the bad black woman—both designed to apologize for and facilitate the continued exploitation of black men and women. Black women perceived this connection very clearly and were early in the forefront of the fight against lynching.[4]

Gerda Lerner, the author of this passage, is one of the few white women writing on the subject of rape during the early 1970s who examined in depth the combined effect of racism and sexism on Black women. The case of Joann Little,[5] tried during the summer of 1975, illustrated Lerner's point. Brought to trial on murder charges, the young Black woman was accused of killing a white guard in a North Carolina jail where she was the only woman inmate. When Joann Little took the stand, she told how the guard had raped her in her cell and how she had killed him in self-defense with the ice pick he had used to threaten her. Throughout the country, her cause was passionately supported by individuals and organizations in the Black community and within the young women's movement, and her acquittal was hailed as an important victory made possible by this mass campaign. In the immediate aftermath of her acquittal, Ms. Little issued several moving appeals on behalf of a Black man named Delbert Tibbs, who awaited execution in Florida because he had been falsely convicted of raping a white woman.

Many Black women answered Joann Little's appeal to support the cause of Delbert Tibbs. But few white women—and certainly few organized groups within the anti-rape movement—followed her suggestion that they agitate for the freedom of this Black man who had been blatantly victimized by Southern racism. Not even when Little's Chief Counsel Jerry Paul announced his decision to represent Delbert Tibbs did many white women dare to stand up in his defense. By 1978, however, when all charges against Tibbs were dismissed, white anti-rape activists had increasingly begun to align themselves with his cause. Their initial reluctance, however, was one of those historical episodes confirming many Black women's suspicions that the anti-rape movement was largely oblivious to their special concerns.

That Black women have not joined the anti-rape movement en masse does not, therefore, mean that they oppose anti-rape measures in general. Before the end of the nineteenth century pioneering Black clubwomen conducted one of the very first organized public protests against sexual abuse. Their eighty-year-old tradition of organized struggle against rape reflects the extensive and exaggerated ways Black women have suffered the threat of sexual violence. One of racism's salient historical features has always been the assumption that white men—especially those who wield economic power—possess an incontestable right of access to Black women's bodies.

Slavery relied as much on routine sexual abuse as it relied on the whip and the lash. Excessive sex urges, whether they existed among individual white men or not, had nothing to do with this virtual institutionalization of rape. Sexual coercion was, rather, an essential dimension of the social relations between slavemaster and slave. In other words, the right claimed by slaveowners and their agents over the bodies of female slaves was a direct expression of their presumed property rights over Black people as a whole. The license to rape emanated from and facilitated the ruthless economic domination that was the gruesome hallmark of slavery.[6]

The pattern of institutionalized sexual abuse of Black women became so powerful that it managed to survive the abolition of slavery. Group rape, perpetrated by the Ku Klux Klan and other

terrorist organizations of the post-Civil War period, became an
uncamouflaged political weapon in the drive to thwart the movement for Black equality. During the Memphis Riot of 1866, for
example, the violence of the mob murders was brutally complemented by the concerted sexual attacks on Black women. In the
riot's aftermath, numerous Black women testified before a Congressional committee about the savage mob rapes they had suffered.[7] This testimony regarding similar events during the Meridian, Mississippi, Riot of 1871 was given by a Black woman named
Ellen Parton:

> I reside in Meridian; have resided here nine years; occupation,
> washing and ironing and scouring; Wednesday night was the last
> night they came to my house; by "they" I mean bodies or compa-
> nies of men; they came on Monday, Tuesday and Wednesday; on
> Monday night they said they came to do us no harm; on Tuesday
> night they said they came for the arms; I told them there was none,
> and they said they would take my word for it; on Wednesday night
> they came and broke open the wardrobe and trunks, and commit-
> ted rape upon me; there were eight of them in the house; I do not
> know how many there were outside. . . .[8]

Of course, the sexual abuse of Black women has not always
manifested itself in such open and public violence. There has
been a daily drama of racism enacted in the countless anonymous
encounters between Black women and their white abusers—men
convinced that their acts were only natural. Such assaults have
been ideologically sanctioned by politicians, scholars and journal-
ists, and by literary artists who have often portrayed Black women
as promiscuous and immoral. Even the outstanding writer Gertrude Stein described one of her Black women characters as possessing ". . . the simple, promiscuous unmorality of the black
people."[9] The imposition of this attitude on white men of the

working class was a triumphant moment in the development of racist ideology.

Racism has always drawn strength from its ability to encourage sexual coercion. While Black women and their sisters of color have been the main targets of these racist-inspired attacks, white women have suffered as well. For once white men were persuaded that they could commit sexual assaults against Black women with impunity, their conduct toward women of their own race could not have remained unmarred. Racism has always served as a provocation to rape, and white women in the United States have necessarily suffered the ricochet fire of these attacks. This is one of the many ways in which racism nourishes sexism, causing white women to be indirectly victimized by the special oppression aimed at their sisters of color.

The experience of the Vietnam War furnished a further example of the extent to which racism could function as a provocation to rape. Because it was drummed into the heads of U.S. soldiers that they were fighting an inferior race, they could be taught that raping Vietnamese women was a necessary military duty. They could even be instructed to "search" the women with their penises.[10] It was the unwritten policy of the U.S. Military Command to systematically encourage rape, since it was an extremely effective weapon of mass terrorism. Where are the thousands upon thousands of Vietnam veterans who witnessed and participated in these horrors? To what extent did those brutal experiences affect their attitudes toward women in general? While it would be quite erroneous to single out Vietnam veterans as the main perpetrators of sexual crimes, there can be little doubt that the horrendous repercussions of the Vietnam experience are still being felt by all women in the United States today.

It is a painful irony that some anti-rape theorists, who ignore the part played by racism in instigating rape, do not hesitate to argue that men of color are especially prone to commit sexual violence against women. In her very impressive study of rape, Susan Brownmiller claims that Black men's historical oppression has placed many of the "legitimate" expressions of male supremacy beyond their reach. They must resort, as a result, to acts of open sexual violence. In her portrayal of "ghetto inhabitants," Brownmiller insists that

> (c)orporate executive dining rooms and climbs up Mount Everest are not usually accessible to those who form the subculture of violence. Access to a female body—through force—is within their ken.[11]

When Brownmiller's book *Against Our Will: Men, Women and Rape* was published, it was effusively praised in some circles. *Time* magazine, which selected her as one of its ten women of the year in 1976, described the book as "... the most rigorous and provocative piece of scholarship that has yet emerged from the feminist movement."[12] In other circles, however, the book has been severely criticized for its part in the resuscitation of the old racist myth of the Black rapist.

It cannot be denied that Brownmiller's book is a pioneering scholarly contribution to the contemporary literature on rape. Yet many of her arguments are unfortunately pervaded with racist ideas. Characteristic of that perspective is her reinterpretation of the 1953 lynching of fourteen-year-old Emmett Till. After this young boy had whistled at a white woman in Mississippi, his maimed body was found at the bottom of the Tallahatchie River. "Till's action," said Brownmiller, "was more than a kid's brash prank."[13]

> Emmett Till was going to show his black buddies that he, and by inference, *they* could get a white woman and Carolyn Bryant was the nearest convenient object. In concrete terms, the accessibility

of *all* white women was on review. . . . And what of the wolf
whistle, Till's 'gesture of adolescent bravado?' . . . The whistle was
no small tweet of hubba-hubba or melodious approval for a well-
turned ankle. . . . It was a deliberate insult just short of physical
assault, a last reminder to Carolyn Bryant that this black boy, Till,
had in mind to possess her.[14]

While Brownmiller deplores the sadistic punishment inflicted on
Emmett Till, the Black youth emerges, nonetheless, as a guilty
sexist—almost as guilty as his white racist murderers. After all, she
argues, both Till and his murderers were exclusively concerned
about their rights of possession over women.

Unfortunately, Brownmiller is not the only contemporary
writer on rape who has suffered the influence of racist ideology.
According to Jean MacKellar, in her book *Rape: The Bait and the
Trap*,

> Blacks raised in the hard life of the ghetto learn that they can get
> what they want only by seizing it. Violence is the rule in the game
> for survival. Women are fair prey: to obtain a woman one subdues
> her.[15]

MacKellar has been so completely mesmerized by racist propaganda that she makes the unabashed claim that 90 percent of all
reported rapes in the United States are committed by Black
men.[16] Inasmuch as the FBI's corresponding figure is 47 percent,[17] it is difficult to believe that MacKellar's statement is not
an intentional provocation.

Most recent studies on rape in the United States have acknowledged the disparity between the actual incidence of sexual assaults
and those which are reported to the police. According to Susan
Brownmiller, for example, reported rapes range anywhere from
one in five to one in twenty.[18] A study published by the New York

Radical Feminists concluded that reported rapes run as low as five percent.[19] In much of the contemporary literature on rape, there is nevertheless a tendency to equate the "police blotter rapist" with the "typical rapist." If this pattern persists, it will be practically impossible to uncover the real social causes of rape.

Diana Russell's *Politics of Rape* unfortunately reinforces the current notion that the typical rapist is a man of color—or, if he is white, a poor or working-class man. Subtitled *The Victims' Perspective*, her book is based on a series of interviews with rape victims in the San Francisco Bay Area. Of the twenty-two cases she describes, twelve—i.e., more than half—involve women who have been raped by Black, Chicano or Native American Indian men. It is revealing that only 26 percent of the original ninety-five interviews she conducted involved men of color.[20] If this dubious process of selection is not enough to evoke deep suspicions of racism, consider the advice she offers to white women:

> . . . (I)f some black men see rape of white women as an act of revenge or as a justifiable expression of hostility toward whites, I think it is equally realistic for white women to be less trusting of black men than many of them are.[21]

Brownmiller, MacKellar and Russell are assuredly more subtle than earlier ideologues of racism. But their conclusions tragically beg comparison with the ideas of such scholarly apologists of racism as Winfield Collins, who published in 1918 a book entitled *The Truth About Lynching and the Negro in the South* (In Which the Author Pleads that the South Be Made Safe for the White Race):

> Two of the Negro's most prominent characteristics are the utter lack of chastity and complete ignorance of veracity. The Negro's sexual laxity, considered so immoral or even criminal in the white

man's civilization, may have been all but a virtue in the habitat of his origin. There, nature developed in him intense sexual passions to offset his high death rate.[22]

Collins resorts to pseudo-biological arguments, while Brownmiller, Russell and MacKellar invoke environmental explanations, but in the final analysis they all assert that Black men are motivated in especially powerful ways to commit sexual violence against women.

One of the earliest theoretical works associated with the contemporary feminist movement that dealt with the subject of rape and race was Shulamith Firestone's *The Dialectic of Sex: The Case For Feminist Revolution*. Racism in general, so Firestone claims, is actually an extension of sexism. Invoking the biblical notion that ". . . the races are no more than the various parents and siblings of the Family of Man,"[23] she develops a construct defining the white man as father, the white woman as wife and mother, and Black people as the children. Transposing Freud's theory of the Oedipus Complex into racial terms, Firestone implies that Black men harbor an uncontrollable desire for sexual relations with white women. They want to kill the father and sleep with the mother.[24] Moreover, in order to "be a man," the Black man must ~~freak away~~ .

> . . . untie himself from his bond with the white female, relating to her if at all only in a degrading way. In addition, due to his virulent hatred and jealousy of her Possessor, the white man, he may lust after her as a thing to be conquered in order to revenge himself on the white man.[25]

Like Brownmiller, MacKellar and Russell, Firestone succumbs to the old racist sophistry of blaming the victim. Whether innocently or consciously, their pronouncements have facilitated the

resurrection of the timeworn myth of the Black rapist. Their
nearsighted historical myopia further prevents them from comprehending
that the portrayal of Black men as rapists reinforces racism's open
invitation to white men to avail themselves sexually of Black
women's bodies. The fictional image of the Black man as rapist
has always strengthened its inseparable companion: the image of
the Black woman as chronically promiscuous. For once the notion
is accepted that Black men harbor irresistible and animal-like
sexual urges, the entire race is invested with bestiality. If Black
men have their eyes on white women as sexual objects, then Black
women must certainly welcome the sexual attentions of white
men. Viewed as "loose women" and whores, Black women's cries
of rape would necessarily lack legitimacy.

During the 1920s a well-known Southern politician declared
that there was no such thing as a "virtuous colored girl" over the
age of fourteen.[26] As it turns out, this white man had two families
—one by his white wife and another by a Black woman. Walter
White, an outstanding anti-lynching leader and Executive Secretary of the NAACP, rightfully accused this man of ". . . explaining
and excusing his own moral derelictions by emphasizing the 'immorality' of women of the 'inferior race.' "[27]

A contemporary Black writer, Calvin Hernton, unfortunately
succumbs to similar falsehood about Black women. In the study
Sex and Racism, he insists that ". . . the Negro woman during
slavery began to develop a depreciatory concept of herself, not
only as a female but as a human being as well."[28] According to
Hernton's analysis, "(A)fter experiencing the ceaseless sexual immorality of the white South,"

> . . . the Negro woman became "promiscuous and loose," and could
> be "had for the taking." Indeed, she came to look upon herself as
> the South viewed and treated her, for she had no other morality
> by which to shape her womanhood.[29]

Hernton's analysis never penetrates the ideological veil which has resulted in the minimizing of the sexual outrages constantly committed against Black women. He falls into the trap of blaming the victim for the savage punishment she was historically forced to endure.

Throughout the history of this country, Black women have manifested a collective consciousness of their sexual victimization. They have also understood that they could not adequately resist the sexual abuses they suffered without simultaneously attacking the fraudulent rape charge as a pretext for lynching. The reliance on rape as an instrument of white-supremacist terror predates by several centuries the institution of lynching. During slavery, the lynching of Black people did not occur extensively— for the simple reason that slaveowners were reluctant to destroy their valuable property. Flogging, yes, but lynching, no. Together with flogging, rape was a terribly efficient method of keeping Black women and men alike in check. It was a routine arm of repression.

Lynchings did occur before the Civil War—but they were aimed more often at white abolitionists, who had no cash value on the market. According to William Lloyd Garrison's *Liberator*, over three hundred white people were lynched over the two decades following 1836.[30] The incidence of lynchings climbed as the anti-slavery campaign gained in power and influence.

> As the slaveholders saw the fight going against them, despite their desperate struggle to check these forces, they more and more resorted to the rope and the faggot.[31]

As Walter White concludes, ". . . the lyncher entered upon the scene as a stalwart defender of the slaveowners' profits."[32]

With the emancipation of the slaves, Black people no longer

possessed a market value for the former slaveholders, and ". . . the lynching industry was revolutionized."[33] When Ida B. Wells researched her first pamphlet against lynching, published in 1895 under the title *A Red Record,* she calculated that over ten thousand lynchings had taken place between 1865 and 1895.

> Not all nor nearly all of the murders done by white men during the past thirty years have come to light, but the statistics as gathered and preserved by white men, and which have not been questioned, show that during these years more than ten thousand Negroes have been killed in cold blood, without the formality of judicial trial and legal execution. And yet, as evidence of the absolute impunity with which the white man dares to kill a Negro, the same record shows that during all these years, and for all these murders, only three white men have been tried, convicted and executed. As no white man has been lynched for the murder of colored people, these three executions are the only instances of the death penalty being visited upon white men for murdering Negroes.[34]

In connection with these lynchings and their countless barbarities, the myth of the Black racist was conjured up. It could only acquire its terrible powers of persuasion within the irrational world of racist ideology. However irrational the myth may be, it was not a spontaneous aberration. On the contrary, the myth of the Black rapist was a distinctly political invention. As Frederick Douglass points out, Black men were not indiscriminately labeled as rapists during slavery. Throughout the entire Civil War, in fact, not a single Black man was publicly accused of raping a white woman.[35] If Black men possessed an animalistic urge to rape, argued Douglass, this alleged rape instinct would have certainly been activated when white women were left unprotected by their men who were fighting in the Confederate Army.

In the immediate aftermath of the Civil War, the menacing specter of the Black rapist had not yet appeared on the historical

scene. But lynchings, reserved during slavery for the white abolitionists, were proving to be a valuable political weapon. Before
lynching could be consolidated as a popularly accepted institution, however, its savagery and its horrors had to be convincingly
justified. These were the circumstances which spawned the myth
of the Black rapist—for the rape charge turned out to be the most
powerful of several attempts to justify the lynching of Black
people. The institution of lynching, in turn, complemented by
the continued rape of Black women, became an essential ingredient of the postwar strategy of racist terror. In this way the brutal
exploitation of Black labor was guaranteed, and after the betrayal
of Reconstruction, the political domination of the Black people
as a whole was assured.

During the first great wave of lynchings, propaganda urging the
defense of white womanhood from Black men's irrepressible rape
instincts was conspicuous for its absence. As Frederick Douglass
observed, the lawless killings of Black people were most often
described as a preventive measure to deter the Black masses from
rising up in revolt.[36] At that time the political function of mob
murders was uncamouflaged. Lynching was undisguised coun-
terinsurgency, a guarantee that Black people would not be able
to achieve their goals of citizenship and economic equality. "During this time," Douglass pointed out,

> . . . the justification for the murder of Negroes was said to be Negro
> conspiracies, Negro insurrections, Negro schemes to murder all the
> white people, Negro plots to burn the town and to commit violence
> generally . . . but never a word was said or whispered about Negro
> outrages upon white women and children.[37]

Later, when it became evident that these conspiracies, plots and
insurrections were fabrications that never materialized, the popular justification for lynching was modified. During the period
following 1872, the years of the rise of such vigilante groups as

the Ku Klux Klan and the Knights of the White Camellia, a new pretext was concocted. Lynchings were represented as a necessary measure to prevent Black supremacy over white people—in other words, to reaffirm white supremacy.[38]

After the betrayal of Reconstruction and the accompanying disfranchisement of Black people, the specter of Black political supremacy as a pretext for lynching became outmoded. Still, as the postwar economic structure took shape, solidifying the superexploitation of Black labor, the number of lynchings continued to rise. This was the historical juncture when the cry of rape emerged as the major justification for lynching. Frederick Douglass' explanation of the political motives underlying the creation of the mythical Black rapist is a brilliant analysis of the way ideology transforms to meet new historical conditions.

> The times have changed and the Negro's accusers have found it necessary to change with them. They have been compelled to invent a new charge to suit the times. The old charges are no longer valid. Upon them the good opinion of the North and of mankind cannot be secured. Honest men no longer believe that there is any ground to apprehend Negro supremacy. Times and events have swept away these old refuges of lies. They were once powerful. They did their work in their day and did it with terrible energy and effect, but they are now cast aside as useless. The lie has lost its ability to deceive. The altered circumstances have made necessary a sterner, stronger and more effective justification of Southern barbarism, and hence we have, according to my theory, to look into the face of a more shocking and blasting charge than either Negro supremacy or Negro insurrection.[39]

This more shocking and blasting charge, of course, was rape. Lynching was now explained and rationalized as a method to avenge Black men's assaults on white Southern womanhood. As one apologist for lynching insisted, it was necessary to find "... a way of meeting the extraordinary condition with extraordinary means—hence lynching in order to hold in check the Negro in the South."[40]

Although the majority of lynchings did not even involve the accusation of sexual assault, the racist cry of rape became a popular explanation which was far more effective than either of the two previous attempts to justify mob attacks on Black people. In a society where male supremacy was all-pervasive, men who were motivated by their duty to defend their women could be excused of any excesses they might commit. That their motive was sublime was ample justification for the resulting barbarities. As Senator Ben Tillman of South Carolina told his Washington colleagues at the beginning of this century,

> (w)hen stern and sad-faced white men put to death a creature in human form who has deflowered a white woman, they have avenged the greatest wrong, the blackest crime . . .[41]

Such crimes, he said, caused civilized men to ". . . revert to the original savage type whose impulses under such circumstances have always been to 'kill, kill, kill.' "[42]

The repercussions of this new myth were enormous. Not only was opposition to individual lynchings stifled—for who would dare to defend a rapist?—white support for the cause of Black equality in general began to wane. By the end of the nineteenth century the largest mass organization of white women—the Women's Christian Temperance Union—was headed by a woman who publicly vilified Black men for their alleged attacks on white women. What is more, Frances Willard went so far as to characterize Black men as especially prone to alcoholism, which in turn exacerbated their instinctual urge to rape.

> The grogshop is the Negro's center of power. Better whisky and more of it is the rallying cry of great, dark-faced mobs. The colored race multiplies like the locusts of Egypt. The grogshop is its center of power. The safety of women, of childhood, the home, is menaced in a thousand localities at this moment, so that men dare not go beyond the sight of their own roof-tree.[43]

The characterization of Black men as rapists wrought incredible confusion within the ranks of progressive movements. Both Frederick Douglass and Ida B. Wells point out in their respective analyses of lynching that as soon as the propagandistic cry of rape became a legitimate excuse for lynching, former white proponents of Black equality became increasingly afraid to associate themselves with Black people's struggle for liberation. They either remained silent or, like Frances Willard, they spoke out aggressively against the sexual crimes indiscriminately attributed to Black men. Douglass described the catastrophic impact of the fabricated rape charge on the movement for Black equality in general:

> It has cooled (the Negro's) friends; it has heated his enemies and arrested at home and abroad, in some measure, the generous efforts that good men were wont to make for his improvement and elevation. It has deceived his friends at the North and many good friends at the South, for nearly all of them, in some measure, have accepted this charge against the Negro as true.[44]

What was the reality behind this terribly powerful myth of the Black rapist? To be sure, there were some examples of Black men raping white women. But the number of actual rapes which occurred was minutely disproportionate to the allegations implied by the myth. As already indicated, during the entire Civil War, there was not a single reported case of a white woman suffering rape at the hands of a slave. While virtually all the Southern white men were on the battlefront, never once was the cry of rape raised. Frederick Douglass argues that the leveling of the rape charge against Black men as a whole was not credible for the simple reason that it implied a radical and instantaneous change in the mental and moral character of Black people.

> History does not present an example of a transformation in the character of any class of men so extreme, so unnatural and so complete as is implied in this charge. The change is too great and the period for it too brief.[45]

Even the real circumstances of most lynchings contradicted the myth of the Black rapist. The majority of mob murders did not even involve the charge of rape. Although the cry of rape was invoked as the popular justification for lynching in general, most lynchings took place for other reasons. In a study published in 1931 by the Southern Commission on the Study of Lynching, it was revealed that between 1889 and 1929 only one-sixth of the mob victims were actually accused of rape: 37.7 percent were charged with murder, 5.8 percent with felonious assault, 7.1 percent of theft, 1.8 percent of insulting a white person and 24.2 percent were accused of miscellaneous charges—the majority of which were astoundingly trivial. According to the Commission's figures, 16.7 percent of lynch victims were accused of rape and 6.7 percent of attempted rape.[46]

Although their arguments were disputed by the facts, most apologists for lynching claimed that only white men's obligation to defend their women could motivate them to commit such savage attacks on Black men. In 1904 Thomas Nelson Page, writing in the *North American Review,* placed the entire burden of lynching on the shoulders of Black men and their unchecked propensity toward sexual crimes.

The crime of lynching is not likely to cease until the crime of
ravishing and murdering women and children is less frequent than
it has been of late. And this crime, which is well-nigh wholly
confined to the negro race, will not greatly diminish until the
negroes themselves take it in hand and stamp it out.[47]

And white men in the South, said Ben Tillman in the U.S.
Senate, would ". . . not submit to (the Negro's) gratifying his lust
on our wives and daughters without lynching him."[48] In 1892,
when Senator Tillman was governor of South Carolina, he had
declared, on the spot where eight Black men had been hanged,
that he would personally lead a lynch mob against any Black man
who dared to rape a white woman. During his term as governor,
he turned over a Black man to a white mob even though the lynch
victim had been publicly absolved by the white woman who had
cried rape.[49]

The colonization of the Southern economy by capitalists from
the North gave lynching its most vigorous impulse. If Black people, by means of terror and violence, could remain the most
brutally exploited group within the swelling ranks of the working
class, the capitalists could enjoy a double advantage. Extra profits
would result from the superexploitation of Black labor, and white
workers' hostilities toward their employers would be defused.
White workers who assented to lynching necessarily assumed a
posture of racial solidarity with the white men who were really
their oppressors. This was a critical moment in the popularization
of racist ideology.

If Black people had simply accepted a status of economic and
political inferiority, the mob murders would probably have sub-
sided. But because vast numbers of ex-slaves refused to discard
their dreams of progress, more than ten thousand lynchings occurred during the three decades following the war.[50] Whoever
challenged the racial hierarchy was marked a potential victim of

the mob. The endless roster of the dead came to include every sort of insurgent—from the owners of successful Black businesses and workers pressing for higher wages to those who refused to be called "boy" and the defiant women who resisted white men's sexual abuses. Yet public opinion had been captured, and it was taken for granted that lynching was a just response to the barbarous sexual crimes against white womanhood. And an important question remained unasked: What about the numerous women who were lynched—and sometimes raped before they were killed by the mob. Ida B. Wells refers to

> . . . the horrible case of the woman in San Antonio, Texas, who had been boxed up in a barrel with nails driven through the sides and rolled down a hill until she was dead.[51]

The *Chicago Defender* published this article on December 18, 1915, under the heading "Rape, Lynch Negro Mother":

> Columbus, Miss., Dec. 17—Thursday a week ago Cordella Stevenson was found early in the morning hanging to the limb of a tree, without any clothing, dead . . . She was hung there from the night before by a bloodthirsty mob who had gone to her home, snatched her from slumber, and dragged her through the streets without any resistance. They carried her to a far-off spot, did their dirt and then strung her up.[52]

Given the central role played by the fictional Black rapist in the shaping of post-slavery racism, it is, at best, irresponsible theorizing to represent Black men as the most frequent authors of sexual violence. At worst, it is an aggression against Black people as a whole, for the mythical rapist implies the mythical whore. Perceiving the rape charge as an attack against the entire Black community, Black women were quick to assume the leadership of the anti-lynching movement. Ida B. Wells-Barnett was the moving force behind a crusade against lynching which was destined to span many decades. In 1892 three acquaintances of this Black newspaperwoman were lynched in Memphis, Tennessee. They were murdered by a racist mob because the store they opened in a Black neighborhood was successfully competing with a white-owned store. Ida B. Wells hastened to speak out against this lynching in the pages of her newspaper, *The Free Speech*. During her trip to New York three months later, the offices of her paper were burned to the ground. Threatened with lynching herself, she decided to remain in the East and to ". . . tell the world for the first time the true story of Negro lynchings, which were becoming more numerous and horrible."[53]

Wells' articles in the *New York Age* motivated Black women to organize a support campaign on her behalf, which eventually led to the establishment of Black women's clubs.[54] As a result of her pioneering efforts, Black women throughout the country became active in the anti-lynching crusade. Ida B. Wells herself traveled from city to city, issuing appeals to ministers, professionals and workers alike to speak out against the outrages of lynch law. During her trips abroad, an important solidarity movement was organized in Britain, which had a marked impact on U.S. public opinion. The extent of her success was such that she incurred the wrath of the *New York Times*. This vicious editorial was published after Wells' 1904 trip to England:

> "Immediately following the day of Miss Wells' return to the United States, a Negro man assaulted a white woman in New York City 'for the purposes of lust and plunder.' . . . The circumstances of his fiendish crime may serve to convince the mulatress missionary that the promulgation in New York just now of her theory of Negro outrages is, to say the least, inopportune."[55]

Mary Church Terrell, the first president of the National Association of Colored Women, was another outstanding Black woman leader who was devoted to the fight against lynching. In 1904 she answered Thomas Nelson Page's virulent article on "The Lynching of Negroes—Its Cause and Prevention." In the *North American Review,* where Page's article had appeared, she published an essay entitled "Lynching From a Negro's Point of View." With compelling logic, Terrell systematically refuted Page's justification of lynching as an understandable response to alleged sexual assaults on white women.[56]

Thirty years after Ida B. Wells had initiated the anti-lynching campaign, an organization called the Anti-Lynching Crusaders was founded. Established in 1922 under the auspices of the NAACP and headed by Mary Talbert, its purpose was to create an integrated women's movement against lynching.

> What will Mary B. Talbert do next? What next will the colored American women do under her leadership? An organization has been effected by colored women to get ONE MILLION WOMEN of all kinds and colors united by December, 1922 against lynching.
> Look out, Mr. Lyncher!
> This class of women generally get what they go after.[57]

This was not the first time Black women had reached out to their white sisters. They were struggling in the tradition of such historical giants as Sojourner Truth and Frances E. W. Harper. Ida B. Wells had personally appealed to white women, as had her contemporary, Mary Church Terrell. And Black clubwomen had collectively attempted to persuade the white women's club movement to direct some of their energies toward the anti-lynching campaign.

White women did not respond to these appeals en masse until

the Association of Southern Women for the Prevention of Lynching was founded in 1930 under the leadership of Jessie Daniel
Ames.[58] The Association set out to repudiate the claim that
lynching was necessary for the protection of Southern womanhood:

> The program of the Southern women has been directed to exposing
> the falsity of the claim that lynching is necessary to their protection
> and to emphasize the real danger of lynching to all the values of
> home and religion.[59]

The small group of women, who attended the Atlanta meeting
where the Association was formed, discussed the role of white
women in the lynchings of the recent period. Women were usually present at the mob gatherings, they pointed out, and in some
instances, were active members of the lynch mobs. Moreover,
those white women who permitted their children to witness the
murders of Black people were indoctrinating them into the racist
ways of the South. Walter White's study of lynching, published
the year before the women's meeting, argued that one of the
worst consequences of these mob murders was the warping of
Southern white children's minds. When White traveled to
Florida to investigate a lynching, a little girl of nine or ten told
him about ". . . the fun we had burning the niggers."[60]

Jessie Daniel Ames and her co-founders of the Association of
Southern Women for the Prevention of Lynching resolved in
1930 to recruit the masses of Southern white women into the
campaign to defeat the racist mobs bent on killing Black people.
Eventually they obtained over forty thousand signatures to the
Association's pledge:

> We declare lynching is an indefensible crime, destructive of all
> principles of government, hateful and hostile to every ideal of

religion and humanity, debasing and degrading to every person involved. . . . (P)ublic opinion has accepted too easily the claim of lynchers and mobsters that they were acting solely in defense of womanhood. In light of facts we dare no longer to permit this claim to pass unchallenged, nor allow those bent upon personal revenge and savagery to commit acts of violence and lawlessness in the name of women. We solemnly pledge ourselves to create a new public opinion in the South, which will not condone, for any reason whatever, acts of mobs or lynchers. We will teach our children at home, at school and at church a new interpretation of law and religion; we will assist all officials to uphold their oath of office; and finally, we will join with every minister, editor, school teacher and patriotic citizen in a program of education to eradicate lynchings and mobs forever from our land.[61]

These courageous white women encountered opposition, hostility and even physical threats on their lives. Their contributions were invaluable within the overall anti-lynching crusade. Without their relentless petition drives, their letter campaigns and their meetings and demonstrations, the tide of lynching would not have been reversed so swiftly. Yet the Association of Southern Women for the Prevention of Lynching was a movement that was forty years late in coming. For four decades or more, Black women had been leading the anti-lynching campaign, and for just about as long, they had appealed to their white sisters to join them. One of the major weaknesses of Susan Brownmiller's study on rape is its absolute disregard of Black women's pioneering efforts in the anti-lynching movement. While Brownmiller rightfully praises Jessie Daniel Ames and the Association of Southern Women, she makes not so much as a passing mention of Ida B. Wells, Mary Church Terrell or Mary Talbert and the Anti-Lynching Crusaders.

While the Association of Southern Women for the Prevention of Lynching was a belated response to their Black sisters' appeals, these women's far-reaching achievements dramatically illustrate white women's special place in the struggle against racism. When Mary Talbert and her Anti-Lynching Crusaders reached out to white women, they felt that white women could more readily identify with the Black cause by virtue of their own oppression as women. Besides, lynching itself, as a terrifying tool of racism, also served to strengthen male dominance.

> Economic dependence, contacts with none save "polite, refined, womanly" pursuits, mental activities in no other field than home life—all these man-imposed restrictions have borne more heavily upon women in the South and have been maintained more rigidly, than in any other part of the country.[62]

Throughout the anti-lynching crusade, the critics of the racist manipulation of the rape charge did not intend to excuse those individual Black men who actually committed the crime of sexual assault. As early as 1894 Frederick Douglass warned that his pronouncements against the myth of the Black rapist were not to be misconstrued as a defense of rape itself.

> I do not pretend that Negroes are saints and angels. I do not deny that they are capable of committing the crime imputed to them, but utterly deny that they are any more addicted to the commission of that crime than is true of any other variety of the human family. . . . I am not a defender of any man guilty of this atrocious crime, but a defender of the coloured people as a class.[63]

The resurgence of racism during the mid-1970s has been accompanied by a resurrection of the myth of the Black rapist. Unfortunately, this myth has sometimes been legitimized by white women associated with the battle against rape. Consider,

for example, Susan Brownmiller's concluding passage of the chapter of her book entitled "A Question of Race":

> Today the incidence of actual rape combined with the looming spec-
> tre of the rapist in the mind's eye, and in particular the mythified
> spectre of the black man as rapist to which the black man in the name
> of his manhood now contributes, must be understood as a control
> mechanism against the freedom, mobility and aspirations of all wo-
> men, white and black. The crossroads of racism and sexism had to be
> a violent meeting place. There is no use pretending it doesn't exist.[64]

Brownmiller's provocative distortion of such historical cases as the
Scottsboro Nine, Willie McGee and Emmett Till are designed to
dissipate any sympathy for Black men who are victims of fraudulent rape charges. As for Emmett Till, she clearly invites us to
infer that if this fourteen-year-old boy had not been shot in the
head and dumped into the Tallahatchie River after he whistled
at one white woman, he would probably have succeeded in raping
another white woman.

Brownmiller attempts to persuade her readers that the absurd
and purposely sensational words of Eldridge Cleaver—who called
rape an "insurrectionary act" against "white society"—are representative. It seems as if she wants to intentionally conjure up in her
readers' imaginations armies of Black men, their penises erect,
charging full speed ahead toward the most conveniently placed
white women. In the ranks of this army are the ghost of Emmett
Till, the rapist Eldridge Cleaver and Imamu Baraka, who once
wrote, "Come up, black dada nihilismus. Rape the white girls.
Rape their fathers. Cut the mothers' throats." But Brownmiller
goes further. Not only does she include men like Calvin Hernton—
whose book is unequivocally sexist—but also, among others,
George Jackson, who never attempted to justify rape. Eldridge
Cleaver's ideas, she argues,

... reflect a strain of thinking among Black male intellectuals and writers that became quite fashionable in the late nineteen sixties and was taken on with astonishing enthusiasm by white male radicals and parts of the white intellectual establishment as a perfectly acceptable excuse of rape committed by black men.[65]

Susan Brownmiller's discussion on rape and race evinces an unthinking partisanship which borders on racism. In pretending to defend the cause of all women, she sometimes boxes herself into the position of defending the particular cause of *white* women, regardless of its implications. Her examination of the Scottsboro Nine case is a revealing example. As Brownmiller herself points out, these nine young men, charged and convicted of rape, spent long years of their lives in prison because two white women perjured themselves on the witness stand. Yet she has nothing but contempt for the Black men and their defense move-ment—and her sympathy for the two white women is glaring.

The left fought hard for its symbols of racial injustice, making bewildered heroes out of a handful of pathetic, semi-literate fellows caught in the jaws of Southern jurisprudence who only wanted to beat the rap.[66]

On the other hand, the two white women, whose false testimony sent the Scottsboro Nine to prison, were

... corraled by a posse of white men who already believed a rape had taken place. Confused and fearful, they fell into line.[67]

No one can deny that the women were manipulated by Alabama racists. However, it is wrong to portray the women as innocent pawns, absolved of the responsibility of having collaborated with the forces of racism. In choosing to take sides with white women, regardless of the circumstances, Brownmiller herself capitulates to racism. Her failure to alert white women about the urgency of combining a fierce challenge to racism with the necessary battle against sexism is an important plus for the forces of racism today.

The myth of the Black rapist continues to carry out the insidious work of racist ideology. It must bear a good portion of the responsibility for the failure of most anti-rape theorists to seek the identity of the enormous numbers of anonymous rapists who remain unreported, untried and unconvicted. As long as their analyses focus on accused rapists who are reported and arrested, thus on only a fraction of the rapes actually committed, Black men—and other men of color—will inevitably be viewed as the villains responsible for the current epidemic of sexual violence. The anonymity surrounding the vast majority of rapes is consequently treated as a statistical detail—or else as a mystery whose meaning is inaccessible.

But why are there so many anonymous rapists in the first place? Might not this anonymity be a privilege enjoyed by men whose status protects them from prosecution? Although white men who are employers, executives, politicians, doctors, professors, etc., have been known to "take advantage" of women they consider their social inferiors, their sexual misdeeds seldom come to light in court. Is it not therefore quite probable that these men of the capitalist and middle classes account for a significant proportion of the unreported rapes? Many of these unreported rapes undoubtedly involve Black women as victims: their historical experience proves that racist ideology implies an open invitation to rape. As the basis of the license to rape Black women during slavery was the slaveholders' economic power, so the class structure of capitalist society also harbors an incentive to rape. It seems, in fact, that men of the capitalist class and their middle-class partners are immune to prosecution because they commit their sexual assaults with the same unchallenged authority that legitimizes their daily assaults on the labor and dignity of working people.

The existence of widespread sexual harassment on the job has never been much of a secret. It is precisely on the job, indeed, that women—especially when they are not unionized—are most vulnerable. Having already established their economic domination over their female subordinates, employers, managers and foremen may attempt to assert this authority in sexual terms. That working-class women are more intensely exploited than their men adds to their vulnerability to sexual abuse, while sexual coercion simultaneously reinforces their vulnerability to economic exploitation.

Working-class men, whatever their color, can be motivated to rape by the belief that their maleness accords them the privilege to dominate women. Yet since they do not possess the social or economic authority—unless it is a white man raping a woman of color—guaranteeing them immunity from prosecution, the incentive is not nearly as powerful as it is for the men of the capitalist class. When working-class men accept the invitation to rape extended by the ideology of male supremacy, they are accepting a bribe, an illusory compensation for their powerlessness.

The class structure of capitalism encourages men who wield power in the economic and political realm to become routine agents of sexual exploitation. The present rape epidemic occurs at a time when the capitalist class is furiously reasserting its authority in face of global and internal challenges. Both racism and sexism, central to its domestic strategy of increased economic exploitation, are receiving unprecedented encouragement. It is not a mere coincidence that as the incidence of rape has arisen, the position of women workers has visibly worsened. So severe are women's economic losses that their wages in relationship to men are lower than they were a decade ago. The proliferation of sexual violence is the brutal face of a generalized intensification of the sexism which necessarily accompanies this economic assault.

Following a pattern established by racism, the attack on women mirrors the deteriorating situation of workers of color and the rising influence of racism in the judicial system, the educational institutions and in the government's posture of studied neglect toward Black people and other people of color. The most dramatic sign of the dangerous resurgence of racism is the new visibility of the Ku Klux Klan and the related epidemic of violent assaults on Blacks, Chicanos, Puerto Ricans and Native Americans. The present rape epidemic bears an extraordinary likeness to this violence kindled by racism.

Given the complexity of the social context of rape today, any attempt to treat it as an isolated phenomenon is bound to founder. An effective strategy against rape must aim for more than the eradication of rape—or even of sexism—alone. The struggle against racism must be an ongoing theme of the anti-rape movement, which must not only defend women of color, but the many victims of the racist manipulation of the rape charge as well. The crisis dimensions of sexual violence constitute one of the facets of a deep and ongoing crisis of capitalism. As the violent face of sexism, the threat of rape will continue to exist as long as the overall oppression of women remains an essential crutch for capitalism. The anti-rape movement and its important current activities—ranging from emotional and legal aid to self-defense and educational campaigns must be situated in a strategic context which envisages the ultimate defeat of monopoly capitalism.

12⟶Racism, Birth Control and Reproductive Rights

When nineteenth-century feminists raised the demand for "voluntary motherhood," the campaign for birth control was born. Its proponents were called radicals and they were subjected to the same mockery as had befallen the initial advocates of woman suffrage. "Voluntary motherhood" was considered audacious, outrageous and outlandish by those who insisted that wives had no right to refuse to satisfy their husbands' sexual urges. Eventually, of course, the right to birth control, like women's right to vote, would be more or less taken for granted by U.S. public opinion. Yet in 1970, a full century later, the call for legal and easily accessible abortions was no less controversial than the issue of "voluntary motherhood" which had originally launched the birth control movement in the United States.

Birth control—individual choice, safe contraceptive methods, as well as abortions when necessary—is a fundamental prerequisite for the emancipation of women. Since the right of birth control is obviously advantageous to women of all classes and races, it would appear that even vastly dissimilar women's groups would have attempted to unite around this issue. In reality, however, the birth control movement has seldom succeeded in uniting women of different social backgrounds, and rarely have the movement's leaders popularized the genuine concerns of working-class women. Moreover, arguments advanced by birth control advocates have sometimes been based on blatantly racist premises. The progressive potential of birth control remains indisputable. But in actuality, the historical record of this movement leaves much to be desired in the realm of challenges to racism and class exploitation.

The most important victory of the contemporary birth control movement was won during the early 1970s when abortions were at last declared legal. Having emerged during the infancy of the new Women's Liberation movement, the struggle to legalize abortions incorporated all the enthusiasm and the militancy of the young movement. By January, 1973, the abortion rights campaign had reached a triumphant culmination. In *Roe* v. *Wade* (410 U.S.) and *Doe* v. *Bolton* (410 U.S.), the U.S. Supreme Court ruled that a woman's right to personal privacy implied her right to decide whether or not to have an abortion.

The ranks of the abortion rights campaign did not include substantial numbers of women of color. Given the racial composition of the larger Women's Liberation movement, this was not at all surprising. When questions were raised about the absence of racially oppressed women in both the larger movement and in the abortion rights campaign, two explanations were commonly proposed in the discussions and literature of the period: women of color were overburdened by their people's fight against racism; and/or they had not yet become conscious of the centrality of sexism. But the real meaning of the almost lily-white complexion of the abortion rights campaign was not to be found in an ostensibly myopic or underdeveloped consciousness among women of color. The truth lay buried in the ideological underpinnings of the birth control movement itself.

The failure of the abortion rights campaign to conduct a historical self-evaluation led to a dangerously superficial appraisal of Black people's suspicious attitudes toward birth control in general. Granted, when some Black people unhesitatingly equated birth control with genocide, it did appear to be an exaggerated —even paranoiac—reaction. Yet white abortion rights activists missed a profound message, for underlying these cries of genocide were important clues about the history of the birth control movement. This movement, for example, had been known to advocate involuntary sterilization—a racist form of mass "birth control." If ever women would enjoy the right to plan their pregnancies, legal and easily accessible birth control measures and abortions would have to be complemented by an end to sterilization abuse.

As for the abortion rights campaign itself, how could women of color fail to grasp its urgency? They were far more familiar than their white sisters with the murderously clumsy scalpels of inept abortionists seeking profit in illegality. In New York, for instance, during the several years preceding the decriminalization of abortions in that state, some 80 percent of the deaths caused by illegal abortions involved Black and Puerto Rican women.[1] Immediately afterward, women of color received close to half of all the legal abortions. If the abortion rights campaign of the early 1970s needed to be reminded that women of color wanted desperately to escape the back-room quack abortionists, they should have also realized that these same women were not about to express pro-abortion sentiments. They were in favor of *abortion rights,* which did not mean that they were proponents of abortion. When Black and Latina women resort to abortions in such large numbers, the stories they tell are not so much about their desire to be free of their pregnancy, but rather about the miserable social conditions which dissuade them from bringing new lives into the world.

Black women have been aborting themselves since the earliest days of slavery. Many slave women refused to bring children into a world of interminable forced labor, where chains and floggings and sexual abuse for women were the everyday conditions of life. A doctor practicing in Georgia around the middle of the last century noticed that abortions and miscarriages were far more common among his slave patients than among the white women he treated. According to the physician, either Black women worked too hard or

... as the planters believe, the blacks are possessed of a secret by which they destroy the fetus at an early stage of gestation ... All country practitioners are aware of the frequent complaints of planters (about the) ... unnatural tendency in the African female to destroy her offspring.[2]

Expressing shock that "... whole families of women fail to have any children,"[3] this doctor never considered how "unnatural" it was to raise children under the slave system. The previously mentioned episode of Margaret Garner, a fugitive slave who killed her own daughter and attempted suicide herself when she was captured by slavecatchers, is a case in point.

She rejoiced that the girl was dead—"now she would never know what a woman suffers as a slave"—and pleaded to be tried for murder. "I will go singing to the gallows rather than be returned to slavery!"[4]

Why were self-imposed abortions and reluctant acts of infanticide such common occurrences during slavery? Not because Black women had discovered solutions to their predicament, but rather because they were desperate. Abortions and infanticides were acts of desperation, motivated not by the biological birth process but by the oppressive conditions of slavery. Most of these women, no doubt, would have expressed their deepest resentment had someone hailed their abortions as a stepping stone toward freedom.

During the early abortion rights campaign it was too frequently assumed that legal abortions provided a viable alternative to the myriad problems posed by poverty. As if having fewer children could create more jobs, higher wages, better schools, etc., etc. This assumption reflected the tendency to blur the distinction between *abortion rights* and the general advocacy of *abortions*. The campaign often failed to provide a voice for women who wanted the *right* to legal abortions while deploring the social conditions that prohibited them from bearing more children.

The renewed offensive against abortion rights that erupted during the latter half of the 1970s has made it absolutely necessary to focus more sharply on the needs of poor and racially oppressed women. By 1977 the passage of the Hyde Amendment in Congress had mandated the withdrawal of federal funding for abortions, causing many state legislatures to follow suit. Black, Puerto Rican, Chicana and Native American Indian women, together with their impoverished white sisters, were thus effectively divested of the right to legal abortions. Since surgical sterilizations, funded by the Department of Health, Education and Welfare, remained free on demand, more and more poor women have been forced to opt for permanent infertility. What is urgently required is a broad campaign to defend the reproductive rights of all women—and especially those women whose economic circumstances often compel them to relinquish the right to reproduction itself.

Women's desire to control their reproductive system is probably as old as human history itself. As early as 1844 the *United States Practical Receipt Book* contained, among its many recipes for food, household chemicals and medicines, "receipts" for "birth preventive lotions." To make "Hannay's Preventive Lotion," for example,

> [t]ake pearlash, 1 part; water, 6 parts. Mix and filter. Keep it in closed bottles, and use it, with or without soap, immediately after connexion.[5]

For "Abernethy's Preventive Lotion,"

> [t]ake bichloride of mercury, 25 parts; milk of almonds, 400 parts; alcohol, 100 parts; rosewater, 1000 parts. Immerse the glands in a little of the mixture. . . . Infallible, if used in proper time.[6]

While women have probably always dreamed of infallible methods of birth control, it was not until the issue of women's rights in general became the focus of an organized movement that reproductive rights could emerge as a legitimate demand. In an essay entitled "Marriage," written during the 1850s, Sarah Grimke argued for a ". . . right on the part of woman to decide *when* she shall become a mother, how often and under what circumstances."[7] Alluding to one physician's humorous observation, Grimke agreed that if wives and husbands alternatively gave birth to their children, ". . . no family would ever have more than three, the husband bearing one and the wife two."[8] But, as she insists, ". . . the *right* to decide this matter has been almost wholly denied to woman."[9]

Sarah Grimke advocated women's right to sexual abstinence. Around the same time the well-known "emancipated marriage" of Lucy Stone and Henry Blackwell took place. These abolitionists and women's rights activists were married in a ceremony that protested women's traditional relinquishment of their rights to their persons, names and property. In agreeing that as husband, he had no right to the "custody of the wife's person,"[10] Henry Blackwell promised that he would not attempt to impose the dictates of his sexual desires upon his wife.

The notion that women could refuse to submit to their husbands' sexual demands eventually became the central idea of the call for "voluntary motherhood." By the 1870s, when the woman suffrage movement had reached its peak, feminists were publicly advocating voluntary motherhood. In a speech delivered in 1873, Virginia Woodhull claimed that

(t)he wife who submits to sexual intercourse against her wishes or desires, virtually commits suicide; while the husband who compels it, commits murder, and ought just as much to be punished for it, as though he strangled her to death for refusing him.[11]

Woodhull, of course, was quite notorious as a proponent of "free love." Her defense of a woman's right to abstain from sexual intercourse within marriage as a means of controlling her pregnancies was associated with Woodhull's overall attack on the institution of marriage.

It was not a coincidence that women's consciousness of their reproductive rights was born within the organized movement for women's political equality. Indeed, if women remained forever burdened by incessant childbirths and frequent miscarriages, they would hardly be able to exercise the political rights they might win. Moreover, women's new dreams of pursuing careers and other paths of self-development outside marriage and motherhood could only be realized if they could limit and plan their pregnancies. In this sense, the slogan "voluntary motherhood" contained a new and genuinely progressive vision of womanhood. At the same time, however, this vision was rigidly bound to the lifestyle enjoyed by the middle classes and the bourgeoisie. The aspirations underlying the demand for "voluntary motherhood" did not reflect the conditions of working-class women, engaged as they were in a far more fundamental fight for economic survival. Since this first call for birth control was associated with goals which could only be achieved by women possessing material wealth, vast numbers of poor and working-class women would find it rather difficult to identify with the embryonic birth control movement.

Toward the end of the nineteenth century the white birth rate in the United States suffered a significant decline. Since no contraceptive innovations had been publicly introduced, the drop in the birth rate implied that women were substantially curtailing their sexual activity. By 1890 the typical native-born white woman was bearing no more than four children.[12] Since U.S. society was becoming increasingly urban, this new birth pattern should not have been a surprise. While farm life demanded large families, they became dysfunctional within the context of city life. Yet this phenomenon was publicly interpreted in a racist and anti-working-class fashion by the ideologues of rising monopoly capitalism. Since native-born white women were bearing fewer children, the specter of "race suicide" was raised in official circles.

In 1905 President Theodore Roosevelt concluded his Lincoln Day Dinner speech with the proclamation that "race purity must be maintained."[13] By 1906 he blatantly equated the falling birth rate among native-born whites with the impending threat of "race suicide." In his State of the Union message that year Roosevelt admonished the well-born white women who engaged in "willful sterility—the one sin for which the penalty is national death, race suicide."[14] These comments were made during a period of accelerating racist ideology and of great waves of race riots and lynchings on the domestic scene. Moreover, President Roosevelt himself was attempting to muster support for the U.S. seizure of the Philippines, the country's most recent imperialist venture.

How did the birth control movement respond to Roosevelt's accusation that their cause was promoting race suicide? The President's propagandistic ploy was a failure, according to a leading historian of the birth control movement, for, ironically, it led to greater support for its advocates. Yet, as Linda Gordon maintains, this controversy ". . . also brought to the forefront those issues that most separated feminists from the working class and the poor."[15]

> This happened in two ways. First, the feminists were increasingly emphasizing birth control as a route to careers and higher education—goals out of reach of the poor with or without birth control. In the context of the whole feminist movement, the race-suicide episode was an additional factor identifying feminism almost exclusively with the aspirations of the more privileged women of the society. Second, the pro-birth control feminists began to popularize the idea that poor people had a moral obligation to restrict the size

of their families, because large families create a drain on the taxes and charity expenditures of the wealthy and because poor children were less likely to be "superior."[16]

The acceptance of the race-suicide thesis, to a greater or lesser extent, by women such as Julia Ward Howe and Ida Husted Harper reflected the suffrage movement's capitulation to the racist posture of Southern women. If the suffragists acquiesced to arguments invoking the extension of the ballot to women as the saving grace of white supremacy, then birth control advocates either acquiesced to or supported the new arguments invoking birth control as a means of preventing the proliferation of the "lower classes" and as an antidote to race suicide. Race suicide could be prevented by the introduction of birth control among Black people, immigrants and the poor in general. In this way, the prosperous whites of solid Yankee stock could maintain their superior numbers within the population. Thus class-bias and racism crept into the birth control movement when it was still in its infancy. More and more, it was assumed within birth control circles that poor women, Black and immigrant alike, had a "moral obligation to restrict the size of their families."[17] What was demanded as a "right" for the privileged came to be interpreted as a "duty" for the poor.

When Margaret Sanger embarked upon her lifelong crusade for birth control—a term she coined and popularized—it appeared as though the racist and anti-working-class overtones of the previous period might possibly be overcome. For Margaret Higgens Sanger came from a working-class background herself and was well acquainted with the devastating pressures of poverty. When her mother died, at the age of forty-eight, she had borne no less than eleven children. Sanger's later memories of her own family's troubles would confirm her belief that working-class women had a special need for the right to plan and space their pregnancies autonomously. Her affiliation, as an adult, with the Socialist movement was a further cause for hope that the birth control campaign would move in a more progressive direction.

When Margaret Sanger joined the Socialist party in 1912, she assumed the responsibility of recruiting women from New York's working women's clubs into the party.[18] *The Call*—the party's paper—carried her articles on the women's page. She wrote a series entitled "What Every Mother Should Know," another called "What Every Girl Should Know," and she did on-the-spot coverage of strikes involving women. Sanger's familiarity with New York's working-class districts was a result of her numerous visits as a trained nurse to the poor sections of the city. During these visits, she points out in her autobiography, she met countless numbers of women who desperately desired knowledge about birth control.

According to Sanger's autobiographical reflections, one of the many visits she made as a nurse to New York's Lower East Side convinced her to undertake a personal crusade for birth control. Answering one of her routine calls, she discovered that twenty-eight-year-old Sadie Sachs had attempted to abort herself. Once the crisis had passed, the young woman asked the attending physician to give her advice on birth prevention. As Sanger relates the story, the doctor recommended that she ". . . tell (her husband) Jake to sleep on the roof."[19]

> I glanced quickly to Mrs. Sachs. Even through my sudden tears I could see stamped on her face an expression of absolute despair. We simply looked at each other, saying no word until the door had closed behind the doctor. Then she lifted her thin, blue-veined hands and clasped them beseechingly. "He can't understand. He's only a man. But you do, don't you? Please tell me the secret, and I'll never breathe it to a soul. Please!"[20]

Three months later Sadie Sachs died from another self-induced abortion. That night, Margaret Sanger says, she vowed to devote all her energy toward the acquisition and dissemination of contraceptive measures.

> I went to bed, knowing that no matter what it might cost, I was finished with palliatives and superficial cures; I resolved to seek out the root of evil, to do something to change the destiny of mothers whose miseries were as vast as the sky.[21]

During the first phase of Sanger's birth control crusade, she maintained her affiliation with the Socialist party—and the campaign itself was closely associated with the rising militancy of the working class. Her staunch supporters included Eugene Debs, Elizabeth Gurley Flynn and Emma Goldman, who respectively represented the Socialist party, the International Workers of the World and the anarchist movement. Margaret Sanger, in turn, expressed the anti-capitalist commitment of her own movement within the pages of its journal, *Woman Rebel,* which was "dedicated to the interests of working women."[22] Personally, she continued to march on picket lines with striking workers and publicly condemned the outrageous assaults on striking workers. In 1914, for example, when the National Guard massacred scores of Chicano miners in Ludlow, Colorado, Sanger joined the labor movement in exposing John D. Rockefeller's role in this attack.[23]

Unfortunately, the alliance between the birth control campaign and the radical labor movement did not enjoy a long life. While Socialists and other working-class activists continued to support the demand for birth control, it did not occupy a central place in their overall strategy. And Sanger herself began to underestimate the centrality of capitalist exploitation in her analysis of poverty, arguing that too many children caused workers to fall into their miserable predicament. Moreover, ". . . women were inadvertently perpetuating the exploitation of the working class," she believed, "by continually flooding the labor market with new workers."[24] Ironically, Sanger may have been encouraged to adopt this position by the neo-Malthusian ideas embraced in some socialist circles. Such outstanding figures of the European socialist movement as Anatole France and Rosa Luxemburg had proposed a "birth strike" to prevent the continued flow of labor into the capitalist market.[25]

When Margaret Sanger severed her ties with the Socialist party for the purpose of building an independent birth control campaign, she and her followers became more susceptible than ever before to the anti-Black and anti-immigrant propaganda of the times. Like their predecessors, who had been deceived by the "race suicide" propaganda, the advocates of birth control began to embrace the prevailing racist ideology. The fatal influence of the eugenics movement would soon destroy the progressive potential of the birth control campaign.

During the first decades of the twentieth century the rising popularity of the eugenics movement was hardly a fortuitous development. Eugenic ideas were perfectly suited to the ideological needs of the young monopoly capitalists. Imperialist incursions in Latin America and in the Pacific needed to be justified, as did the intensified exploitation of Black workers in the South and immigrant workers in the North and West. The pseudo-scientific racial theories associated with the eugenics campaign furnished dramatic apologies for the conduct of the young monopolies. As a result, this movement won the unhesitating support of such leading capitalists as the Carnegies, the Harrimans and the Kelloggs.[26]

By 1919 the eugenic influence on the birth control movement was unmistakably clear. In an article published by Margaret Sanger in the American Birth Control League's journal, she defined "the chief issue of birth control" as "more children from the fit, less from the unfit."[27] Around this time the ABCL heartily welcomed the author of *The Rising Tide of Color Against White World Supremacy* into its inner sanctum.[28] Lothrop Stoddard, Harvard professor and theoretician of the eugenics movement, was offered a seat on the board of directors. In the pages of the ABCL's journal, articles by Guy Irving Birch, director of the American Eugenics Society, began to appear. Birch advocated birth control as a weapon to

> . . . prevent the American people from being replaced by alien or Negro stock, whether it be by immigration or by overly high birth rates among others in this country.[29]

By 1932 the Eugenics Society could boast that at least twenty-six states had passed compulsory sterilization laws and that thousands of "unfit" persons had already been surgically prevented from reproducing.[30] Margaret Sanger offered her public approval of this development. "Morons, mental defectives, epileptics, illiterates, paupers, unemployables, criminals, prostitutes and dope fiends" ought to be surgically sterilized, she argued in a radio talk.[31] She did not wish to be so intransigent as to leave them with no choice in the matter; if they wished, she said, they should be able to choose a lifelong segregated existence in labor camps.

Within the American Birth Control League, the call for birth control among Black people acquired the same racist edge as the call for compulsory sterilization. In 1939 its successor, the Birth Control Federation of America, planned a "Negro Project." In the Federation's words,

> (t)he mass of Negroes, particularly in the South, still breed carelessly and disastrously, with the result that the increase among Negroes, even more than among whites, is from that portion of the population least fit, and least able to rear children properly.[32]

Calling for the recruitment of Black ministers to lead local birth control committees, the Federation's proposal suggested that Black people should be rendered as vulnerable as possible to their birth control propaganda. "We do not want word to get out," wrote Margaret Sanger in a letter to a colleague,

> . . . that we want to exterminate the Negro population and the minister is the man who can straighten out that idea if it ever occurs to any of their more rebellious members.[33]

This episode in the birth control movement confirmed the ideological victory of the racism associated with eugenic ideas. It had been robbed of its progressive potential, advocating for people of color not the individual right to *birth control,* but rather the racist strategy of *population control.* The birth control campaign would be called upon to serve in an essential capacity in the execution of the U.S. government's imperialist and racist population policy.

The abortion rights activists of the early 1970s should have examined the history of their movement. Had they done so, they might have understood why so many of their Black sisters adopted a posture of suspicion toward their cause. They might have understood how important it was to undo the racist deeds of their predecessors, who had advocated birth control as well as compulsory sterilization as a means of eliminating the "unfit" sectors of the population. Consequently, the young white feminists might have been more receptive to the suggestion that their campaign for abortion rights include a vigorous condemnation of sterilization abuse, which had become more widespread than ever.

It was not until the media decided that the casual sterilization of two Black girls in Montgomery, Alabama, was a scandal worth reporting that the Pandora's box of sterilization abuse was finally flung open. But by the time the case of the Relf sisters broke, it was practically too late to influence the politics of the abortion rights movement. It was the summer of 1973 and the Supreme Court decision legalizing abortions had already been announced in January. Nevertheless, the urgent need for mass opposition to sterilization abuse became tragically clear. The facts surrounding the Relf sisters' story were horrifyingly simple. Minnie Lee, who was twelve years old, and Mary Alice, who was fourteen, had been unsuspectingly carted into an operating room, where surgeons irrevocably robbed them of their capacity to bear children.[34] The surgery had been ordered by the HEW-funded Montgomery Community Action Committee after it was discovered that Depo-Provera, a drug previously administered to the girls as a birth prevention measure, caused cancer in test animals.[35]

After the Southern Poverty Law Center filed suit on behalf of the Relf sisters, the girls' mother revealed that she had unknowingly "consented" to the operation, having been deceived by the social workers who handled her daughters' case. They had asked Mrs. Relf, who was unable to read, to put her "X" on a document, the contents of which were not described to her. She assumed, she said, that it authorized the continued Depo-Provera injections. As she subsequently learned, she had authorized the surgical sterilization of her daughters.[36]

In the aftermath of the publicity exposing the Relf sisters' case, similar episodes were brought to light. In Montgomery alone, eleven girls, also in their teens, had been similarly sterilized. HEW-funded birth control clinics in other states, as it turned out, had also subjected young girls to sterilization abuse. Moreover, individual women came forth with equally outrageous stories. Nial Ruth Cox, for example, filed suit against the state of North Carolina. At the age of eighteen—eight years before the suit—officials had threatened to discontinue her family's welfare payments if she refused to submit to surgical sterilization.[37] Before she assented to the operation, she was assured that her infertility would be temporary.[38]

Nial Ruth Cox's lawsuit was aimed at a state which had diligently practiced the theory of eugenics. Under the auspicies of the Eugenics Commission of North Carolina, so it was learned, 7,686 sterilizations had been carried out since 1933. Although the operations were justified as measures to prevent the reproduction of "mentally deficient persons," about 5,000 of the sterilized persons ha been Black.[39] According to Brenda Feigen Fasteau, the ACLU attorney representing Nial Ruth Cox, North Carolina's recent record was not much better.

> As far as I can determine, the statistics reveal that since 1964, approximately 65% of the women sterilized in North Carolina were Black and approximately 35% were white.[40]

As the flurry of publicity exposing sterilization abuse revealed, the neighboring state of South Carolina had been the site of further atrocities. Eighteen women from Aiken, South Carolina, charged that they had been sterilized by a Dr. Clovis Pierce during the early 1970s. The sole obstetrician in that small town, Pierce had consistently sterilized Medicaid recipients with two or more children. According to a nurse in his office, Dr. Pierce insisted that pregnant welfare women "will have to submit (sic!) to voluntary sterilization" if they wanted him to deliver their babies.[41] While he was ". . . tired of people running around and having babies and paying for them with my taxes,"[42] Dr. Pierce received some $60,000 in taxpayers' money for the sterilizations he performed. During his trial he was supported by the South Carolina Medical Association, whose members declared that doctors ". . . have a moral and legal right to insist on sterilization permission before accepting a patient, if it is done on the initial visit."[43]

Revelations of sterilization abuse during that time exposed the complicity of the federal government. At first the Department of Health, Education and Welfare claimed that approximately 16,-000 women and 8,000 men had been sterilized in 1972 under the auspices of federal programs.[44] Later, however, these figures underwent a drastic revision. Carl Shultz, director of HEW's Population Affairs Office, estimated that between 100,000 and 200,000 sterilizations had actually been funded that year by the federal government.[45] During Hitler's Germany, incidentally, 250,000 sterilizations were carried out under the Nazis' Hereditary Health Law.[46] Is it possible that the record of the Nazis, throughout the years of their reign, may have been almost equaled by U.S. government-funded sterilizations in the space of a single year?

Given the historical genocide inflicted on the native population of the United States, one would assume that Native American Indians would be exempted from the government's sterilization campaign. But according to Dr. Connie Uri's testimony in a Senate committee hearing, by 1976 some 24 percent of all Indian women of childbearing age had been sterilized.[47] "Our blood lines are being stopped," the Choctaw physician told the Senate committee, "Our unborn will not be born . . . This is genocidal to our people."[48] According to Dr. Uri, the Indian Health Services Hospital in Claremore, Oklahoma, had been sterilizing one out of every four women giving birth in that federal facility.[49]

Native American Indians are special targets of government propaganda on sterilization. In one of the HEW pamphlets aimed at Indian people, there is a sketch of a family with *ten children* and *one horse* and another sketch of a family with *one child* and *ten horses*. The drawings are supposed to imply that more children mean more poverty and fewer children mean wealth. As if the ten horses owned by the one-child family had been magically conjured up by birth control and sterilization surgery.

The domestic population policy of the U.S. government has an undeniably racist edge. Native American, Chicana, Puerto Rican and Black women continue to be sterilized in disproportionate numbers. According to a National Fertility Study conducted in 1970 by Princeton University's Office of Population Control, 20 percent of all married Black women have been permanently sterilized.[50] Approximately the same percentage of Chicana women had been rendered surgically infertile.[51] Moreover, 43 percent of the women sterilized through federally subsidized programs were Black.[52]

The astonishing number of Puerto Rican women who have been sterilized reflects a special government policy that can be traced back to 1939. In that year President Roosevelt's Interdepartmental Committee on Puerto Rico issued a statement attributing the island's economic problems to the phenomenon of overpopulation.[53] This committee proposed that efforts be undertaken to reduce the birth rate to no more than the level of the death rate.[54] Soon afterward an experimental sterilization campaign was undertaken in Puerto Rico. Although the Catholic Church initially opposed this experiment and forced the cessation of the program in 1946, it was converted during the early 1950s to the teachings and practice of population control.[55] In this period over 150 birth control clinics were opened, resulting in a 20 percent decline in population growth by the mid-1960s.[56] By the 1970s over 35 percent of all Puerto Rican women of childbearing age had been surgically sterilized.[57] According to Bonnie Mass, a serious critic of the U.S. government's population policy,

> . . . if purely mathematical projections are to be taken seriously, if the present rate of sterilization of 19,000 monthly were to continue, then the island's population of workers and peasants could be extinguished within the next 10 or 20 years . . . (establishing)

for the first time in world history a systematic use of population
control capable of eliminating an entire generation of people.[58]

During the 1970s the devastating implications of the Puerto
Rican experiment began to emerge with unmistakable clarity. In
Puerto Rico the presence of corporations in the highly automated
metallurgical and pharmaceutical industries had exacerbated the
problem of unemployment. The prospect of an ever-larger army
of unemployed workers was one of the main incentives for the
mass sterilization program. Inside the United States today, enormous numbers of people of color—and especially racially oppressed youth—have become part of a pool of permanently
unemployed workers. It is hardly coincidental, considering the
Puerto Rican example, that the increasing incidence of sterilization has kept pace with the high rates of unemployment. As
growing numbers of white people suffer the brutal consequences
of unemployment, they can also expect to become targets of the
official sterilization propaganda.

The prevalence of sterilization abuse during the latter 1970s
may be greater than ever before. Although the Department of
Health, Education and Welfare issued guidelines in 1974, which
were ostensibly designed to prevent involuntary sterilizations, the
situation has nonetheless deteriorated. When the American Civil
Liberties Union's Reproductive Freedom Project conducted a
survey of teaching hospitals in 1975, they discovered that 40
percent of those institutions were not even aware of the regula-
tions issued by HEW.[59] Only 30 percent of the hospitals examined by the ACLU were even attempting to comply with the
guidelines.[60]

The 1977 Hyde Amendment has added yet another dimension
to coercive sterilization practices. As a result of this law passed by
Congress, federal funds for abortions were eliminated in all cases
but those involving rape and the risk of death or severe illness.

According to Sandra Salazar of the California Department of Public Health, the first victim of the Hyde Amendment was a twenty-seven-year-old Chicana woman from Texas. She died as a result of an illegal abortion in Mexico shortly after Texas discontinued government-funded abortions. There have been many more victims—women for whom sterilization has become the only alternative to the abortions, which are currently beyond their reach. Sterilizations continue to be federally funded and free, to poor women, on demand.

Over the last decade the struggle against sterilization abuse has been waged primarily by Puerto Rican, Black, Chicana and Native American women. Their cause has not yet been embraced by the women's movement as a whole. Within organizations representing the interests of middle-class white women, there has been a certain reluctance to support the demands of the campaign against sterilization abuse, for these women are often denied their individual rights to be sterilized when they desire to take this step. While women of color are urged, at every turn, to become permanently infertile, white women enjoying prosperous economic conditions are urged, by the same forces, to reproduce themselves. They therefore sometimes consider the "waiting period" and other details of the demand for "informed consent" to sterilization as further inconveniences for women like themselves. Yet whatever the inconveniences for white middle-class women, a fundamental reproductive right of racially oppressed and poor women is at stake. Sterilization abuse must be ended.

13 ✍ The Approaching Obsolescence of Housework: A Working-Class Perspective

The countless chores collectively known as "housework"—cooking, washing dishes, doing laundry, making beds, sweeping, shopping, etc.—apparently consume some three to four thousand hours of the average housewife's year.[1] As startling as this statistic may be, it does not even account for the constant and unquantifiable attention mothers must give to their children. Just as a woman's maternal duties are always taken for granted, her never-ending toil as a housewife rarely occasions expressions of appreciation within her family. Housework, after all, is virtually invisible: "No one notices it until it isn't done—we notice the unmade bed, not the scrubbed and polished floor."[2] Invisible, repetitive, exhausting, unproductive, uncreative—these are the adjectives which most perfectly capture the nature of housework.

The new consciousness associated with the contemporary women's movement has encouraged increasing numbers of women to demand that their men provide some relief from this drudgery. Already, more men have begun to assist their partners around the house, some of them even devoting equal time to household chores. But how many of these men have liberated themselves from the assumption that housework is "women's work"? How many of them would not characterize their housecleaning activities as "helping" their women partners?

If it were at all possible simultaneously to liquidate the idea that housework is women's work and to redistribute it equally to men and women alike, would this constitute a satisfactory solution? Freed from its exclusive affiliation with the female sex, would housework thereby cease to be oppressive? While most women would joyously hail the advent of the "househusband," the desexualization of domestic labor would not really alter the oppressive nature of the work itself. In the final analysis, neither women nor men should waste precious hours of their lives on work that is neither stimulating, creative nor productive.

One of the most closely guarded secrets of advanced capitalist societies involves the possibility—the real possibility—of radically transforming the nature of housework. A substantial portion of the housewife's domestic tasks can actually be incorporated into the industrial economy. In other words, housework need no longer be considered necessarily and unalterably private in character. Teams of trained and well-paid workers, moving from dwelling to dwelling, engineering technologically advanced cleaning machinery, could swiftly and efficiently accomplish what the present-day housewife does so arduously and primitively. Why the shroud of silence surrounding this potential of radically redefining the nature of domestic labor? Because the capitalist economy is structurally hostile to the industrialization of housework. Socialized housework implies large government subsidies in order to guarantee accessibility to the working-class families whose need for such services is most obvious. Since little in the way of profits would result, industrialized housework—like all unprofitable enterprises—is anathema to the capitalist economy. Nonetheless, the rapid expansion of the female labor force means that more and more women are finding it increasingly difficult to excel as housewives according to the traditional standards. In other words, the industrialization of housework, along with the socialization of housework, is becoming an objective social need. Housework as individual women's private responsibility and as female labor performed under primitive technical conditions, may finally be approaching historical obsolescence.

Although housework as we know it today may eventually become a bygone relic of history, prevailing social attitudes continue to associate the eternal female condition with images of brooms and dustpans, mops and pails, aprons and stoves, pots and pans. And it is true that women's work, from one historical era to another, has been associated in general with the homestead. Yet female domestic labor has not always been what it is today, for like all social phenomena, housework is a fluid product of human history. As economic systems have arisen and faded away, the scope and quality of housework have undergone radical transformations.

As Frederick Engels argued in his classic work on the *Origin of the Family, Private Property and the State*,[3] sexual inequality as we know it today did not exist before the advent of private property. During early eras of human history the sexual division of labor within the system of economic production was complementary as opposed to hierarchical. In societies where men may have been responsible for hunting wild animals and women, in turn, for gathering wild vegetables and fruits, both sexes performed economic tasks that were equally essential to their community's survival. Because the community, during those eras, was essentially an extended family, women's central role in domestic affairs meant that they were accordingly valued and respected as productive members of the community.

The centrality of women's domestic tasks in pre-capitalist cultures was dramatized by a personal experience during a jeep trip I took in 1973 across the Masai Plains. On an isolated dirt road in Tanzania, I noticed six Masai women enigmatically balancing an enormous board on their heads. As my Tanzanian friends explained, these women were probably transporting a house roof to a new village which they were in the process of constructing. Among the Masai, as I learned, women are responsible for all domestic activities, thus also for the construction of their nomadic people's frequently relocated houses. Housework, as far as Masai women are concerned, entails not only cooking, cleaning, child-rearing, sewing, etc., but house-building as well. As important as their men's cattle-raising duties may be, the women's "housework" is no less productive and no less essential than the economic contributions of Masai men.

Within the pre-capitalist, nomadic economy of the Masai, women's domestic labor is as essential to the economy as the cattle-raising jobs performed by their men. As producers, they enjoy a correspondingly important social status. In advanced capitalist societies, on the other hand, the service-oriented domestic labor of housewives, who can seldom produce tangible evidence of their work, diminishes the social status of women in general. When all is said and done, the housewife, according to bourgeois ideology, is, quite simply, her husband's lifelong servant.

The source of the bourgeois notion of woman as man's eternal servant is itself a revealing story. Within the relatively short history of the United States, the "housewife" as a finished historical product is just a little more than a century old. Housework, during the colonial era, was entirely different from the daily work routine of the housewife in the United States today.

> A woman's work began at sunup and continued by firelight as long as she could hold her eyes open. For two centuries, almost everything that the family used or ate was produced at home under her direction. She spun and dyed the yarn that she wove into cloth and cut and hand-stitched into garments. She grew much of the food her family ate, and preserved enough to last the winter months. She made butter, cheese, bread, candles, and soap and knitted her family's stockings.[4]

In the agrarian economy of pre-industrial North America, a woman performing her household chores was thus a spinner, weaver and seamstress as well as a baker, butter-churner, candle-maker and soap-maker. And et cetera, et cetera, et cetera. As a matter of fact,

> . . . the pressures of home production left very little time for the tasks that we would recognize today as housework. By all accounts, pre-industrial revolution women were sloppy housekeepers by today's standards. Instead of the daily cleaning or the weekly cleaning, there was the *spring* cleaning. Meals were simple and repetitive; clothes were changed infrequently; and the household wash was allowed to accumulate, and the washing done once a month, or in some households once in three months. And, of course, since each wash required the carting and heating of many buckets of water, higher standards of cleanliness were easily discouraged.[5]

Colonial women were not "house-cleaners" or "housekeepers" but rather full-fledged and accomplished workers within the home-based economy. Not only did they manufacture most of the products required by their families, they were also the guardians of their families' and their communities' health.

> It was [the colonial woman's] responsibility to gather and dry wild herbs used . . . as medicines; she also served as doctor, nurse, and midwife within her own family and in the community.[6]

Included in the *United States Practical Receipt Book*—a popular colonial recipe book—are recipes for foods as well as for household chemicals and medicines. To cure ringworm, for example, "obtain some blood-root . . . slice it in vinegar, and afterwards wash the place affected with the liquid."[7]

The economic importance of women's domestic functions in

colonial America was complemented by their visible roles in economic activity outside the home. It was entirely acceptable, for example, for a woman to become a tavern keeper.

> Women also ran sawmills and gristmills, caned chairs and built furniture, operated slaughterhouses, printed cotton and other cloth, made lace, and owned and ran dry-goods and clothing stores. They worked in tobacco shops, drug shops (where they sold concoctions they made themselves), and general stores that sold everything from pins to meat scales. Women ground eyeglasses, made netting and rope, cut and stitched leather goods, made cards for wool carding, and even were housepainters. Often they were the town undertakers . . .[8]

The postrevolutionary surge of industrialization resulted in a proliferation of factories in the northeastern section of the new country. New England's textile mills were the factory system's successful pioneers. Since spinning and weaving were traditional female domestic occupations, women were the first workers recruited by the mill-owners to operate the new power looms. Considering the subsequent exclusion of women from industrial production in general, it is one of the great ironies of this country's economic history that the first industrial workers were women.

As industrialization advanced, shifting economic production from the home to the factory, the importance of women's domestic work suffered a systematic erosion. Women were the losers in a double sense: as their traditional jobs were usurped by the burgeoning factories, the entire economy moved away from the home, leaving many women largely bereft of significant economic roles. By the middle of the nineteenth century the factory provided textiles, candles and soap. Even butter, bread and other food products began to be mass-produced.

By the end of the century, hardly anyone made their own starch
or boiled their laundry in a kettle. In the cities, women bought their
bread and at least their underwear ready-made, sent their children
out to school and probaby some clothes out to be laundered, and
were debating the merits of canned foods . . . The flow of industry
had passed on and had left idle the loom in the attic and the soap
kettle in the shed."9

As industrial capitalism approached consolidation, the cleavage
between the new economic sphere and the old home economy
became ever more rigorous. The physical relocation of economic
production caused by the spread of the factory system was undoubtedly a drastic transformation. But even more radical was the
generalized revaluation of production necessitated by the new
economic system. While home-manufactured goods were valuable primarily because they fulfilled basic family needs, the importance of factory-produced commodities resided overwhelmingly
in their exchange value—in their ability to fulfill employers' demands for profit. This revaluation of economic production revealed—beyond the physical separation of home and factory—a
fundamental *structural* separation between the domestic home
economy and the profit-oriented economy of capitalism. Since
housework does not generate profit, domestic labor was naturally
defined as an inferior form of work as compared to capitalist wage
labor.

An important ideological by-product of this radical economic
transformation was the birth of the "housewife." Women began
to be ideologically redefined as the guardians of a devalued domestic life. As ideology, however, this redefinition of women's place
was boldly contradicted by the vast numbers of immigrant women
flooding the ranks of the working class in the Northeast. These
white immigrant women were wage earners first and only secon-
darily housewives. And there were other women—millions of

women—who toiled away from home as the unwilling producers of the slave economy in the South. The reality of women's place in nineteenth-century U.S. society involved white women, whose days were spent operating factory machines for wages that were a pittance, as surely as it involved Black women, who labored under the coercion of slavery. The "housewife" reflected a partial reality, for she was really a symbol of the economic prosperity enjoyed by the emerging middle classes.

Although the "housewife" was rooted in the social conditions of the bourgeoisie and the middle classes, nineteenth-century ideology established the housewife and the mother as universal models of womanhood. Since popular propaganda represented the vocation of *all* women as a function of their roles in the home, women compelled to work for wages came to be treated as alien visitors within the masculine world of the public economy. Having stepped outside their "natural" sphere, women were not to be treated as full-fledged wage workers. The price they paid involved long hours, substandard working conditions and grossly inadequate wages. Their exploitation was even more intense than the exploitation suffered by their male counterparts. Needless to say, sexism emerged as a source of outrageous super-profits for the capitalists.

The structural separation of the public economy of capitalism and the private economy of the home has been continually reinforced by the obstinate primitiveness of household labor. Despite the proliferation of gadgets for the home, domestic work has remained qualitatively unaffected by the technological advances brought on by industrial capitalism. Housework still consumes thousands of hours of the average housewife's year. In 1903 Charlotte Perkins Gilman proposed a definition of domestic labor which reflected the upheavals which had changed the structure and content of housework in the United States:

> ... The phrase "domestic work" does not apply to a special kind of work, but to a certain grade of work, a state of development through which all kinds pass. All industries were once "domestic," that is, were performed at home and in the interests of the family. All industries have since that remote period risen to higher stages, except one or two which have never left their primal stage.[10]

"The home," Gilman maintains, "has not developed in proportion to our other institutions." The home economy reveals

> ... the maintenance of primitive industries in a modern industrial community and the confinement of women to these industries and their limited area of expression.[11]

Housework, Gilman insists, vitiates women's humanity:

> She is feminine, more than enough, as man is masculine, more than enough; but she is not human as he is human. The house-life does not bring out our humanness, for all the distinctive lines of human progress lie outside.[12]

The truth of Gilman's statement is corroborated by the historical experience of Black women in the United States. Throughout this country's history, the majority of Black women have worked outside their homes. During slavery, women toiled alongside their men in the cotton and tobacco fields, and when industry moved into the South, they could be seen in tobacco factories, sugar refineries and even in lumber mills and on crews pounding steel for the railroads. In labor, slave women were the equals of their men. Because they suffered a grueling sexual equality at work, they enjoyed a greater sexual equality at home in the slave quarters than did their white sisters who were "housewifes."

As a direct consequence of their outside work—as "free" women no less than as slaves—housework has never been the central focus of Black women's lives. They have largely escaped the psychological damage industrial capitalism inflicted on white middle-class housewives, whose alleged virtues were feminine weakness and wifely submissiveness. Black women could hardly strive for weakness; they had to become strong, for their families and their communities needed their strength to survive. Evidence of the accumulated strengths Black women have forged through work, work and more work can be discovered in the contributions of the many outstanding female leaders who have emerged within the Black community. Harriet Tubman, Sojourner Truth, Ida Wells and Rosa Parks are not exceptional Black women as much as they are epitomes of Black womanhood.

Black women, however, have paid a heavy price for the strengths they have acquired and the relative independence they have enjoyed. While they have seldom been "just housewives," they have always done their housework. They have thus carried the double burden of wage labor and housework—a double burden which always demands that working women possess the persevering powers of Sisyphus. As W. E. B. DuBois observed in 1920:

> ... some few women are born free, and some amid insult and scarlet letters achieve freedom; but our women in black had freedom thrust contemptuously upon them. With that freedom they are buying an untrammeled independence and dear as is the price they pay for it, it will in the end be worth every taunt and groan.[13]

Like their men, Black women have worked until they could work no more. Like their men, they have assumed the responsibilities of family providers. The unorthodox feminine qualities of assertiveness and self-reliance—for which Black women have been frequently praised but more often rebuked—are reflections of their labor and their struggles outside the home. But like their white sisters called "housewives," they have cooked and cleaned and have nurtured and reared untold numbers of children. But unlike the white housewives, who learned to lean on their husbands for economic security, Black wives and mothers, usually workers as well, have rarely been offered the time and energy to become experts at domesticity. Like their white working-class sisters, who also carry the double burden of working for a living and servicing husbands and children, Black women have needed relief from this oppressive predicament for a long, long time.

For Black women today and for all their working-class sisters, the notion that the burden of housework and child care can be shifted from their shoulders to the society contains one of the radical secrets of women's liberation. Child care should be socialized, meal preparation should be socialized, housework should be industrialized—and all these services should be readily accessible to working-class people.

The shortage, if not absence, of public discussion about the feasibility of transforming housework into a social possibility bears witness to the blinding powers of bourgeois ideology. It is not even the case that women's domestic role has received no attention at all. On the contrary, the contemporary women's movement has represented housework as an essential ingredient of women's oppression. There is even a movement in a number of capitalist countries, whose main concern is the plight of the housewife. Having reached the conclusion that housework is degrading and oppressive primarily because it is *unpaid* labor, this movement has raised the demand for wages. A weekly government paycheck, its activists argue, is the key to improving the housewife's status and the social position of women in general.

The Wages for Housework Movement originated in Italy, where its first public demonstration took place in March, 1974.

Addressing the crowd assembled in the city of Mestre, one of the speakers proclaimed:

> Half the world's population is unpaid—this is the biggest class contradiction of all! And this is our struggle for wages for housework. It is *the* strategic demand; at this moment it is the most revolutionary demand for the whole working class. If we win, the class wins, if we lose, the class loses.[14]

According to this movement's strategy, wages contain the key to the emancipation of housewives, and the demand itself is represented as the central focus of the campaign for women's liberation in general. Moreover, the housewife's struggle for wages is projected as the pivotal issue of the entire working-class movement.

The theoretical origins of the Wages for Housework Movement can be found in an essay by Mariarosa Dalla Costa entitled "Women and the Subversion of the Community."[15] In this paper, Dalla Costa argues for a redefinition of housework based on her thesis that the private character of household services is actually an illusion. The housewife, she insists, only appears to be ministering to the private needs of her husband and children, for the real beneficiaries of her services are her husband's present employer and the future employers of her children.

> (The woman) has been isolated in the home, forced to carry out work that is considered unskilled, the work of giving birth to, raising, disciplining, and servicing the worker for production. Her role in the cycle of production remained invisible because only the product of her labor, the *laborer,* was visible.[16]

The demand that housewives be paid is based on the assumption that they produce a commodity as important and as valuable as the commodities their husbands produce on the job. Adopting Dalla Costa's logic, the Wages for Housework Movement defines housewives as creators of the labor-power sold by their family members as commodities on the capitalist market.

Dalla Costa was not the first theorist to propose such an analysis of women's oppression. Both Mary Inman's *In Woman's Defense* (1940)[17] and Margaret Benston's "The Political Economy of Women's Liberation" (1969)[18] define housework in such a way as to establish women as a special class of workers exploited by capitalism called "housewives." That women's procreative, child-rearing and housekeeping roles make it possible for their family members to work—to exchange their labor-power for wages—can hardly be denied. But does it automatically follow that women in general, regardless of their class and race, can be fundamentally defined by their domestic functions? Does it automatically follow that the housewife is actually a secret worker inside the capitalist production process?

If the industrial revolution resulted in the structural separation of the home economy from the public economy, then housework cannot be defined as an integral component of capitalist production. It is, rather, related to production as a *precondition.* The employer is not concerned in the least about the way labor-power is produced and sustained, he is only concerned about its availability and its ability to generate profit. In other words, the capitalist production process presupposes the existence of a body of exploitable workers.

> The replenishment of (workers') labor-power is not a part of the process of social production but a prerequisite to it. It occurs *outside* of the labor process. Its function is the maintenance of human existence which is the ultimate purpose of production in all societies.[19]

In South African society, where racism has led economic exploitation to its most brutal limits, the capitalist economy betrays its structural separation from domestic life in a characteristically violent fashion. The social architects of Apartheid have simply determined that Black labor yields higher profits when domestic life is all but entirely discarded. Black men are viewed as labor units whose productive potential renders them valuable to the capitalist class. But their wives and children

> . . . are superfluous appendages—non-productive, the women being nothing more than adjuncts to the procreative capacity of the black male labor unit.[20]

This characterization of African women as "superfluous appendages" is hardly a metaphor. In accordance with South African law, unemployed Black women are banned from the white areas (87 percent of the country!), even, in most cases, from the cities where their husbands live and work.

Black domestic life in South Africa's industrial centers is viewed by Apartheid supporters as superfluous and unprofitable. But it is also seen as a threat.

> Government officials recognize the homemaking role of the women and fear their presence in the cities will lead to the establishment of a stable black population.[21]

The consolidation of African families in the industrialized cities is perceived as a menace because domestic life might become a base for a heightened level of resistance to Apartheid. This is undoubtedly the reason why large numbers of women holding residence permits for white areas are assigned to live in sex-segregated hostels. Married as well as single women end up living in these projects. In such hostels, family life is rigorously prohibited—husbands and wives are unable to visit one another and neither mother nor father can receive visits from their children.[22]

This intense assault on Black women in South Africa has already taken its toll, for only 28.2 percent are currently opting for marriage.[23] For reasons of economic expediency and political security, Apartheid is eroding—with the apparent goal of destroying—the very fabric of Black domestic life. South African capitalism thus blatantly demonstrates the extent to which the capitalist economy is utterly dependent on domestic labor.

The deliberate dissolution of family life in South Africa could not have been undertaken by the government if it were truly the case that the services performed by women in the home are an essential constituent of wage labor under capitalism. That domestic life can be dispensed with by the South African version of capitalism is a consequence of the separation of the private home economy and the public production process which characterizes capitalist society in general. It seems futile to argue that on the basis of capitalism's internal logic, women ought to be paid wages for housework.

Assuming that the theory underlying the demand for wages is hopelessly flawed, might it not be nonetheless politically desirable to insist that housewives be paid. Couldn't one invoke a moral imperative for women's right to be paid for the hours they devote to housework? The idea of a paycheck for housewives would probably sound quite attractive to many women. But the attraction would probably be short-lived. For how many of those women would actually be willing to reconcile themselves to deadening, never-ending household tasks, all for the sake of a wage? Would a wage alter the fact, as Lenin said, that

> . . . petty housework crushes, strangles, stultifies and degrades (the woman), chains her to the kitchen and to the nursery, and wastes her labor on barbarously unproductive, petty, nerve-racking, stultifying and crushing drudgery.[24]

It would seem that government paychecks for housewives would further legitimize this domestic slavery.

Is it not an implicit critique of the Wages for Housework Movement that women on welfare have rarely demanded compensation for keeping house. Not "wages for housework" but rather "a guaranteed annual income for all" is the slogan articulating the immediate alternative they have most frequently proposed to the dehumanizing welfare system. What they want in the long run, however, is jobs and affordable public child care. The guaranteed annual income functions, therefore, as unemployment insurance pending the creation of more jobs with adequate wages along with a subsidized system of child care.

The experiences of yet another group of women reveal the problematic nature of the "wages for housework" strategy. Cleaning women, domestic workers, maids—these are the women who know better than anyone else what it means to receive wages for housework. Their tragic predicament is brilliantly captured in the film by Ousmane Sembene entitled *La Noire de . . .*[25] The main character is a young Senegalese woman who, after a search for work, becomes a governess for a French family living in Dakar. When the family returns to France, she enthusiastically accompanies them. Once in France, however, she discovers she is responsible not only for the children, but for cooking, cleaning, washing and all the other household chores. It is not long before her initial enthusiasm gives way to depression—a depression so profound that she refuses the pay offered her by her employers. Wages cannot compensate for her slavelike situation. Lacking the means to return to Senegal, she is so overwhelmed by her despair that she chooses suicide over an indefinite destiny of cooking, sweeping, dusting, scrubbing . . .

In the United States, women of color—and especially Black women—have been receiving wages for housework for untold decades. In 1910, when over half of all Black females were working outside their homes, one-third of them were employed as paid domestic workers. By 1920 over one-half were domestic servants, and in 1930 the proportion had risen to three out of five.[26] One of the consequences of the enormous female employment shifts during World War II was a much-welcomed decline in the number of Black domestic workers. Yet in 1960 one-third of all Black women holding jobs were still confined to their traditional occupations.[27] It was not until clerical jobs became more accessible to Black women that the proportion of Black women domestics headed in a definitely downward direction. Today the figure hovers around 13 percent.[28]

The enervating domestic obligations of women in general provide flagrant evidence of the power of sexism. Because of the added intrusion of racism, vast numbers of Black women have had to do their own housekeeping and other women's home chores as well. And frequently, the demands of the job in a white woman's home have forced the domestic worker to neglect her own home and even her own children. As paid housekeepers, they have been called upon to be surrogate wives and mothers in millions of white homes.

During their more than fifty years of organizing efforts, domestic workers have tried to redefine their work by rejecting the role of the surrogate housewife. The housewife's chores are unending and undefined. Household workers have demanded in the first place a clear delineation of the jobs they are expected to perform. The name itself of one of the houseworkers' major unions today —Household Technicians of America—emphasizes their refusal to function as surrogate housewives whose job is "just housework." As long as household workers stand in the shadow of the housewife, they will continue to receive wages which are more closely related to a housewife's "allowance" than to a worker's paycheck. According to the National Committee on Household Employment, the average, full-time household technician earned only $2,732 in 1976, two-thirds of them earning under $2,000.[29] Although household workers had been extended the protection of the minimum wage law several years previously, in 1976 an astounding 40 percent still received grossly substandard wages. The Wages for Housework Movement assumes that if women were paid for being housewives, they would accordingly enjoy a higher social status. Quite a different story is told by the age-old struggles of the paid household worker, whose condition is more miserable than any other group of workers under capitalism.

Over 50 percent of all U.S. women work for a living today, and they constitute 41 percent of the country's labor force. Yet countless numbers of women are currently unable to find decent jobs. Like racism, sexism is one of the great justifications for high female unemployment rates. Many women are "just housewives" because in reality they are unemployed workers. Cannot, therefore, the "just housewife" role be most effectively challenged by demanding jobs for women on a level of equality with men and by pressing for the social services (child care, for example) and job benefits (maternity leaves, etc.) which will allow more women to work outside the home?

The Wages for Housework Movement discourages women from seeking outside jobs, arguing that "slavery to an assembly line is not liberation from slavery to the kitchen sink."[30] The campaign's spokeswomen insist, nonetheless, that they don't advocate the continued imprisonment of women within the isolated environment of their homes. They claim that while they refuse to work on the capitalist market per se, they do not wish to assign to women the permanent responsibility for housework. As a U.S. representative of this movement says:

> ... we are not interested in making our work more efficient or more productive for capital. We are interested in reducing our work, and ultimately refusing it altogether. But as long as we work in the

home for nothing, no one really cares how long or how hard we work. For capital only introduces advanced technology to cut the costs of production after wage gains by the working class. Only if we make our work cost (i.e., only if we make it uneconomical) will capital "discover" the technology to reduce it. At present, we often have to go out for a second shift of work to afford the dishwasher that should cut down our housework.[31]

Once women have achieved the right to be paid for their work, they can raise demands for higher wages, thus compelling the capitalists to undertake the industrialization of housework. Is this a concrete strategy for women's liberation or is it an unrealizable dream?

How are women supposed to conduct the initial struggle for wages? Dalla Costa advocates the *housewives' strike:*

> We must reject the home, because we want to unite with other women, to struggle against all situations which presume that women will stay at home . . . To abandon the home is already a form of struggle, since the social services we perform there would then cease to be carried out in those conditions.[32]

But if women are to leave the home, where are they to go? How will they unite with other women? Will they really leave their homes motivated by no other desire than to protest their housework? Is it not much more realistic to call upon women to "leave home" in search of outside jobs—or at least to participate in a massive campaign for decent jobs for women? Granted, work under the conditions of capitalism is brutalizing work. Granted, it is uncreative and alienating. Yet with all this, the fact remains that on the job, women can unite with their sisters—and indeed with their brothers—in order to challenge the capitalists at the point of production. As workers, as militant activists in the labor movement, women can generate the real power to fight the main-stay and beneficiary of sexism which is the monopoly capitalist system.

If the wages-for-housework strategy does little in the way of providing a long-range solution to the problem of women's op-pression, neither does it substantively address the profound dis-content of contemporary housewives. Recent sociological studies have revealed that housewives today are more frustrated by their lives than ever before. When Ann Oakley conducted interviews for her book *The Sociology of Housework*, [33] she discovered that even the housewives who initially seemed unbothered by their housework eventually expressed a very deep dissatisfaction. These comments came from a woman who held an outside factory job:

> (Do you like housework?) I don't mind it . . . I suppose I don't mind housework because I'm not at it all day. I go to work and I'm only on housework half a day. If I did it all day I wouldn't like it— woman's work is never done, she's on the go all the time—even before you go to bed, you've still got something to do—emptying ashtrays, wash a few cups up. You're still working. It's the same thing every day; you can't sort of say you're not going to do it, because you've got to do it—like preparing a meal: it's got to be done because if you don't do it, the children wouldn't eat . . . I suppose you get used to it, you just do it automatically. . . . I'm happier at work than I am at home.

> (What would you say are the worst things about being a house-wife?) I suppose you get days when you feel you get up and you've got to do the same old things—you get bored, you're stuck in the same routine. I think if you ask any housewife, if they're honest, they'll turn around and say they feel like a drudge half the time— everybody thinks when they get up in the morning "Oh no, I've got the same old things to do today, till I go to bed tonight." It's doing the same things—boredom.[34]

Would wages diminish this boredom? This woman would certainly say no. A full-time housewife told Oakley about the compulsive nature of housework:

> The worst thing is I suppose that you've got to do the work because you *are* at home. Even though I've got the option of not doing it, I don't really feel I *could* not do it because I feel I *ought* to do it.[35]

In all likelihood, receiving wages for doing this work would aggravate this woman's obsession.

Oakley reached the conclusion that housework—particularly when it is a full-time job—so thoroughly invades the female personality that the housewife becomes indistinguishable from her job.

> The housewife, in an important sense, *is* her job: separation between subjective and objective elements in the situation is therefore intrinsically more difficult.[36]

The psychological consequence is frequently a tragically stunted personality haunted by feelings of inferiority. Psychological liberation can hardly be achieved simply by paying the housewife a wage.

Other sociological studies have confirmed the acute disillusionment suffered by contemporary housewives. When Myra Ferree[37] interviewed over a hundred women in a working community near Boston, "almost twice as many housewives as employed wives said they were dissatisfied with their lives." Needless to say, most of the working women did not have inherently fulfilling jobs: they were waitresses, factory workers, typists, supermarket and department store clerks, etc. Yet their ability to leave the isolation of their homes, "getting out and seeing other people," was as important to them as their earnings. Would the housewives who felt they were "going crazy staying at home" welcome the idea of being paid for driving themselves crazy? One woman complained that "staying at home all day is like being in jail"—would wages tear down the walls of her jail? The only realistic escape path from this jail is the search for work outside the home.

Each one of the more than 50 percent of all U.S. women who work today is a powerful argument for the alleviation of the burden of housework. As a matter of fact, enterprising capitalists have already begun to exploit women's new historical need to emancipate themselves from their roles as housewives. Endless profit-making fast-food chains like McDonald's and Kentucky Fried Chicken bear witness to the fact that more women at work means fewer daily meals prepared at home. However unsavory and unnutritious the food, however exploitative of their workers, these fast-food operations call attention to the approaching obsolescence of the housewife. What is needed, of course, are new social institutions to assume a good portion of the housewife's old duties. This is the challenge emanating from the swelling ranks of women in the working class. The demand for universal and subsidized child care is a direct consequence of the rising number of working mothers. And as more women organize around the demand for more jobs—for jobs on the basis of full equality with men—serious questions will increasingly be raised about the future viability of women's housewife duties. It may well be true that "slavery to an assembly line" is not in itself "liberation from the kitchen sink," but the assembly line is doubtlessly the most powerful incentive for women to press for the elimination of their age-old domestic slavery.

The abolition of housework as the private responsibility of individual women is clearly a strategic goal of women's liberation. But the socialization of housework—including meal preparation and child care—presupposes an end to the profit-motive's reign over the economy. The only significant steps toward ending domestic slavery have in fact been taken in the existing socialist countries. Working women, therefore, have a special and vital interest in the struggle for socialism. Moreover, under capitalism, campaigns for jobs on an equal basis with men, combined with movements for institutions such as subsidized public child care, contain an explosive revolutionary potential. This strategy calls into question the validity of monopoly capitalism and must ultimately point in the direction of socialism.

Notes

1. Ulrich Bonnell Phillips, *American Negro Slavery: A Survey of the Supply, Employment, and Control of Negro Labor as Determined by the Plantation Regime* (New York and London: D. Appleton, 1918). See also Phillips' article "The Plantation as a Civilizing Factor," *Sewanee Review,* XII (July, 1904), reprinted in Ulrich Bonnell Phillips, *The Slave Economy of the Old South: Selected Essays in Economic and Social History,* edited by Eugene D. Genovese (Baton Rouge: Louisiana State University Press, 1968). The following passage is included in this article:

The conditions of our problem are as follows:

1. A century or two ago the negroes were savages in the wilds of Africa. 2. Those who were brought to America, and their descendants, have acquired a certain amount of civilization, and are now in some degree fitted for life in modern civilized society. 3. This progress of the negroes has been in very large measure the result of their association with civilized white people. 4. An immense mass of the negroes is sure to remain for an indefinite period in the midst of a civilized white nation. The problem is, How can we best provide for their peaceful residence and their further progress in this nation of white men and how can we best guard against their lapsing back into barbarism? As a possible solution for a large part of the problem, I suggest the plantation system. (p. 83)

2. Observations on the special predicament of Black women slaves can be found in numerous books, articles and anthologies authored and edited by Herbert Aptheker, including *American Negro Slave Revolts* (New York: International Publishers, 1970. First edition: 1948); *To Be Free: Studies in American Negro History* (New York: International Publishers, 1969. First edition: 1948); *A Documentary History of the Negro People in the United States,* Vol. 1 (New York: The Citadel Press, 1969. First edition: 1951). In February, 1948, Aptheker published an article entitled "The Negro Woman" in *Masses and Mainstream,* Vol. 11, No. 2.

3. Eugene D. Genovese, *Roll, Jordan, Roll: The World the Slaves Made* (New York: Pantheon Books, 1974).

4. John W. Blassingame, *The Slave Community: Plantation Life in the An-*

tebellum South (London and New York: Oxford University Press, 1972).

5. Robert W. Fogel and Stanley Engerman, *Time on the Cross: The Economics of Slavery in the Antebellum South,* 2 volumes. (Boston: Little, Brown & Co., 1974.)

6. Herbert Gutman, *The Black Family in Slavery and Freedom, 1750–1925* (New York: Pantheon Books, 1976).

7. Stanley Elkins, *Slavery: A Problem in American Institutional and Intellectual Life,* third edition, revised (Chicago and London: University of Chicago Press, 1976).

8. See Daniel P. Moynihan, *The Negro Family: The Case for National Action,* Washington, D.C.: U.S. Department of Labor, 1965. Reprinted in Lee Rainwater and William L. Yancey, *The Moynihan Report and the Politics of Controversy* (Cambridge, Mass.: MIT Press, 1967).

9. See W. E. B. DuBois, "The Damnation of Women," Chapter VII of *Darkwater* (New York: Harcourt, Brace and Howe, 1920).

10. Kenneth M. Stampp, *The Peculiar Institution: Slavery in the Antebellum South* (New York: Vintage Books, 1956), p. 343.

11. *Ibid.,* p. 31; p. 49; p. 50; p. 60.

12. Mel Watkins and Jay David, editors, *To Be a Black Woman: Portraits in Fact and Fiction* (New York: William Morrow and Co., Inc., 1970), p. 16. Quoted from Benjamin A. Botkin, editor, *Lay My Burden Down: A Folk History of Slavery* (Chicago: University of Chicago Press, 1945).

13. Barbara Wertheimer, *We Were There: The Story of Working Women in America* (New York: Pantheon Books, 1977), p. 109.

14. *Ibid.,* p. 111. Quoted from Lewis Clarke, *Narrative of the Sufferings of Lewis and Milton Clarke, Sons of a Soldier of the Revolution* (Boston: 1846), p. 127.

15. Stampp, *op. cit.,* p. 57.

16. Charles Ball, *Slavery in the United States: A Narrative of the Life and Adventures of Charles Ball, a Black Man* (Lewistown, Pa.: J. W. Shugert, 1836), pp. 150–151. Quoted in Gerda Lerner, editor, *Black Women in White America: A Documentary History* (New York: Pantheon Books, 1972), p. 48.

17. Moses Grandy, *Narrative of the Life of Moses Grandy: Late a Slave in the United States of America* (Boston: 1844), p. 18. Quoted in E. Franklin Frazier, *The Negro Family in the United States* (Chicago: University of Chicago Press, 1969. First edition: 1939).

18. *Ibid.*

19. Robert S. Starobin, *Industrial Slavery in the Old South* (London, Oxford, New York: Oxford University Press, 1970), pp. 165ff.

20. *Ibid.,* pp. 164–165.

21. *Ibid.,* p. 165.

22. *Ibid.,* pp. 165–166.

23. "Iron works and mines also directed slave women and children to lug trams and to push lumps of ore into crushers and furnaces." *Ibid.*, p. 166.

24. Karl Marx, *Das Kapital, Kritik der politischen Ökonomie,* Erster Band (Berlin, D.D.R.: Dietz Verlag, 1965), pp. 415–416: "In England werden gelegentlich statt der Pferde immer noch Weiber zum Ziehn usw, bei den Kanalbooten verwandt, weil die zur Produktion von Pferden und Maschinen erheischte Arbeit ein mathematisch gegebenes Quantum, die zur Erhaltung von Weibern der Surplus-population dagegen unter aller Berechnung steht." Translation: *Capital,* Vol. 1 (New York: International Publishers, 1968), p. 391.

25. Starobin, *op. cit.,* p. 166: "Slaveowners used women and children in several ways in order to increase the competitiveness of southern products. First, slave women and children cost less to capitalize and to maintain than prime males. John Ewing Calhoun, a South Carolina textile manufacturer, estimated that slave children cost two-thirds as much to maintain as adult slave cotton millers. Another Carolinian estimated that the difference in cost between female and male slave labor was even greater than that between slave and free labor. Evidence from businesses using slave women and children supports the conclusion that they could reduce labor costs substantially."

26. Frederick Law Olmsted, *A Journey in the Back Country* (New York: 1860), pp. 14–15. Quoted in Stampp, *op. cit.,* p. 34.

27. Karl Marx, *Grundrisse der Kritik der politischen Ökonomie* (Berlin, D.D.R.: Dietz Verlag, 1953), p. 266. "Die Arbeit ist das lebendige, gestaltende Feuer; die Vergänglichkeit der Dinge, ihre Zeitlichkeit, als ihre Formung durch die lebendige Zeit."

28. Quoted in Robert Staples, editor, *The Black Family: Essays and Studies* (Belmont, Cal.: Wadsworth Publishing Company, Inc., 1971), p. 37. See also John Bracey, Jr., August Meier, Elliott Rudwick, editors, *Black Matriarchy: Myth or Reality* (Belmont, Cal.: Wadsworth Publishing Company, Inc., 1971), p. 140.

29. Bracey *et al., op. cit.,* p. 81. Lee Rainwater's article "Crucible of Identity: The Negro Lower-Class Family" was originally published in *Daedalus,* Vol. XCV (Winter, 1966), pp. 172–216.

30. *Ibid.,* p. 98.

31. *Ibid.*

32. Frazier, *op. cit.*

33. *Ibid.,* p. 102

34. Gutman, *op. cit.*

35. The first chapter of his book is entitled "Send Me Some of the Children's Hair," a plea made by a slave husband in a letter to his wife from whom he had been forcibly separated by sale: "Send me some of the children's hair in a separate paper with their names on the paper. . . . The woman is not born that feels as near to me as you do. You feel this day like myself. Tell them they must

remember they have a good father and one that cares for them and one that
thinks about them every day. . . . Laura I do love you the same. My love to you
never have failed. Laura, truly, I have got another wife, and I am very sorry, that
I am. You feels and seems to me as much like my dear loving wife, as you ever
did Laura. You know my treatment to a wife and you know how I am about my
children. You know I am one man that do love my children." (pp. 6–7)

36. *Ibid.* See Chapters 3 and 4.

37. *Ibid.,* pp. 356–357.

38. Elkins, *op. cit.,* p. 130.

39. Stampp, *op. cit.,* p. 344.

40. Angela Y. Davis, "The Black Woman's Role in the Community of
Slaves," *Black Scholar,* Vol. III, No. 4 (December, 1971).

41. Genovese, *Roll, Jordan, Roll.* See Part II, especially the sections entitled
"Husbands and Fathers" and "Wives and Mothers."

42. *Ibid.,* p. 500.

43. *Ibid.*

44. *Ibid.*

45. Aptheker, *op. cit.* See pages 145, 169, 173, 181, 182, 201, 207, 215, 239,
241–242, 251, 259, 277, 281, 287.

46. Frederick Douglass, *The Life and Times of Frederick Douglass* (New
York: Collier; London: Collier-Macmillan Ltd., 1962). Reprinted from the
revised edition of 1892. See especially Chapters 5 and 6.

47. *Ibid.,* p. 46. "One of the first circumstances that opened my eyes to the
cruelties and wickedness of slavery and its hardening influences upon my old
master was his refusal to interpose his authority to protect and shield a young
woman, a cousin of mine, who had been most cruelly abused and beaten by his
overseer in Tuckahoe. This overseer, a Mr. Plummer, was, like most of his class,
little less than a human brute, and, in addition to his general profligacy and
repulsive coarseness, he was a miserable drunkard, a man not fit to have the
management of a drove of mules. In one of his moments of drunken madness
he committed the outrage which brought the young woman in question down
to my old master's for protection. . . . Her neck and shoulders were covered with
scars, newly made, and, not content with marring her neck and shoulders with
a cowhide, the cowardly wretch had dealt her a blow on the head with a hickory
club, which cut a horrible gash, and left her face literally covered with blood."

48. *Ibid.,* pp. 48–49.

49. *Ibid.,* p. 52.

50. Wertheimer, *op. cit.,* pp. 113–114. Gerda Lerner's version of this escape
is slightly different: "On Christmas Eve, 1855, six young slaves, availing themselves of a holiday and their master's horses and carriage, left Loudoun Co,
Virginia, and traveling day and night through snow and cold, arrived in Columbia two days later. Barnaby Grigby was a twenty-six year old mulatto; his

wife, Elizabeth, who had had a different owner than her husband, was twenty-four years old. Her sister, Ann Wood, was engaged to the leader of the group, Frank Wanzer. Ann was twenty-two, good-looking and smart. Frank was trying to escape from a particularly bad master. There were two more young men in the group." Lerner, *op. cit.*, p. 57.

51. Sarah M. Grimke's testimony in Theodore D. Weld, *American Slavery As It Is: Testimony of a Thousand Witnesses* (New York: American Anti-Slavery Society, 1839). Quoted in Lerner, *op. cit.*, p. 19.

52. *Ibid.*

53. Aptheker, "The Negro Woman," p. 11.

54. *Ibid.*, pp. 11–12.

55. Aptheker, "Slave Guerilla Warfare," in *To Be Free*, p. 11.

56. Aptheker, *American Negro Slave Revolts*, p. 259.

57. *Ibid.*, p. 280.

58. Lerner, *op. cit.*, pp. 32–33: "[In Natchez, Louisiana, there were] two schools taught by colored teachers. One of these was a slave woman who had taught a midnight school for a year. It was opened at eleven or twelve o'clock at night, and closed at two o'clock a.m. . . . Milla Granson, the teacher, learned to read and write from the children of her indulgent master in her old Kentucky home. Her number of scholars was twelve at a time, and when she had taught these to read and write she dismissed them, and again took her apostolic number and brought them up to the extent of her ability, until she had graduated hundreds. A number of them wrote their own passes and started for Canada." Quoted from Laura S. Haviland, *A Woman's Life-Work, Labors and Experiences* (Chicago: Publishing Association of Friends, 1889), pp. 300–301.

59. Alex Haley, *Roots: The Saga of an American Family* (Garden City, New York: Doubleday and Co., 1976). See Chapters 66 and 67.

60. Sarah Bradford, *Harriet Tubman: The Moses of Her People* (New York: Corinth Books, 1961. Reprinted from the 1886 edition). Ann Petry, *Harriet Tubman, Conductor on the Underground Railroad* (New York: Pocket Books, 1971. First edition: 1955).

61. Arlene Eisen-Bergman, *Women in Vietnam* (San Francisco: People's Press, 1975), p. 63.

62. *Ibid.*, p. 62. "When we went through the villages and searched people, the women would have all their clothes taken off and the men would use their penises to probe them to make sure they didn't have anything hidden anywhere; and this was raping, but it was done as searching." Quoted from Sgt. Scott Camil, First Marine Division, in VVAW, *Winter Soldier Investigation* (Boston: Beacon Press, 1972), p. 13.

63. *Ibid.*, p. 71. Quoted from *Winter Soldier Investigation*, p. 14.

64. Blassingame, *op. cit.*, p. 83.

65. Genovese, *Roll, Jordan, Roll*, p. 415.

66. *Ibid.,* p. 419.
67. Gayl Jones, *Corregidora* (New York: Random House, 1975).
68. Frazier, *op. cit.,* p. 69.
69. *Ibid.,* p. 53.
70. *Ibid.,* p. 70.
71. Harriet Beecher Stowe, *Uncle Tom's Cabin* (New York: New American Library, Signet Books, 1968), p. 27.
72. *Ibid.,* p. 61.
73. *Ibid.,* p. 72.

CHAPTER 2

1. Douglass, *op. cit.,* p. 469.
2. *Ibid.,* p. 472.
3. *Ibid.*
4. *Ibid.*
5. Stowe, *op. cit.* Frederick Douglass included the following comments in his autobiography: "In the midst of these fugitive slave troubles came the book known as *Uncle Tom's Cabin,* a work of marvelous depth and power. Nothing could have better suited the moral and human requirements of the hour. Its effect was amazing, instantaneous, and universal. No book on the subject of slavery had so generally and favorably touched the American heart. It combined all the power and pathos of preceding publications of the kind, and was hailed by many as an inspired production. Mrs. Stowe at once became an object of interest and admiration." (Douglass, *op. cit.,* p. 282)
6. Stowe, *op. cit.,* p. 107.
7. See Barbara Ehrenreich and Deirdre English, "Microbes and the Manufacture of Housework," Chapter 5 of *For Her Own Good: 150 Years of the Experts' Advice to Women* (Garden City, N. Y.: Anchor Press/Doubleday, 1978). Also Ann Oakley, *Woman's Work: The Housewife Past and Present* (New York: Vintage Books, 1976).
8. See Eleanor Flexner, *Century of Struggle: The Women's Rights Movement in the U.S.* (New York: Atheneum, 1973). Also Mary P. Ryan, *Womanhood in America* (New York: New Viewpoints, 1975).
9. See Aptheker, *Nat Turner's Slave Rebellion* (New York: Humanities Press, 1966); Harriet H. Robinson, *Loom and Spindle or Life Among the Early Mill Girls* (Kailua, Hawaii: Press Pacifica, 1976). Also Wertheimer, *op. cit.,* and Flexner, *op. cit.*
10. Robinson, *op. cit.,* p. 51.
11. See discussion of this tendency to equate the institution of marriage with that of slavery in Pamela Allen, "Woman Suffrage: Feminism and White Supremacy," Chapter V of Robert Allen, *Reluctant Reformers*

NOTES   253

(Washington, D.C.: Howard University Press, 1974), pp. 136ff.

12. Wertheimer, *op. cit.*, p. 106.

13. See Flexner, *op. cit.*, pp. 38–40. Also Samuel Sillen, *Women Against Slavery* (New York: Masses and Mainstream, Inc., 1955), pp. 11–16.

14. Sillen, *op. cit.*, p. 13.

15. *Ibid.*

16. *Ibid.*, p. 14.

17. *Liberator*, January 1, 1831. Quoted in William Z. Foster, *The Negro People in American History* (New York: International Publishers, 1970), p. 108.

18. Sillen, *op. cit.*, p. 17.

19. *Ibid.*

20. The first woman to speak publicly in the United States was the Scottish-born lecturer and writer Frances Wright (see Flexner, *op. cit.*, pp. 27–28). When the Black woman Maria W. Stewart delivered four lectures in Boston in 1832, she became the first native-born woman to speak publicly (see Lerner, *op. cit.*, p. 83).

21. Flexner, *op. cit.*, p. 42. See the text of the constitution of the Philadelphia Female Anti-Slavery Society in Judith Papachristou, editor, *Women Together: A History in Documents of the Women's Movement in the United States* (New York: Alfred A. Knopf, Inc., A Ms. Book, 1976), pp. 4–5.

22. Sillen, *op. cit.*, p. 20.

23. *Ibid.*, pp. 21–22.

24. *Ibid.*, p. 25.

25. Flexner, *op. cit.*, p. 51.

26. *Ibid.*

27. Elizabeth Cady Stanton, Susan B. Anthony and Matilda Joslyn Gage, *History of Woman Suffrage*, Vol. 1 (1848–1861) (New York: Fowler and Wells, 1881), p. 52.

28. Quoted in Papachristou, *op. cit.*, p. 12. See Gerda Lerner's analysis of the pastoral letter in her work *The Grimke Sisters from South Carolina: Pioneers for Women's Rights and Abolition* (New York: Schocken Books, 1971), p. 189.

29. Quoted in Papachristou, *op. cit.*, p. 12.

30. *Ibid.*

31. Sarah Grimke began publishing her *Letters on the Equality of the Sexes* in July, 1837. They appeared in the *New England Spectator* and were reprinted in the *Liberator*. See Lerner, *The Grimke Sisters*, p. 187.

32. Quoted in Alice Rossi, editor, *The Feminist Papers* (New York: Bantam Books, 1974), p. 308.

33. *Ibid.*

34. Quoted in Flexner, *op. cit.*, p. 48. Also quoted and discussed in Lerner, *The Grimke Sisters*, p. 201.

35. Angelina Grimke, *Appeal to the Women of the Nominally Free States.*

Issued by an Anti-Slavery Convention of American Women and Held by Adjournment from the 9th to the 12th of May, 1837 (New York: W. S. Dorr, 1838), pp. 13–14.

36. *Ibid.*, p. 21.

37. Flexner, *op. cit.*, p. 47.

38. Lerner, *The Grimke Sisters*, p. 353.

CHAPTER 3

1. Stanton *et al.*, *History of Woman Suffrage*, Vol. 1, p. 62.

2. *Ibid.*, p. 60 (note).

3. Judith Hole and Ellen Levine, "The First Feminists," in Anne Koedt, Ellen Levine and Anita Rapone, editors, *Radical Feminism* (New York: Quadrangle, 1973), p. 6.

4. Elizabeth Cady Stanton, *Eighty Years and More: Reminiscences 1815–1897* (New York: Schocken Books, 1917). See Chapter V.

5. Stanton *et al.*, *History of Woman Suffrage*, Vol. 1, p. 62.

6. *Ibid.*, p. 61.

7. *Ibid.*

8. *Ibid.*

9. Charles Remond, "The World Anti-Slavery Conference, 1840," *Liberator*, (October 16, 1840). Reprinted in Aptheker, *A Documentary History*, Vol. 1, p. 196.

10. *Ibid.*

11. *Ibid.*

12. Stanton *et al.*, *History of Woman Suffrage*, Vol. 1, p. 53.

13. Stanton, *Eighty Years and More*, p. 33.

14. *Ibid.*, pp. 147–148.

15. Douglass, *op. cit.*, p. 473.

16. Flexner, *op. cit.*, p. 76. See also Allen, *op. cit.*, p. 133.

17. *North Star*, July 28, 1848. Reprinted in Philip Foner, editor, *The Life and Writings of Frederick Douglass*, Vol. 1 (New York: International Publishers, 1950), p. 321.

18. S. Jay Walker, "Frederick Douglass and Woman Suffrage," *Black Scholar*, Vol. IV, Nos. 6–7 (March–April, 1973), p. 26.

19. Stanton, *Eighty Years and More*, p. 149.

20. *Ibid.*

21. Miriam Gurko, *The Ladies of Seneca Falls: The Birth of the Women's Rights Movement* (New York: Schocken Books, 1976), p. 105.

22. See "Declaration of Sentiments" in Papachristou, *op. cit.*, pp. 24–25.

23. *Ibid.*, p. 25.

24. *Ibid.*

25. Rosalyn Baxandall, Linda Gordon, Susan Reverby, editors, *America's Working Women: A Documentary History—1600 to the Present* (New York: Random House, 1976), p. 46.

26. Wertheimer, *op. cit.*, p. 66.

27. *Ibid.*, p. 67.

28. Baxandall *et al.*, *op. cit.*, p. 66.

29. Wertheimer, *op. cit.*, p. 74.

30. *Ibid.*, p. 103.

31. *Ibid.* p. 104.

32. Papachristou, *op. cit.*, p. 26.

33. Lerner, *The Grimke Sisters*, p. 335.

34. Wertheimer, *op. cit.*, p. 104.

35. Lerner, *The Grimke Sisters*, p. 159.

36. *Ibid.*, p. 158.

37. For the text of Maria Stewart's 1833 speech, see Lerner, *Black Women in White America*, pp. 563ff.

38. Lerner, *Black Women in White America*, p. 83. Also Flexner, *op. cit.*, pp. 44–45.

39. Aptheker, *A Documentary History*, Vol. 1, p. 89.

40. Douglass, *op. cit.*, p. 268.

41. Walker, *op. cit.*, p. 26.

42. Foner, *The Life and Writings of Frederick Douglass*, Vol. 2, p. 19.

43. Stanton *et al.*, *History of Woman Suffrage*, Vol. 1, pp. 115–117.

44. *Ibid.*

45. *Ibid.*

46. *Ibid.*

47. *Ibid.*

48. *Ibid.*

49. *Ibid.*

50. *Ibid.*

51. *Ibid.*

52. *Ibid.*

53. *Ibid.*

54. *Ibid.*

55. *Ibid.*, pp. 567–568 (complete text of speech). Also see Lerner, *Black Women in White America*, pp. 566ff.

56. John Hope Franklin, *From Slavery to Freedom* (New York: Vintage Books, 1969), p. 253.

57. Sillen, *op. cit.*, p. 86. See also section on Harper.

58. Foster, *op. cit.*, pp. 115–116.

59. Flexner, *op. cit.*, p. 108.

60. *Ibid.*

61. Foster, *op. cit.*, p. 261.
62. Gurko, *op. cit.*, p. 211.
63. Lerner, *The Grimke Sisters*, p. 353.
64. *Ibid.*, p. 354.
65. *Ibid.*
66. *Ibid.*

CHAPTER 4

1. Elizabeth Cady Stanton, Susan B. Anthony and Matilda Joslyn Gage, editors, *History of Woman Suffrage*, Vol. 2 (1861–1876) (Rochester, N. Y.: Charles Mann, 1887), pp. 94–95 (note).
2. *Ibid.*, p. 172.
3. *Ibid.*, p. 159.
4. *Ibid.*, p. 188.
5. *Ibid.*, p. 216.
6. Stanton, *Eighty Years and More*, p. 240.
7. *Ibid.*, pp. 240–241.
8. *Ibid.*, p. 241.
9. Gurko, *op. cit.*, p. 213.
10. *Ibid.*
11. Stanton *et al.*, *History of Woman Suffrage*, Vol. 2, p. 214.
12. Flexner, *op. cit.*, p. 144.
13. Allen, *op. cit.*, p. 143.
14. Foner, *The Life and Writings of Frederick Douglass*, Vol. 4, p. 167. This passage comes from a speech entitled "The Need for Continuing Anti-Slavery Work" delivered by Douglass at the Thirty-second Annual Meeting of the American Anti-Slavery Society, May 9, 1865. Originally published in the *Liberator*, May 26, 1865.
15. *Ibid.*, p. 17.
16. *Ibid.*, p. 41.
17. Aptheker, *A Documentary History*, Vol. 2, pp. 553–554. "Memphis Riots and Massacres." Report No. 101, House of Representatives, 39th Cong., 1st Sess. (Serial #1274), pp. 160–161, 222–223.
18. Foster, *op. cit.*, p. 261.
19. W. E. B. DuBois, *Black Reconstruction in America* (Cleveland and New York: Meridian Books, 1964), p. 670.
20. *Ibid.*, p. 671.
21. *Ibid.*, p. 672.
22. According to Philip Foner, "Douglass objected to Susan Anthony's praise of James Brooks' championship of woman suffrage in Congress, pointing out that it was simply 'the trick of the enemy to assail and endanger the right of

black men.' Brooks, former editor of the *New York Express*, a viciously anti-Negro, pro-slavery paper, was playing up to the leaders of the women's movement in order to secure their support in opposing Negro suffrage. Douglass warned that if the women did not see through these devices of the former slaveowners and their northern allies, 'there would be trouble in our family.' " (Foner, *The Life and Writings of Frederick Douglass*, Vol. 4, pp. 41–42)

23. Stanton *et al.*, *History of Woman Suffrage*, Vol. 2, p. 245.

24. Stanton, *Eighty Years and More*, p. 256.

25. Gurko, *op. cit.*, p. 223.

26. *Ibid.*, pp. 223–224.

27. *Ibid.*, p. 221. Also Stanton, *Eighty Years and More*, p. 256.

28. Stanton *et al.*, *History of Woman Suffrage*, Vol. 2, p. 382.

29. Foner, *The Life and Writings of Frederick Douglass*, Vol. 4, p. 44.

30. *Ibid.*

31. *Ibid.*

32. Stanton et al., *History of Woman Suffrage*, Vol. 2, p. 222. See also Lerner, *Black Women in White America*, p. 569.

33. Foner, *The Life and Writings of Frederick Douglass*, Vol. 4, p. 212 (letter to Josephine Sophie White Griffin, Rochester, September 27, 1968).

34. Stanton *et al.*, *History of Woman Suffrage*, Vol. 2, p. 928. Sojourner Truth was criticizing Henry Ward Beecher's approach to the suffrage question. See Allen's analysis, *op. cit.*, p. 148.

35. Stanton *et al.*, *History of Woman Suffrage*, Vol. 2, p. 391. Frances E. W. Harper warned the gathering of the dangers of racism by describing a situation in Boston where sixty white women walked off the job to protest the hiring of one Black woman. (p. 392)

36. Allen, *op. cit.*, p. 145.

37. Stanton *et al.*, *History of Woman Suffrage*, Vol. 2, p. 214. See also Allen, *op. cit.*, p. 146.

CHAPTER 5

1. DuBois, *Darkwater*, p. 113.

2. Wertheimer, *op. cit.*, p. 228.

3. Aptheker, *A Documentary History*, Vol. 2, p. 747. "Tenant Farming in Alabama, 1889" from *The Journal of Negro Education* XVII (1948), pp. 46ff.

4. Aptheker, *A Documentary History*, Vol. 2, p. 689. Texas State Convention of Negroes, 1883.

5. *Ibid.*, p. 690.

6. Aptheker, *A Documentary History*, Vol. 2, p. 704. Founding Convention of Afro-American League, 1890.

7. DuBois, *Black Reconstruction in America*, p. 698.

8. *Ibid.*

9. *Ibid.*, p. 699.

10. *Ibid.*, p. 698.

11. Aptheker, *A Documentary History of the Negro People in the United States*, Vol. 1 (Secaucus, N.J.: The Citadel Press, 1973), p. 46. "A Southern Domestic Worker Speaks," *The Independent*, Vol. LXXII (January 25, 1912).

12. *Ibid.*, p. 46.

13. *Ibid.*, p. 47.

14. *Ibid.*, p. 50.

15. *Ibid.*

16. *Ibid.*, p. 49.

17. *Ibid.*

18. *Ibid.*

19. *Ibid.*

20. Lerner, *Black Women in White America*, p. 462. "The Colored Women's Statement to the Women's Missionary Council, American Missionary Association."

21. Aptheker, *A Documentary History*, Vol. 1, p. 49.

22. DuBois, *Darkwater*, p. 116.

23. *Ibid.*, p. 115.

24. Isabel Eaton, "Special Report on Negro Domestic Service" in W. E. B. DuBois, *The Philadelphia Negro* (New York: Schocken Books, 1967. First edition: 1899), p. 427.

25. *Ibid.*

26. *Ibid.*, p. 428.

27. *Ibid.*

28. *Ibid.*, p. 465.

29. *Ibid.*, p. 484.

30. *Ibid.*, p. 485.

31. *Ibid.*

32. *Ibid.*, p. 484.

33. *Ibid.*, p. 449. Eaton presents evidence which ". . . points to the probability that among women in domestic service at least, there is no difference between 'white pay and black pay,' . . ."

34. Lerner, *Black Women in White America*, pp. 229–231. Louise Mitchell, "Slave Markets Typify Exploitation of Domestics," *The Daily Worker*, May 5, 1940.

35. Gerda Lerner, *The Female Experience: An American Documentary* (Indianapolis: Bobbs-Merrill, 1977), p. 269.

36. *Ibid.*, p. 268.

37. Wertheimer, *op. cit.*, pp. 182–183.

38. Lerner, *Black Women in White America*, p. 232.

39. Inez Goodman, "A Nine-Hour Day for Domestic Servants," *The Independent,* Vol. LIX (February 13, 1902). Quoted in Baxandall *et al., op. cit.,* pp. 213–214.

40. Lerner, *The Female Experience,* p. 268.

41. Jacquelyne Johnson Jackson, "Black Women in a Racist Society," in Charles Willie et al., editors, *Racism and Mental Health* (Pittsburgh: University of Pittsburgh Press, 1973), p. 236.

42. *Ibid.*

43. DuBois, *Darkwater,* p. 115.

CHAPTER 6

1. DuBois, *Black Reconstruction in America,* Chapter V.

2. *Ibid.,* p. 122.

3. *Ibid.,* p. 124.

4. *Ibid.*

5. *Ibid.*

6. *Ibid.,* p. 123.

7. Douglass, *op. cit.,* p. 79.

8. *Ibid.*

9. Watkins and David, *op. cit.,* p. 18.

10. Aptheker, *A Documentary History,* Vol. 1, p. 493.

11. *Ibid.,* p. 19.

12. *Ibid.*

13. Wertheimer, *op. cit.,* pp. 35–36.

14. Lerner, *Black Women in White America,* p. 76.

15. See Chapter 2.

16. Foner, *The Life and Writings of Frederick Douglass,* Vol. 4, p. 553 (note 16).

17. *Ibid.,* pp. 371ff.

18. *Ibid.,* p. 372.

19. *Ibid.*

20. *Ibid.,* p. 371.

21. *Ibid.*

22. Flexner, *op. cit.,* p. 99.

23. *Ibid.,* pp. 99–101.

24. Foner, *op. cit.,* Vol. 4, p. 373.

25. Aptheker, *A Documentary History,* Vol. 1, pp. 157–158.

26. *Ibid.*

27. William Goodell, *The American Slave Code* (New York: American and Foreign Anti-Slavery Society, 1853), p. 321. Quoted in Elkins, *op. cit.,* p. 60.

28. *Ibid.*

29. Genovese, *Roll, Jordan, Roll,* p. 565.

30. Lerner, *Black Women in White America,* pp. 27ff. and pp. 99ff.

31. *Ibid.,* pp. 32ff.

32. DuBois, *Black Reconstruction in America,* p. 123.

33. Lerone Bennett, *Before the Mayflower* (Baltimore: Penguin Books, 1969), p. 181.

34. Foster, *op. cit.,* p. 321.

35. DuBois, *Black Reconstruction in America,* p. 638.

36. Lerner, *Black Women in White America,* p. 102.

37. *Ibid.,* p. 103.

38. *Ibid.*

39. *Ibid.,* pp. 104–105.

40. Franklin, *op. cit.,* p. 308.

41. DuBois, *Black Reconstruction in America,* p. 667.

CHAPTER 7

1. Ida B. Wells, *Crusade for Justice: The Auto-Biography of Ida B. Wells,* edited by Alfreda M. Duster (Chicago and London: University of Chicago Press, 1970), pp. 228–229.

2. *Ibid.*

3. *Ibid.,* p. 230.

4. *Ibid.*

5. See Aileen Kraditor, editor, *Up From the Pedestal: Selected Writings in the History of American Feminism* (Chicago: Quadrangle, 1968), For a documentary presentation of the "expediency argument," see Part II, Chapters 5 and 6.

6. Herbert Aptheker, *Afro-American History: The Modern Era* (New York: The Citadel Press, 1971), p. 100.

7. *Ibid.*

8. Wells, *op. cit.,* p. 100.

9. *Ibid.,* p. 229.

10. Susan B. Anthony and Ida Husted Harper, editors, *History of Woman Suffrage,* Vol. 4 (Rochester: 1902), p. 246.

11. *Ibid.*

12. Stanton *et al., History of Woman Suffrage,* Vol. 2, p. 930.

13. *Ibid.,* p. 931.

14. *Ibid.*

15. *Ibid.,* p. 248.

16. Anthony and Harper, *History of Woman Suffrage,* Vol. 4, p. 216 (note).

17. Aptheker, *A Documentary History,* Vol. 2, p. 813.

18. Anthony and Harper, *History of Woman Suffrage,* Vol. 4, p. 328.

19. *Ibid.,* p. 333.

20. *Ibid.*

21. *Ibid.*, p. 343.

22. Aileen S. Kraditor, *The Ideas of the Woman Suffrage Movement* (New York: Doubleday/Anchor, 1971), p. 143.

23. Wells, *op. cit.*, p. 100.

24. Aptheker, *A Documentary History*, Vol. 2, pp. 796–797; p. 798.

25. *Ibid.*, p. 789.

26. *Ibid.*, pp. 789–790.

27. *Ibid.*, p. 790.

28. *Ibid.*, p. 799.

29. Ida Husted Harper, editor, *History of Woman Suffrage*, Vol. 5 (New York: J. J. Little and Ives Co., 1902), p. 5.

30. *Ibid.*

31. *Ibid.*

32. *Ibid.*, p. 6.

33. *Ibid.*, p. 80.

34. *Ibid.*, p. 81.

35. Papachristou, *op. cit.*, p. 144.

36. *Ibid.*

37. *Ibid.*

38. *Ibid.*

39. John Hope Franklin and Isidore Starr, editors, *The Negro in Twentieth Century America* (New York: Vintage Books, 1967), pp. 68–69.

40. *Ibid.*, p. 40.

41. Papachristou, *op. cit.*, p. 144.

42. Harper, *History of Woman Suffrage*, Vol. 5, p. 83.

43. *Ibid.*

44. *Ibid.*

CHAPTER 8

1. Lerner, *Black Women in White America*, pp. 447–450.

2. Wells, *op. cit.*, p. 271.

3. *Ibid.*

4. William L. O'Neill, *The Woman Movement: Feminism in the United States and England* (Chicago: Quadrangle, 1969), pp. 47ff.

5. *Ibid.*, p. 48.

6. *Ibid.*

7. *Ibid.*, pp. 48–49.

8. Wertheimer, *op. cit.*, p. 195.

9. Wells, *op. cit.*, p. 78.

10. *Ibid.*

11. *Ibid.*, pp. 78–79.

12. *Ibid.*, p. 81.

13. *Ibid.*

14. *Ibid.*

15. *Ibid.*

16. *Ibid.*, p. 83.

17. *Ibid.*, p. 117.

18. *Ibid.*, p. 121.

19. *Ibid.*, pp. 121–122.

20. *Ibid.*

21. *Ibid.*

22. *Ibid.*

23. *Ibid.*

24. *Ibid.*, p. 242.

25. *Ibid.*

26. Lerner, *Black Women in White America,* pp. 575–576.

27. *Ibid.*, p. 576.

28. *Ibid.*, pp. 575–576.

29. *Ibid.*, p. 444.

30. Wells, *op. cit.*, p. 78.

31. *Ibid.*

32. Lerner, *Black Women in White America,* pp. 206ff.

33. Wells, *op. cit.*, p. 260.

CHAPTER 9

1. Baxandall *et al.*, *op. cit.*, p. 83.

2. *Ibid.*

3. Wertheimer, *op. cit.*, p. 161.

4. *Ibid.*

5. Philip S. Foner, *Organized Labor and the Black Worker 1619–1973* (New York: International Publishers, 1973), p. 34 (note).

6. *Ibid.*

7. "The Ballot-Bread, Virtue, Power," *Revolution,* January 8, 1868. Quoted in William L. O'Neill, *Everyone Was Brave: The Rise and Fall of Feminism in America* (Chicago: Quadrangle, 1971), p. 19.

8. Wertheimer, *op. cit.*, p. 166; p. 167.

9. "Proceedings, National Labor Union, August 1869," *Workingman's Advocate* Vol. VI, No. 5 (September 4, 1869). Quoted in Baxandall *et al.*, *op. cit.*, pp. 109–114.

10. *Ibid.*, p. 113.

11. O'Neill, *Everyone was Brave,* p. 20.

12. Ida Husted Harper, *The Life and Work of Susan B. Anthony,* Vol. 2 (Indianapolis, 1898). Quoted in Miriam Schneir, *Feminism: The Essential Historical Writings* (New York: Vintage Books, 1972), pp. 139–140.

13. Schneir, *op. cit.*, pp. 138–142.

14. "Proceedings, National Labor Union, . . ." Quoted in Baxandall *et al., op. cit.*, p. 111.

15. "Susan B. Anthony's Constitutional Argument" (1873). Quoted in Kraditor, *Up From the Pedestal, op. cit.*, p. 249.

16. *Ibid.*

17. Harper, *History of Woman Suffrage*, Vol. 5, p. 352.

18. Lerner, *Black Women in White America*, p. 446.

19. *Ibid.*

20. *Ibid.*

21. Kraditor, *The Ideas of the Woman Suffrage Movement*, p. 169.

22. W. E. B. DuBois, *A.B.C. of Color* (New York: International Publishers, 1963), p. 56.

23. *Ibid.*, p. 57.

24. *Ibid.*, p. 58.

25. Kraditor, *The Ideas of the Woman Suffrage Movement*, p. 168.

26. Editorial, *The Crisis*, IV (September, 1912), 234. Quoted in Aptheker, *A Documentary History*, Vol. 1, p. 56.

27. *Ibid.*, pp. 56–57.

28. *The Crisis*, X (August, 1915), 178–192. Quoted in Aptheker, *A Documentary History*, Vol. 1, pp. 94–116.

29. *Ibid.*, pp. 108ff.

30. *Ibid.*, p. 104.

31. *Ibid.*, pp. 314–315.

CHAPTER 10

1. William Z. Foster, *History of the Communist Party of the United States* (New York: International Publishers, 1952), pp. 28ff.

2. *Ibid.*, Chapter 5.

3. Bruce Dancis, "Socialism and Women in the United States, 1900–1912," *Socialist Revolution*, No. 27, Vol. VI, No. 1 (January–March, 1976), p. 85.

4. Wertheimer, *op. cit.*, pp. 281–284.

5. Foster, *History of the Communist Party*, p. 113.

6. *Ibid.*, p. 125.

7. Foster, *The Negro People*, p. 403.

8. Foner, *Organized Labor and the Black Worker*, p. 107.

9. Foster, *History of the Communist Party*, p. 264.

10. Carolyn Asbaugh, *Lucy Parsons: American Revolutionary* (Chicago:

Charles H. Kerr Publishing Co., 1976. Published for the Illinois Labor History Society).

11. *Ibid.*, pp. 30–33.

12. *Ibid.*, p. 112.

13. *Ibid.*, p. 117.

14. *Ibid.*, p. 136.

15. *Ibid.*, pp. 65–66.

16. *Ibid.*, p. 66.

17. *Ibid.*, p. 217.

18. *Ibid.*

19. A brief description of the Tom Mooney case can be found in Foster, *History of the Communist Party,* p. 131 and p. 380. For the Scottsboro case, see Foster, *History of the Communist Party,* p. 286, and Foster, *The Negro People,* pp. 482–483; Angelo Herndon case: *History of the Communist Party,* p. 288, and *The Negro People,* p. 461 and p. 483.

20. Asbaugh, *op. cit.,* p. 261.

21. *Ibid.*, p. 267.

22. Joseph North, "Communist Women." *Political Affairs* Vol. LI, No. 3 (March, 1971), p. 31.

23. Ella Reeve Bloor, *We Are Many: An Autobiography* (New York: International Publishers, 1940), p. 224.

24. *Ibid.*, p. 250.

25. *Ibid.*

26. *Ibid.*, p. 254.

27. *Ibid.*

28. *Ibid.*, p. 255.

29. *Ibid.*

30. *Ibid.*

31. *Ibid.*, p. 256.

32. *Ibid.*

33. Al Richmond, *Native Daughter: The Story of Anita Whitney* (San Francisco: Anita Whitney 75th Anniversary Committee, 1942). See Chapter 4.

34. *Ibid.*, p. 70.

35. *Ibid.*, p. 78.

36. *Ibid.*, p. 94.

37. *Ibid.*, p. 95.

38. *Ibid.*, pp. 95–96.

39. *Ibid.*, p. 139.

40. *Ibid.*, p. 198.

41. Elizabeth Gurley Flynn, *The Rebel Girl: An Autobiography* (New York: International Publishers, 1973). p. 53.

42. *Ibid.*, p. 62.

43. Richard O. Boyer, "Elizabeth Gurley Flynn," *Masses and Mainstream* (May, 1952) p. 7.

44. *Ibid.*, p. 12.

45. Mary Heaton Vorse, *A Footnote to Folly: Reminiscences* (New York: Farrar & Rinehart, Inc., 1935), pp. 3–4.

46. *Ibid.*, p. 9.

47. Flynn, *op. cit.*, p. 232.

48. *Ibid.*, p. 233.

49. *Ibid.* See also Foster, *History of the Communist Party*, p. 116.

50. Foner, *Organized Labor and the Black Worker*, p. 198.

51. Flynn, *The Rebel Girl.* See editor's note, p. 10.

52. Elizabeth Gurley Flynn, "1948—A Year of Inspiring Anniversaries for Women," *Political Affairs*, Vol. XXVII, No. 3 (March, 1948), p. 264.

53. *Ibid.*, p. 262.

54. Elizabeth Gurley Flynn, *The Alderson Story: My Life As a Political Prisoner* (New York: International Publishers, 1972), p. 9.

55. *Ibid.*, p. 17.

56. *Ibid.*, pp. 17–18.

57. *Ibid.*, p. 32.

58. *Ibid.*, p. 176.

59. *Ibid.*, p. 180.

60. *Ibid.*

61. North, *op. cit.*, p. 29.

62. This article was reprinted in *Political Affairs*, Vol. LIII, No. 3 (March, 1974).

63. *Ibid.*, p. 33.

64. *Ibid.*

65. *Ibid.*, p. 35.

66. *Ibid.*

67. *Ibid.*

68. *Ibid.*, p. 41.

69. *Ibid.*, p. 35.

70. Flynn, *The Alderson Story*, p. 118.

71. *Ibid.*, p. 211.

CHAPTER 11

1. Nancy Gager and Cathleen Schurr, *Sexual Assault: Confronting Rape in America* (New York: Grosset & Dunlap, 1976), p. 1.

2. Michael Meltsner, *Cruel and Unusual: The Supreme Court and Capital Punishment* (New York: Random House, 1973), p. 75.

3. "The Racist Use of Rape and the Rape Charge." A Statement to the

Women's Movement From a Group of Socialist Women (Louisville, Ky: Socialist Women's Caucus, 1974), pp. 5–6.

4. Lerner, *Black Women in White America*, p. 193.

5. See Angela Davis, "JoAnne Little—The Dialectics of Rape." *Ms. Magazine*, Vol. III, No. 12 (June, 1975).

6. See Chapter 1.

7. Aptheker, *A Documentary History*, Vol. 2, pp. 552ff.

8. Lerner, *Black Women in White America*, pp. 185–186.

9. Gertrude Stein, *Three Lives* (New York: Vintage Books, 1970. First edition: 1909), p. 86.

10. Eisen-Bergman, *op. cit.*, Part I, Chapter 5.

11. Susan Brownmiller, *Against Our Will: Men, Women and Rape* (New York: Simon and Schuster, 1975), p. 194.

12. "A Dozen Who Made a Difference," *Time*, Vol. 107, No. 1 (January 5, 1976), p. 20.

13. Brownmiller, *op. cit.*, p. 247.

14. *Ibid.*

15. Jean MacKellar, *Rape: The Bait and the Trap* (New York: Crown Publishers, 1975), p. 72.

16. *Ibid.* "In sum, for every reported rape in which the offender is a white man, there are nine by blacks. Black men, who constitute about a tenth of the U.S. male population, are involved in 90 percent of the reported rapes."

17. Brownmiller, *op. cit.*, p. 213.

18. *Ibid.*, p. 175.

19. Noreen Connell and Cassandra Wilson, editors, *Rape: The First Sourcebook for Women* by New York Radical Feminists (New York: New American Library, 1974), p. 151.

20. Diana Russell, *The Politics of Rape: The Victim's Perspective* (New York: Stein & Day, 1975).

21. *Ibid.*, p. 163.

22. Winfield H. Collins, *The Truth About Lynching and the Negro in the South* (In Which the Author Pleads that the South Be Made Safe for the White Race) (New York: Neale Publishing Co., 1918), pp. 94–95.

23. Shulamith Firestone, *The Dialectic of Sex: The Case for Feminist Revolution* (New York: Bantam Books, 1971), p. 108.

24. *Ibid.*, p. 108ff.

25. *Ibid.*, p. 110.

26. Walter White, *Rope and Faggot: A Biography of Judge Lynch* (New York: Alfred A. Knopf, Inc., 1929), p. 66.

27. *Ibid.*

28. Calvin Hernton, *Sex and Racism in America* (New York: Grove Press, 1965), p. 125.

29. *Ibid.*, p. 124.

30. White, *op. cit.*, p. 91.

31. *Ibid.*, p. 92.

32. *Ibid.*, p. 86.

33. *Ibid.*, p. 94.

34. Ida B. Wells-Barnett, *On Lynching* (New York: Arno Press & New York Times, 1969), p. 8.

35. Frederick Douglass, "The Lesson of the Hour" (pamphlet published in 1894). Reprinted under the title "Why is the Negro Lynched" in Foner, *The Life and Writings of Frederick Douglass*, Vol. 4, pp. 498–499.

36. *Ibid.*, p. 501.

37. *Ibid.*

38. *Ibid.*

39. *Ibid.*, p. 502.

40. Collins, *op. cit.*, p. 58.

41. Gager and Schurr, *op. cit.*, p. 163.

42. *Ibid.*

43. Wells-Barnett, *On Lynching*, p. 59.

44. Foner, *The Life and Writings of Frederick Douglass*, Vol. 4, p. 503.

45. *Ibid.*, p. 499.

46. *Lynchings and What They Mean*, General Findings of the Southern Commission on the Study of Lynching (Atlanta: 1931), p. 19.

47. Quoted in Lerner, *Black Women in White America*, pp. 205–206.

48. Franklin and Starr, *op. cit.*, p. 67.

49. Wells-Barnett, *On Lynching*, p. 57.

50. *Ibid.*, p. 8.

51. Wells, *Crusade for Justice*, p. 149.

52. Ralph Ginzburg, *One Hundred Years of Lynchings* (New York: Lancer Books, 1969), p. 96.

53. Wells, *Crusade for Justice*, p. 63.

54. See Chapter 8.

55. Wells, *Crusade for Justice*, p. 218.

56. Lerner, *Black Women in White America*, pp. 205–211.

57. *Ibid.*, p. 215.

58. See Jessie Daniel Ames, *The Changing Character of Lynching, 1931–1941* (New York: AMS Press, 1973).

59. *Ibid.*, p. 19.

60. White, *op. cit.*, p. 3.

61. Ames, *op. cit.*, p. 64.

62. White, *op. cit.*, p. 159.

63. Foner, *Life and Writings of Frederick Douglass*, Vol. 4, p. 496.

64. Brownmiller, *op. cit.*, p. 255.

65. *Ibid.*, pp. 248–249.
66. *Ibid.*, p. 237.
67. *Ibid.*, p. 233.

CHAPTER 12

1. Edwin M. Gold *et al.*, "Therapeutic Abortions in New York City: A Twenty-Year Review" in *American Journal of Public Health*, Vol. LV (July, 1965), pp. 964–972. Quoted in Lucinda Cisla, "Unfinished Business: Birth Control and Women's Liberation," in Robin Morgan, editor, *Sisterhood is Powerful: An Anthology of Writings From the Women's Liberation Movement* (New York: Vintage Books, 1970), p. 261. Also quoted in Robert Staples, *The Black Woman in America* (Chicago: Nelson Hall, 1974), p. 146.

2. Gutman, *op. cit.*, pp. 80–81 (note).
3. *Ibid.*
4. Aptheker, "The Negro Woman," p. 12.
5. Quoted in Baxandall *et al.*, *op. cit.*, p. 17.
6. *Ibid.*
7. Lerner, *The Female Experience*, op. cit., p. 91.
8. *Ibid.*
9. *Ibid.*
10. "Marriage of Lucy Stone under Protest" appeared in *History of Woman Suffrage*, Vol. 1. Quoted in Schneir, *op. cit.*, p. 104.
11. Speech by Virginia Woodhull, "The Elixir of Life." Quoted in Schneir, *op. cit*, p. 153.
12. Mary P. Ryan, *Womanhood in America from Colonial Times to the Present* (New York: Franklin Watts, Inc., 1975), p. 162.
13. Melvin Steinfeld, *Our Racist Presidents* (San Ramon, California: Consensus Publishers, 1972), p. 212.
14. Bonnie Mass, *Population Target: The Political Economy of Population Control in Latin America* (Toronto, Canada: Women's Educational Press, 1977), p. 20.
15. Linda Gordon, *Woman's Body, Woman's Right: Birth Control in America* (New York: Penguin Books, 1976), p. 157.
16. *Ibid.*, p. 158.
17. *Ibid.*
18. Margaret Sanger, *An Autobiography* (New York: Dover Press, 1971), p. 75.
19. *Ibid.*, p. 90.
20. *Ibid.*, p. 91.
21. *Ibid.*, p. 92.
22. *Ibid.*, p. 106.

23. Mass, *op. cit.*, p. 27.

24. Dancis, *op. cit.*, p. 96.

25. David M. Kennedy, *Birth Control in America: The Career of Margaret Sanger* (New Haven and London: Yale University Press, 1976), pp. 21–22.

26. Mass, *op. cit.*, p. 20.

27. Gordon, *op. cit.*, p. 281.

28. Mass, *op. cit.*, p. 20.

29. Gordon, *op. cit.*, p. 283.

30. Herbert Aptheker, "Sterilization, Experimentation and Imperialism," *Political Affairs*, Vol. LIII, No. 1 (January, 1974), p. 44.

31. Gena Corea, *The Hidden Malpractice* (New York: A Jove/HBJ Book, 1977), p. 149.

32. Gordon, *op. cit.*, p. 332.

33. *Ibid.*, pp. 332–333.

34. Aptheker, "Sterilization," p. 38. See also Anne Braden, "Forced Sterilization: Now Women Can Fight Back," *Southern Patriot*, September, 1973.

35. *Ibid.*

36. Jack Slater, "Sterilization, Newest Threat to the Poor," *Ebony*, Vol. XXVIII, No. 12 (October, 1973), p. 150.

37. Braden, *op. cit.*

38. Les Payne, "Forced Sterilization for the Poor?" *San Francisco Chronicle*, February 26, 1974.

39. Harold X., "Forced Sterilization Pervades South," *Muhammed Speaks*, October 10, 1975.

40. Slater, *op. cit.*

41. Payne, *op. cit.*

42. *Ibid.*

43. *Ibid.*

44. Aptheker, "Sterilization," p. 40.

45. Payne, *op. cit.*

46. Aptheker, "Sterilization," p. 48.

47. Arlene Eisen, "They're Trying to Take Our Future—Native American Women and Sterilization," *The Guardian*, March 23, 1972.

48. *Ibid.*

49. *Ibid.*

50. Quoted in a pamphlet issued by the Committee to End Sterilization Abuse, Box A244, Cooper Station, New York 10003.

51. *Ibid.*

52. *Ibid.*

53. Gordon, *op. cit.*, p. 338.

54. *Ibid.*

55. Mass, *op. cit.*, p. 92.

56. *Ibid.*, p. 91.
57. Gordon, *op. cit.*, p. 401. See also pamphlet issued by CESA.
58. Mass, *op. cit.*, p. 108.
59. Rahemah Aman, "Forced Sterilization," *Union Wage*, March 4, 1978.
60. *Ibid.*

CHAPTER 13

1. Oakley, *op. cit.*, p. 6.
2. Barbara Ehrenreich and Deirdre English, "The Manufacture of Housework," in *Socialist Revolution*, No. 26, Vol. 5, No. 4 (October–December 1975), p. 6.
3. Frederick Engels, *Origin of the Family, Private Property and the State*, edited, with an introduction, by Eleanor Burke Leacock (New York: International Publishers, 1973). See Chapter II. Leacock's introduction to this edition contains numerous enlightening observations on Engels' theory of the historical emergence of male supremacy.
4. Wertheimer, *op. cit.*, p. 12.
5. Ehrenreich and English, "The Manufacture of Housework," p. 9.
6. Wertheimer, *op. cit.*, p. 12.
7. Quoted in Baxandall *et al.*, *op. cit.*, p. 17.
8. Wertheimer, *op. cit.*, p. 13.
9. Ehrenreich and English, "The Manufacture of Housework," p. 10.
10. Charlotte Perkins Gilman, *The Home: Its Work and Its Influence* (Urbana, Chicago, London: University of Illinois Press, 1972. Reprint of the 1903 edition), pp. 30–31.
11. *Ibid.*, p. 10.
12. *Ibid.*, p. 217.
13. DuBois, *Darkwater*, p. 185.
14. Speech by Polga Fortunata. Quoted in Wendy Edmond and Suzie Fleming, editors, *All Work and No Pay: Women, Housework and the Wages Due!* (Bristol, England: Falling Wall Press, 1975), p. 18.
15. Mariarosa Dalla Costa and Selma James, *The Power of Women and the Subversion of the Community* (Bristol, England: Falling Wall Press, 1973).
16. *Ibid.*, p. 28.
17. Mary Inman, *In Woman's Defense* (Los Angeles: Committee to Organize the Advancement of Women, 1940). See also Inman, *The Two Forms of Production Under Capitalism* (Long Beach, Cal.: Published by the Author, 1964).
18. Margaret Benston, "The Political Economy of Women's Liberation," *Monthly Review*, Vol. XXI, No. 4 (September, 1969).
19. "On the Economic Status of the Housewife." Editorial Comment in *Political Affairs*, Vol. LIII, No. 3 (March, 1974), p. 4.

20. Hilda Bernstein, *For Their Triumphs and For Their Tears: Women in Apartheid South Africa* (London: International Defence and Aid Fund, 1975), p. 13.

21. Elizabeth Landis, "Apartheid and the Disabilities of Black Women in South Africa," *Objective: Justice*, Vol. VII, No. 1 (January–March, 1975), p. 6. Excerpts from this paper were published in *Freedomways*, Vol. XV, No. 4, 1975.

22. Bernstein, *op. cit.*, p. 33.

23. Landis, *op. cit.*, p. 6.

24. V. I. Lenin, "A Great Beginning," pamphlet published in July, 1919. Quoted in *Collected Works*, Vol. 29 (Moscow: Progress Publishers, 1966), p. 429.

25. Released in the United States under the title *Black Girl.*

26. Jackson, *op. cit.*, pp. 236–237.

27. Victor Perlo, *Economics of Racism U.S.A., Roots of Black Inequality* (New York: International Publishers, 1975), p. 24.

28. Staples, *The Black Woman in America*, p. 27.

29. *Daily World*, July 26, 1977, p. 9.

30. Dalla Costa and James, *op. cit.*, p. 40.

31. Pat Sweeney, "Wages for Housework: The Strategy for Women's Liberation," *Heresies*, January, 1977, p. 104.

32. Dalla Costa and James, *op. cit.*, p. 41.

33. Ann Oakley, *The Sociology of Housework* (New York: Pantheon Books, 1974).

34. *Ibid.*, p. 65.

35. *Ibid.*, p. 44.

36. *Ibid.*, p. 53.

37. *Psychology Today*, Vol. X, No. 4 (September, 1976), p. 76.

ABOUT THE AUTHOR

ANGELA Y. DAVIS studied at Brandeis University and at Goethe University in Frankfurt, Germany. She lives in California and teaches Black Philosophy and Aesthetics as well as courses in women's studies.